ADVANCE PRAISE

Candid, cleverly written, and wonderfully upbeat in its delivery, *Do Not Write a Book . . . Until You Read This One* offers one-stop publishing knowledge. Few books about the industry are as wise and refreshingly direct as this one, without literary stuffiness or salesy hyperbole. Each page provides a publishing framework and actionable steps for authors who recognize their books as a business, not a vanity moment. If you want an outstanding alternative to fast-talking coaches, get schooled by Ally and Bridgett. Their book already has earned a prominent spot on my bookshelf, and I will refer it to all my clients.

Judy Ellis
President, Daybreak Lit

From the first page of *Do Not Write a Book . . . Until You Read this One*, you'll feel as though you've gained a personal concierge to navigate the intricate world of book publishing. The authors excel at transforming the daunting into the doable with their knack for simplifying complex issues into digestible, actionable advice. Geared specifically for aspiring nonfiction authors—especially those in the business realm— this book offers comprehensive, engaging guidance. It's more than just a good read; it's a road map to your writing success. If you're serious about converting your expertise or story into a compelling book, consider this your indispensable guide.

Jennifer Columbe
Chief Operations Guru, Blue House Solutions
Author, *Escaping Chaos*

In their book *Do Not Write a Book . . . Until You Read This One*, Bridgett and Ally have created the all-inclusive go-to guide on how to add "author" to your résumé. In today's highly competitive world, personal branding is the key to breaking through the crowd and creating competitive differentiation. And what better way to do that than to share your expertise with the world through the publishing of a book? While I always dreamed of publishing, the thought was daunting and overwhelming. I only wish I had this book available to me when I first embarked on the journey. *Do Not Write a Book . . . Until You Read This One* breaks down the process, provides the pros and cons of self-publishing versus using a publishing company, and gives strategies for marketing and tips on how to avoid the most common mistakes, especially if you are leveraging AI. So, if you are thinking about writing your own book, I highly recommend that you read this book first. I know that it will inspire you and give you the confidence to fulfill your dream.

Heidi Solomon-Orlick
Founder and CEO, GirlzWhoSell

This book has it all! It's educational, informative, and written in an easy-to-understand style. Learn from the experts how to write, publish, promote, and profit from writing a book. The chapters are positive and encouraging while also pointing out challenges that can occur.

Writing a book might be the "easy" part, but the "hard" part is knowing how to publish and market a book, which are essential for success in today's world. With an even, comprehensive approach to the various options that authors should consider, this book provides a wealth of details and lets the reader decide what routes to pursue.

As an editor, I was especially impressed with chapter 5 about the drafting, editing, and revising of a document. The tips for self-editing are excellent, and the various types of professional editing are explained in a clear, concise manner. I wish all my clients would read and follow these guidelines!

Ally Berthiaume and Bridgett McGowen-Hawkins have impressive backgrounds and extensive writing and publishing experience, and they share their vast expertise throughout this book. They have compiled answers to all the questions that first-time and seasoned authors want to know.

Joni Wilson
Editor

As an aspiring author, I've always dreamed of seeing my words in print, but little did I know that writing a book is not just an artistic endeavor—it's also a business. That's the powerful lesson I've learned from this book, a book that has completely transformed my perspective on the world of publishing.

The book reflects on a powerful premise: writing a book is no longer enough to ensure its success. With the changing landscape of the publishing industry, authors must embrace their roles as entrepreneurs. Ally and Bridgett dive deep into the various aspects of this transformation, covering everything from the cover to mastering the art of self-promotion. This book underscores the reality that writing a book is only the first step in a much larger journey. With the right mindset and strategies, anyone can turn their passion for writing into a successful and sustainable business.

I wholeheartedly recommend this book to anyone who dreams of seeing their book not only on the shelves but also in the hands of eager readers. Ally and Bridgett's invaluable insights will empower you to take control of your writing destiny, turning your passion into a prosperous lifestyle. Writing and marketing a book is indeed a business, and this book is your ultimate guide to mastering it.

Bogdan Matei
Graphic Designer

Ally and Bridgett have created a must-read book for anyone who intends to publish. *Do Not Write a Book . . . Until You Read This One* is an informative yet enjoyable read about writing, publishing, and marketing your book to success. Clarity flows from its pages. This book has become an essential tool in my reference library. As a book coach, I will save time by recommending this book to my clients! The book not only tells you how to write your book and get it done but also takes a deep dive into what makes authorship profitable and successful. The appendices alone are worth buying! If you intend to write a book that more than one person will read, you have to get this book!

Tanya Brockett
Host of *Write Something Worthy Podcast*
Ghostwriter and Book Coach, Hallagen Ink

If only I had read this *before* I wrote my book . . . I would have avoided some of the pitfalls Ally and Bridgett so eloquently speak to. Thinking about how writing a book is a small business and the author is the CEO hit me over the head like a ton of bricks. The authors have done an outstanding job of pinpointing why this matters, noting key considerations, anchoring back to the power of purpose, and ensuring that each chapter is full of actionable takeaways. It has me tempted to write another book . . . just when I swore off doing so. It's that good!

Amy Volas
Founder and CEO, Avenue Talent Partners

As a leadership performance coach who has written hundreds of blog posts and contributed writing to anthology projects but not yet written my own book, I find Berthiaume and McGowen-Hawkins's book immensely valuable. *Do Not Write a Book . . . Until You Read This One* takes the reader deeper than the usual steps provided by other coaches and books that try to direct the reader through the publishing process. This book steps back before that to put you in the right mindset and guide you through the pain points of book writing. It's a step-by-step guide through the mindset of considering what your book can be and bringing it to the masses—just like it deserves to be if you believe in your message and value enough. It preempts the execution to build up and reinforce a solid foundation of awareness, clarity, and commitment. And who better to walk that path with you than two authors and publishers with years of experience who have taken that journey themselves and coached others in doing the same? As you read the book, it's clear that their experience intermeshes with their love and passion for books.

That's what we aspiring authors need—the technical support and a push of the heart, which both serve as the main pillars of this book. That passion sustains you in what can honestly be, from what I've seen, an often tedious and exhausting, but tremendously worthwhile and fulfilling adventure, of writing your own book.

John M. Jaramillo
Leadership Performance Coach
Host of *The Book Leads* Podcast

Ally and Bridgett are the dynamic duo you didn't know you needed! Not only is their energy infectious, but their expertise and knowledge on what it takes to be a successful author is both deep and wide. The moment they told me they were cowriting a book on how to craft, publish, and become a profitable author, I smiled and said to myself, "Of course they are!" I love their analogy of seeing your book as an "elevated business card" alongside their ideas of how to create multiple streams of income with a timeless asset that showcases your expertise and unique method. I'm excited to dig deep into the rest of the book. Their impact has only just begun!

Ravi Rajani
Speaker, Coach, and Consultant

This gem of a book is loaded with nuggets of wisdom that will enrich the publishing knowledge of all writers who are navigating the new normal of what it takes to get a book into the marketplace. Berthiaume and McGowen-Hawkins's "tell it like it is" writing style engages the reader from the get-go. These ladies are not afraid to get jiggy with it! From part 1: Your Book Is Your Business to part 4: Calling in the Pros, Ally and Bridgett offer their experience, share their publishing mistakes, and provide a true master class in the reality of today's book marketing landscape. Highly recommend.

Mary Catherine Jones
Executive Producer, Voice Over Vermont Audiobook Production

Having written, published, and used both of my books as marketing tools to grow my business, this guide is a must-read for business owners who desire to write a nonfiction book *and* use it as a business-building tool. *Do Not Write a Book . . . Until You Read This One* includes a practical, step-by-step process to help you discover how to write a book that positions you as an expert—and what to do with that book once it is written. One of the most valuable pieces of this guide (and what sets it apart from others) is the in-depth discussion from Ally and Bridgett about the mindset you must adopt as the CEO of your book—if you want that book to live far beyond your bookshelf once it's published.

M. Shannon Hernandez
Founder, Joyful Business Revolution™

As a first-time author, I've had the pleasure of working with industry experts Ally and Bridgett to get my award-winning book into the world. This dynamic duo has combined their collective genius to give the nonfiction indie author the inside track on the need-to-know details and pro tips that will make their book stand out in a crowd. *Do Not Write a Book . . . Until You Read This One* is a must-have for the business owner who is contemplating writing their first book.

Susan Lynch
Author, *Life After Kevin*

Berthiaume and McGowen-Hawkins's advice through this book is right on. As a publisher, the number one problem I see with new authors is underfunding the book journey. Authoring a book is a transformative journey that requires the same dedication and entrepreneurial spirit as starting a small business—which this book accurately solidifies. As the author, you step into the role of the CEO of your book, wielding the power to shape the narrative and turn it into a success story. Just like any business venture, investing both time and resources is crucial. From writing and developmental editing to audience building and publishing, it's essential to budget wisely, prioritizing development, launch strategies, and ongoing sales. As *Do Not Write a Book . . . Until You Read This One* promotes, embrace the challenge, be prepared to promote your book, and watch your creation thrive as it impacts readers' lives. This book will make a great reference for any nonfiction writer to consult along their path to publication.

Juliet Clark
Best-Selling Author, *The Author Success Handbook*
Founder, Superbrand Publishing

Do Not Write a Book . . . Until You Read This One is written in a style I appreciate. It is direct, witty, and full of tips to save a writer a lot of time when it comes to their book project. It is meant to be read in order and includes breakdowns in each section to solidify the relevant information. Any aspiring author would be wise to invest in this book to clarify their idea and to save time, money, and possibly embarrassment down the line. Concise and in-your-face advice—such as "are you ready to invest?"—is what I wish I'd been asked before my first book. It's more than money. As *Do Not Write a Book . . . Until You Read This One* clearly shares, the writer is the spokesperson and CEO of their upcoming book. Are we ready to be the marketing expert, too? The media advice is clear, up-to-date, and honestly like a present from the authors. Grab this book and share it with your writing groups so you can be the hero with this straightforward treasure of detailed assistance.

Lisa David Olson
Author, Interactive Speaker, Trainer, Three-Time TEDx Speaker,
and Host of the *Stranger Connections* Podcast

Do Not Write a Book . . . Until You Read This One is a terrific resource guide that you will refer to time and time again. I loved extending my thinking to move past the traditional life cycle of writing to publishing. Bridgett and Ally let you know that you're the CEO of your book and should act accordingly to ensure ongoing success with your authority and legacy. They say it's a lifetime commitment to promoting your book. I can't say enough about the many thoughtful takeaways to provoke strategic thinking for future books. Of course, as an already-published author of several books, I immediately went to the chapter on making money on my book. I don't want to give away the book's content, so you'll have to purchase the book to get the insights. Let me say that this book is worth your while and investment.

Simone E. Morris
CEO and Founder, Simone Morris Enterprises LLC

Do Not Write a Book . . . Until You Read This One is a great guide for any new author. The layout of the book and its chapters has an easy flow, which makes it a breeze to read and understand. Each chapter explains one part of the process so that new authors or someone struggling with the writing process can relax and write their book. It will definitely help a lot of people become authors.

Chanin Storm, MFA
International Author and College Writing Professor

DO NOT WRITE A BOOK . . .

UNTIL YOU READ THIS ONE

DO NOT WRITE A BOOK...

UNTIL YOU READ THIS ONE

THE ONLY GUIDE YOU NEED TO PEN, PUBLISH, AND PROFIT FROM YOUR NONFICTION BOOK

A. Y. BERTHIAUME
BRIDGETT McGOWEN-HAWKINS

press 49

Press 49
4980 South Alma School Road
Suite 2-493
Chandler, Arizona 85248

Volume pricing is available to bulk orders placed by corporations, associations, and others. For bulk order details and for media inquiries, please contact Press 49 at info@press49.com or 833.PRESS49 (833.773.7749).

FIRST EDITION

Library of Congress Control Number: 2023917405
ISBN: 978-1-953315-28-1 (hardcover)
ISBN: 978-1-953315-34-2 (e-book)

LAN002000 LANGUAGE ARTS & DISCIPLINES/Writing/Authorship
LAN027000 LANGUAGE ARTS & DISCIPLINES/Publishers & Publishing Industry
LAN005020 LANGUAGE ARTS & DISCIPLINES/Writing/Business Aspects
REF000000 REFERENCE/General

Cover design by Artichoked Creative.
Interior design by Medlar Publishing Solutions Pvt Ltd., India.

Printed in the United States of America.

To the brilliant minds
who are called to write a powerful book
and don't want to "just get it done"
but who want to get it done right.
We've got your back.
This one's for you.

TABLE OF CONTENTS

PART 1: YOUR BOOK IS YOUR BUSINESS

PART 2: THE MAKINGS OF A GOOD BOOK

APPENDICES

HOW TO USE (AND NOT USE) THIS BOOK

Writing a nonfiction book is no small undertaking. We know this—not just from writing the book on it but from personal experience. Whether your aim is to elevate your profile, share your thought leadership, and/or promote your business, writing a book "is a thing." So, before we begin, we want you to know that (1) you *can* do this, (2) this kind of critical and monumental project will take time, and (3) we've got you.

Figuring out this how-to-write-a-book-and-get-it-published landscape while also doing it right is a process that most unseasoned or first-time authors find is much like navigating one's way in the dark. The light at the end of the tunnel is this book. But first, a word of caution: you will not read this book in one sitting and then go out into the world to slay. Well, you can, but that's *so* not our recommendation. This book is a guide, it is a reference, and it is a how-to all in one. Read a few pages, make your notes, sit and think, do some work. Rinse and repeat.

With every step you take to bring your book to life, this book needs to be by your side. Before you write your first draft, check this book. Before you hire a writing coach, an editor, a graphic designer, a publisher, or anybody else, check this book. Before you do *anything* with your own book, check with this book first.

DO'S AND DON'TS TO USING THIS BOOK

Here's the short version:

DO: Get jiggy with this book.
DON'T: Put this book in the corner.

We want *Do Not Write a Book . . . Until You Read This One* to be one of those books that does not look perfect and pristine after you've read it. Please dog-ear the pages, underline and highlight key ideas, write down your thoughts (it's why we left you lines at the end of each chapter) . . . We know librarians everywhere would tell you not to do any of those things, and, of course, if you checked this book out from a library, please don't. We don't want you to be on the hook for damaging public property. But assuming that you bought this book to always have and to hold, then proceed with marking it up, Post-it®-noting it, and even leaving it on your desk by your keyboard for quick and easy reference. We would be honored. And when you've fully consumed this book from cover to cover, you will be fully equipped to pen, publish, and profit from your *own* book—one that you can be immensely proud of.

KNOWING YOUR WAY AROUND THE BOOK

We also want to note that we've organized this book's content in an intentional way, so we don't recommend skipping chapters—at least not the first time through, especially if you're a first-time author. We've purposely begun the book with part 1: Your Book Is Your Business so that you get the full 30,000-foot view and guiding perspective we want you to have before you truly jump into writing a book.

Naturally, from there, we go into part 2: The Makings of a Good Book so that once you understand how your book is a business, you can then focus on the book itself. And because you can't make money off your book until you *have* a book, part 3: Publishing, Marketing, and Making Money from Your Book comes next. Rounding out the book is our last section, part 4: Calling in the Pros, so you know who you need and how to find them to make parts 1–3 possible for you in real time.

THE LITTLE BITS AND PIECES

You'll notice a number of fun things called out throughout the chapters. We want to give you the heads-up so that you know what these are and our intention behind them. You'll find, listed below, a number of fun bits and callouts that appear throughout these pages:

Did You Catch That?

These are one to two sentences we've highlighted for added emphasis and because we hope you'll write that stuff down or commit it to memory. If you post them to social media, then we'd love that, too. Just make sure you tag us so we can give you a virtual high-five for sharing the love (and the knowledge)!

Pro Tip

These are recommendations, suggestions, or best practices for you to produce a better book. It's our professional advice.

IN OUR EXPERT OPINION

These feature boxes contain content that likely goes against the grain and conventional thought. This is us being really real with y'all about our opinions on certain things that we see inside the industry.

What Does That Mean?

These are places for us to go a little deeper in explaining something that might not be automatically known because it's industry jargon or knowledge.

You might also see included some tables and charts that we felt might be helpful, with information that we think is best presented in a visual format.

Last but not least, you'll see at the end of each chapter sections called Takeaways and To-Dos. *Do* go through them and actually attempt the next steps we suggest; you and your book will be better for them. Like everything else in this book, we've intentionally included these takeaways and to-dos. We want this book to be an easy-to-use, digestible reference and actionable guide for you. Those ending chapter bits are meant to help you synthesize the chapter material and give you bite-sized action items to move you in the right direction with your own book.

DON'T FORGET THE BACK

We didn't develop a robust group of appendices for our health or our ego. We added checklists, budgets, step-by-step guides, and resources to make your job of being a successful author way easier. Who wants to go down the Google rabbit hole all the time and have to move around multiple websites to gather information? Maybe that's your jam, but because you have this book, we're thinking that it's not. So, we culled through everything we know about writing, publishing, and making your book your business and pulled together a wealth of material, carefully selecting the best of the best, to give you what we believe you need (and will eventually realize you want) that goes perfectly with everything we discuss in the main body of this book. So, when you get to the conclusion, don't just "turn the dial." Spend some time reviewing the abundance of information just a few more pages away that's meant to help you and your book become stars.

REVIEW, PRAISE, REFER, OR BUY AGAIN

When you get done reading this book and if you decide it's been an informative, eye-opening, and resourceful read, do us a favor, okay? Please leave a review—preferably a praiseworthy one—online where you bought the book. Then, if you know other aspiring authors in your life, recommend this book to them or, by all means, buy another copy and send it right to their door.

WHY YOU DON'T WANT TO WRITE A BOOK UNTIL YOU READ THIS ONE

There's nothing quite like holding a copy of your new book in your hands after months of dedication, devotion, and determination to produce a fine piece of work. We get as excited about holding our clients' books as we do our own. It's an amazing feeling of accomplishment and awe-inducing to see the final product. Just think, that book that began as a mere abstract spark of an idea or an internal whisper (*"write a book . . ."*) morphed into words and paragraphs on a blank page all the way to its final metamorphosis with beautiful covers, thick pages, and that brand-new book smell (one of our favorite smells). (Don't pretend like you haven't sniffed a new book . . . and liked it.)

This transformational process from idea to final book is a mystery to most, especially first-time authors like yourself. Why wouldn't it be? Any time we do anything for the first time, we don't know what we don't know. That's why we've set out to demystify the process of penning, publishing, and profiting from your book. We want you to know as much as possible before you step foot on this book-writing path so you can avoid common mistakes and misconceptions about writing, publishing, and making money off your book.

IS THIS BOOK RIGHT FOR YOU?

Before we dive into the nitty-gritty, we want to make sure you're in the right place and that this book is destined to serve you in all the ways we intend. This book is for you if . . .

- you're a business owner, entrepreneur, or seasoned professional looking to spotlight and share your expertise using a nonfiction book as the vehicle.
- you're a person who appreciates both creativity and strategy and is looking to understand how those two things come together when writing a book.
- you're a mover and shaker, a master doer, and *will* execute on what you read here.
- you're a believer in quality over speed and are looking to understand the greater impact your book can have on your corner of the world.
- you identify with one of these statements:
    - You've written a book, you think you did a pretty good job, and now you're ready to do it again, but you want to know *unequivocally* that you will get it right this next time around.
    - You've never written a book, but you know you need to get to it.
    - You have a finished manuscript, or are working on one, and are wondering in what direction to go, what you need to do, what pitfalls to avoid, and how to make sure you set up yourself and your book for success.

GETTING IT DONE RIGHT

So often we hear from our clients that they want to write a book or that they have the idea for a book, but they don't really know all the little pieces that blossom from a blank page to a meaty manuscript to a polished product that sits on the shelf somewhere ready for purchase. We've set out to produce a book that holds people's hands and sheds light on the path to publication so that they're not feeling their way in the dark. We want people to take writing and publishing their book seriously because this is a long-term engagement. *Do Not Write a Book . . . Until You Read This One* is the only guide you will need to get your nonfiction book done and get it done right.

Now, when we say "get your book done," we mean soup to nuts. We're talking about the stuff that happens before you write a single word all the way to what you do after your precious thought-baby is out there in the big vast world. And when we say "get it done right," we mean that we want you to be successful, and we believe there are certain perspectives you must have and considerations you must make to do so.

Do Not Write a Book . . . Until You Read This One tells you exactly what you need to do before, during, and after you write your book; what makes for a good book; and how to monetize it. You'll learn how to get your book published, how to market it, and how to find the experts to do the work for you. *Do Not Write a Book . . . Until You Read This One* tells you about the benefits of and drawbacks to various avenues of publishing: traditional, hybrid, independent, and self-publishing. *Do Not Write a Book . . . Until You Read This One* even tells you how to make money off your book without selling one copy of it.

SERVING YOU WITH THE BEST OF THE BEST

If you think we are promising too much, don't worry—we're not. We've specifically curated the information we share inside these pages to serve many aspiring or novice authors who need a better handle on the full writing and publishing journey.

There are all kinds of information out there—free and otherwise—that will give you bits and pieces on how to write, publish, and market your book, but there is no single source that explicitly spells out for you what it takes to get your book done and get it done right—at least not one that doesn't require you to jump through hoops or navigate a bunch of bells and whistles, or without someone giving you a bit of guidance and then trying to sell you a program, or that doesn't make all kinds of promises that may or may not pan out. Then, there's information that's downright misleading or that gives you false hope as an author.

What we want to do is keep it real for you. This book is pragmatic and honest and includes actionable takeaways and great resources. We've tried to keep it informative and fun without a ton of extra fluff because we don't want you to have to work too hard to pick up what we are laying down.

We, the authors, combine our years of experience—which, at the time of this writing, is 36 years—in writing, editing, book coaching, ghost-writing, speaking (to monetize books), and publishing to give you a no-nonsense road map that most publishing industry pros won't sit down and tell you all at once.

We are authors ourselves and have worked with award-winning and bestselling nonfiction authors from a multitude of backgrounds, have seen and heard the challenges authors face, and know what it takes to navigate the seemingly complicated, confusing, and, at times, competitive world of publishing.

We tell you what we wish we'd known when we wrote our first books or what we wish someone would have told us. We tell you what we tell our clients. And we tell you exactly what you need to know to get it done, get it done right, and make your book your business.

Whatever we don't get around to telling you, we are happy to share at another time and place because—let's be real—we could talk about this stuff for days and there's so much more to say than what we've said here.

If, by the time you're done reading this book, you're like, "Uh . . . I don't want to do all this by myself," we encourage you to reach out. Writing and publishing a book shouldn't be done in isolation, and we wouldn't want you to ride along this journey alone. A party is always better with at least one other person, and we'd be honored if we were picked as your wingwomen. You can read up on us in the About the Authors section at the back of the book. For now, get ready to find out how to get your book done and how to get it done right.

PART 1

YOUR BOOK IS YOUR BUSINESS

CHAPTER 1

THE PUBLISHING LANDSCAPE AND OTHER THINGS TO KNOW FIRST

Once you publish a book, that book becomes a part of your world. Your book is a nonphysiological extension of you—your credibility, reputability, authority, thought leadership, personality, opinion, expertise, and methodology . . . You know this even if you've never consciously considered it. In a lot of ways, once you have your book, you are promoting and selling yourself (not the other way around). (More on that in chapter 8.)

Then, once you get your book into the hands of readers, you want them to promote and sell you (and your book), too. You want them to become unpaid advertising simply by loving what you've created. Think about any book you have loved and respected or that you frequently refer to or recommend to someone else. Think of any book you've told yourself you want to write the equivalent of but about x, y, or z. These books have left their mark and, therefore, so have their authors. When you recommend that book to a friend or colleague or when you envision writing a similar book for whatever reason, you're endorsing that book and encouraging others to check it out and buy it. You want your reader to do the same for you. You want them to share your book's title and where to find it with everyone they know.

So, to have a great book that best represents you and makes others want to recommend it to their inner circle, you've got to write a great book. Writing a great book begins with intention—being intentionally committed to writing a high-quality book you can be proud of. We call this the ABCD mindset. **A**pproach your **B**ook with a **C**ommitment to **D**oing it right. To follow the ABCD mindset, you've got to know what makes a great book and how to go about penning, publishing, and profiting from a great book. Luckily, that's what *this* entire book is about.

> **Did You Catch That?**
>
> The ABCD mindset to writing a high-quality book you can be proud of: Approach your **B**ook with a **C**ommitment to **D**oing it right.

THE ABCD MINDSET AND MAKING YOUR BOOK YOUR BUSINESS

Your book is your business, and we mean that in two ways. First, your book needs you. It needs you to call the shots, make decisions, and do your best to ensure that it's a high-quality final product to place in the hands of its dear readers. Second, "your book is your business" means you should treat your book *like* a business. Becoming an author doesn't just mean you finish the manuscript, get it published, then call it done. You're going to have to up your game and think bigger and more strategically.

If you think we're coming across a little intense and dishing out some tough love, you're right. We are. And the reason for this is that we are tired of sitting by watching people get this writing, editing, publishing process wrong when we know it doesn't have to be that way. With the right information, direction, and resources, you can put a great book out into the world. You do not have to bumble and fumble your way through the process, feigning ignorance when you arrive at a subpar finished product. And we've seen enough people spinning their wheels, following misleading advice, and ending up all over the map trying to figure out this penning-publishing-profiting thing. It doesn't have to be that way.

We promise that our real talk is all for the sake of your (and your book's) success. Your book is the compilation of your thoughts, your ideas, your framework or methodology, your story . . . so your book is *very much* your business and needs to be treated as one. You'll get more of this dish the further we get into part 1: Your Book Is Your Business.

We feel strongly about this notion of doing your book right. You have an opportunity to do more than just put a book out; you have an opportunity to do it in a truly impressive way. You owe it to yourself as well as to your book and your legacy. How many times have you bought a friend's or colleague's book after seeing them parade it around on social media, knowing you have no intention of reading it beyond the front cover because, quite frankly, it looks and sounds like crap? There are enough titles out there that are garbage. Yes, we said (or wrote) that. Garbage. Pure trash. Pura basura! (You didn't know we are bilingual, did you?) We don't want your book to fall inside the waste pile.

Let's agree that that's not the path you will take. You have the opportunity to do more than just put out a book without thinking or caring about what it will look like and how it will sound.

Do it right, or don't do it all. But let's opt for the former.

First, you will commit to doing an amazing job with your book from start to finish. (Well, there really is no finish line, but don't worry about that for now. We will cover more on that later in the book.)

Next, you will put in the work to write, rewrite, then write again and again until you've nailed your message. (This isn't just talk or a "do as I say, not as I do" moment. *Do Not Write a Book . . . Until You Read This One* underwent more revisions than you can imagine.)

After that, you will get your book out into the marketplace in such a fantastic way that if someone takes one glance at your book versus one that's been published by one of the Big Five publishers, they won't know the difference. They won't know you weren't picked up by Penguin Random House unless they look at the imprint.

Then, you will market your book like it's the hottest ticket in town since Beyoncé's last concert tour hit the scene. And you'll *keep* marketing it. (Hint: Look at the title of chapter 8.)

In short, we are tired of people not wanting to get this right. Or maybe we're wrong, and they *do* want to get it right but just don't know how. Well, Ally and Bridgett are on the scene now. With our expert guidance, you can now do everything in your power to write well-thought-out, carefully curated content that makes people want to read your book and tell others about it. But there is so much more to this than conquering the doom of the blank page and getting your manuscript written. Once it's written, you have to get it published.

A PUBLISHING INDUSTRY PRIMER

We will not go into much depth here because publishing and its various models are discussed in great detail later in the book. For now, we want you to know what does and does not happen in the publishing space so you can be prepared for what comes once your manuscript is ready. You need to understand the publishing landscape before we begin diving into details. No matter if you work with a traditional, hybrid, or independent (indie) publisher or if you do the work yourself and self-publish, you will need to understand the publishing industry.

▶ **What Does That Mean?** ▶▶

TRADITIONAL, HYBRID, INDIE, OR SELF-PUBLISH

There are several ways to publish, and each has advantages and disadvantages, which we cover in more detail in chapter 9 (and review again in appendix A: The Pros and Cons of Each Publishing Route). Here is the CliffsNotes version of the most common avenues to bring your book to the marketplace:

- *Self/DIY: You do everything (or find everyone to do all the things for you)*
- *Indie: Someone else does mostly everything and allows you to retain 100 percent creative license; you pay them*
- *Hybrid: A cross between indie and traditional, the publisher does everything, but they may insist on extensive edits to your manuscript before they will publish you; you pay them*
- *Traditional: The oldest publishing route and the one most people know (think Penguin Random House and the like), traditional publishing is super competitive, you need an agent (usually), and you might not have much creative control over your project; you don't have to pay them*

Key Players and Mission

The book publishing industry is a combination of all the activities, processes, and actors involved in producing and distributing books and e-books. Authors create content. Editors improve the content. Literary agents accept and review the content with the goal of locating what has great promise of being profitable for traditional publishers, then represent and protect authors' interests. And publishers get books out into the world. No surprise there, right?

All publishers typically divide their operations as follows: editorial, design, production, publicity, sales, distribution, contracts, rights (e.g., translation, foreign republishing, and licensing), and administration. Outside of internal operations, it's a must that publishers also work with printers, information processors, and distributors. Printers create multiple copies of a book (of course, you likely already knew that, but we are making no assumptions here); information processors make books available electronically (think e-books); and distributors, such as Amazon Kindle Direct Publishing (KDP) and IngramSpark, make books available to online and brick-and-mortar retailers and are also responsible for packing and shipping books to consumers, such as individual purchasers, book sellers, and libraries.

If you self-publish, you will interface with all of these publishing partners, and the ones with which you will have an ongoing relationship long after your book publishes are your distributors. Amazon KDP is the distributor and the path that most self-published authors take; however, IngramSpark has a greater reach and is the distributor you should select if you have to choose only one. When you use IngramSpark as your distributor, your book will be available for purchase not just on Amazon's sites but also on other online retailers' sites. That's a win, right?! When you upload your files to Amazon KDP, your book is only available on Amazon's site, limiting your book's reach (more on this in chapter 9).

Speed

Sit back and relax because the industry can move pretty slowly. You will want to know something—*anything*—soon after submitting your proposal to an agent or a traditional publisher or after submitting your manuscript to a hybrid or indie publisher, but things don't work like that. It can take weeks or even months for you to hear back. This goes for reviewing your proposal and editing your manuscript, too. Your project is not the only one on the publisher's plate—not that that's what you want to hear. Plus, it takes time to edit. Editors do not tend to work on a manuscript in one sitting. It can take several hours over the course of several days or several weeks. It takes time to design. It takes time to typeset. It takes time to proofread—and on and on, and there's little you can do to control the time. So, the excitement you had with finally being able to hand over your masterpiece will have to take a pause until you hear back, which can be more time than you may have anticipated.

> **Did You Catch That?**
>
> *The publishing industry can move pretty slowly.*

People

There are several people involved with getting one book to market. Just as a car on an assembly line will have the hands of all sorts of people on it before it finally arrives at the local dealer's lot, the same goes for your book. There are assistants, editors, designers, typesetters, and proofreaders—to name a few. And each one is viewing your book through a different lens. They may not be as in love with your ideas as you are. Be prepared for that, but do know that they are there (or should be there) to perform their jobs to the best of their abilities while producing a book for you that makes you beam with pride (more on that in chapter 14).

Goals

Different publishers and publishing partners will have different goals in mind that may or may not align with your goals or benefit you and your book. Keep this on your radar throughout the entire process of getting your book done. If you are one of the very few "lucky" ones to get offered a contract from a traditional publisher, before you sign on the dotted line and do your happy dance, have a legal professional review it to make sure it's a good deal for you, too! (You'll later find out when we discuss the pros and cons of the different publishing models in chapter 9 why it's not necessarily "all that" to get picked up by a traditional publisher. You'll also find a recap of this information inside appendix A: The Pros and Cons of Each Publishing Route.) You may find that it's better to be a big deal with a smaller publisher than to be just another name on the roster of a larger publisher. Think about it: who is a publisher going to pay the most attention to? Check the small print, find out everything you can about a publishing company before deciding to move forward, and make sure that part of the company's goals includes making you a priority.

Did You Catch That?

Different publishers and publishing partners will have different goals in mind that may or may not align with your goals or benefit you and your book. Keep this on your radar throughout the entire process of getting your book done.

Broader Thinking and the Connection to Success

The publishing industry and your readers expect you to do more than just write a book. Start thinking about multiple business aspects to your book and additional revenue streams. (More on that in chapter 2.) Spend time with others—editors, authors, distributors, publishers—in the industry. Watch trends, and pay attention to what equates success in the industry.

Reader Love and Criticism

Your agent (not everyone will have one . . . more on that later), editor, reviewers, and publisher may think your book is the bee's knees, but readers may think otherwise. It's a strange idea, but it happens. Publishing industry professionals are looking at your book with an eye that is vastly different from that of a reader. Be ready for the fact that not every reader will love everything you put out there even if everyone else in the industry can't stop singing your book's praises. Focus on the ones who love you.

Getting Paid and the Start of Getting Paid

It doesn't matter if you work with a publisher or if you self-publish, it takes time before the checks come rolling in, and don't plan on paying your mortgage with your royalties because the income can be relatively sporadic. The only consistency will be the payout date—that's about it. It can be several months from the time you publish before you see a royalty payment, and the amounts will vary depending on—you guessed it!—how well your book does in the marketplace. Some publishers pay royalties on an annual basis, while others pay on a quarterly or biannual basis. (When you self-publish, payouts are scheduled on a more frequent basis, but again, it takes more than just the act of publishing for you to actually see those payouts. People have to know about it in order to buy it. Much more on all of that later in the book.) The biggest checks will be the ones you see when your book is newly released. The numbers will taper off as your book ages unless you put in the work to keep your book relevant. (More on the truth about your return on investment [ROI] and royalty calculations and expectations in chapter 10.)

> **Did You Catch That?**
>
> *Don't plan on paying your mortgage with your royalties because the income is relatively sporadic.*

But because we are on the topic of keeping your book relevant, we would be remiss if we did not stress the importance of marketing because that's *how* you keep your book relevant and how you start the ball rolling with getting paid. Marketing begins before your book even publishes. (You will likely see that exact same sentence again later in the book. It's not that we lack creativity. It's just that it is what it is, friend.) The sales will not automatically come pouring in the day your book drops—not unless you have been talking and talking and talking about it well before its publication date. Yes, make a big deal about your book finally coming to life on the day it actually publishes, but first, create as much interest, buzz, and excitement *beforehand* to let people know that the big day is coming. Doing so is a must because it gets those early sales rolling in (more on marketing is covered in chapter 8).

WHAT'S WRONG WITH PUBLISHING

We won't mince words here—any and everybody can get published, and at the time of this writing, any and everything is allowed in the publishing space. And that, my friends, is a problem. That's why we are so insistent on putting out quality. Now, have we made mistakes in publishing? Yes. Do we wish we hadn't? Absolutely. Can we fix what's wrong with publishing with one book? Not likely. But are we going to try? Um . . . that may be a bit ambitious.

On the flip side, while some crappy work is indeed out there, a big problem is that too many great manuscripts never see the light of day. This is because the authors are waiting for an agent or a big house publisher to get back with them, and they never do. So, authors just keep waiting and hoping for the moment they hear back, or, even worse, they shut down and don't try another route because they are blinded by the anticipated promise of the notoriety associated with getting signed by a large publisher or they are unaware of the other options available to them and how to pursue them.

Back to the crappy work for a second, though. That's a *huge* problem we cannot overlook. (And we need you to read *huge* in the same voice Oprah would use to emphasize a point.) With so many self-publishing options, it is easy to have a lack of attention to all the details, and there is a higher probability of unpolished content getting out into the marketplace. Remember what we wrote earlier: do it right, or don't do it all. But opt for the former. People will spend more time thinking about their book tour and what they will wear than what they spend on getting their book looked over with a fine-tooth comb. We're not saying don't look fly at your book signings, but don't show up with your outfit looking better than your book.

Next, the industry can be confusing. Authors should not have to jump through hoops to figure out how publishing works. It should be straight-forward and clear for anyone to navigate. If it's too easy, then it's not worth doing—is that a thing? We are throwing that one out the window. By the mere fact of all the work it takes to get your manuscript done, everything else should be a little simpler. Wouldn't you agree?

It shouldn't just be big names who can get published. Sure, they have the clout and the following to bring in the sales, but that's not all that makes for a great book. If you go against the grain, if you believe in an important cause that needs more attention, if you have formulated a better or more inventive way to get stuff done, then you deserve to be a published author.

But how do you know if you deserve to be an author? And is it even time for you to write a book? We're so glad you asked.

KNOWING IF THE TIME IS RIGHT FOR YOU

Unless you're preparing to launch a rocket into outer space and you require several conditions to be just so, there is no perfect and precise moment when angels will start singing, notifying you that it's time to write and release your book. Well, you may get that sign, and if you do, then, by all means, follow it! But for the rest of you, if you want to know as closely as you can—within a few inches of without a doubt—here are seven signs that it's time to put pen to paper (or fingertips to keyboard). If any one of these resonates with you, then it's time to write and publish your book. If more than one resonates, then it was time to write and publish your book . . . yesterday.

1. People already love everything you say and do.

Your social media posts are blowing up! Your email inbox is blowing up! Your DMs are blowing up! You could—not that you would—post a picture of a head of lettuce, and everyone would eat it up (no pun intended). Your posts and responses are filled with content that's fresh, challenging, and funny or includes no-nonsense truths that others won't dare to utter. You keep it real, give encouragement, and share innovative thinking. You have exciting plans, a powerful personal perspective, and motivation that screams, "Get up. Get out. Get to it. You can do it!" Your posts consistently garner all kinds of attention, reactions, and responses from your followers, and all the better if you are able to effortlessly crank out material, not having to think twice about what you're writing. And it's gorgeous! Your content flows from your heart, and others find it to be downright irresistible.

2. Others have written on your topic, but you see gaps or are simply unimpressed.

You know that your solution is just as good, if not better, than what's already in the marketplace. You find yourself regularly referencing your methodology or your process in conversations. You read, watch, or listen to others who are in the same space and say to yourself, "I can do that. Hell, I can do better than that!" You give your opinion on a matter, backing it up with what you have experienced, learned, or created, as well as what you have tested and know works. You wish for that one source you can direct people to that you know will unequivocally give the advice and answers that are superior to the content that's already out there.

3. You're tired of seeing people make mistakes.

It is so hard to watch people make missteps that you know are 100 percent avoidable if they simply put in place what you've been practicing, teaching (even preaching at times!), and coaching others on. You want to give them a proven plan or take them under your wing to show them what's possible and how it's done. You know that if they had your system or your method—if they knew what you know—then they could be a success. You just know it.

4. Your ideas are too big for the current platforms you're using to get them out.

Blogging is not enough. A LinkedIn post is not enough. A Facebook reel is not enough. A selfie on The Gram is not enough. A TikTok video is not enough. Moreover, not everyone who needs your expertise is on your mailing list, is subscribed to your blog, or sees your content on social media. Plus, there's only so much you can put in any of those posts, and you have a new idea that comes to you what seems like every few seconds. Your brilliance is outgrowing the current space you're using to publish it. It's bursting at the seams! It needs a new home where all of it is beautifully organized and in one place for easy consumption by all.

5. You're damn good at what you do.

You're always being asked to solve a specific problem. You are called upon for a certain skill set, and the best part is you consistently crush it! Simply put, you're phenomenal at what you do, and what you do helps people. Your business makes good money at helping people with a specific challenge, and you have become regarded as a thought leader in a niche, with industry peers even looking to you as an authority. The bottom line is you're exceptional at what you do. You know it, and others know it.

6. You're looking for the next big thing.

You are ready to dominate and stand out from your competition because you already know you are different from others who do the same thing, but you need something that will make it crystal clear that you're not more of the same. Plus, there's a "been there, done that" résumé that you're working with; it's time to go where you've never gone before. Yes, a book is scary and opens you up to scrutiny and judgment, but you're tough, and you're ready for it. Only the best people are willing to put themselves out there—to take risks. And weren't you told that to be a success, you must do what scares you? You've checked off everything else and mastered them all. This is your next big thing. Feel the fear, and—you know the rest of the statement—do it anyway.

7. You are getting signs from everywhere else that writing your book just makes sense.

You attend events, see others with their own books, and you think to yourself, "That could be me." Or perhaps you are constantly told by family, friends, colleagues, and clients that you should write a book. You give great advice. Friends reach out with questions. You've heard the phrase "pick your brain" more times than you care to count. And if only you had a dollar for every time you've heard someone ask you if you have a book. The signs are all around you. All that's left to do is do what makes sense. (To assess if it really, really, really *is* time to do this thing, we have put together an incredible list of questions that you seriously need to ask yourself in appendix C: Interview Yourself: Ten Questions to Ask Yourself before You Start Your Book. Go! Go do it now!)

THE BIGGEST PITFALLS TO AVOID

Now that you're pumped at the prospect of doing the next big thing (that would be writing and publishing your book, right?), let's pump your brakes and look at the biggest mistake we see authors make. Don't let this be you. Make note of these five biggest pitfalls to avoid, then get ready for more on them in the chapters to come.

1. You are not strategic about the idea of writing a book.

How to avoid it: Conduct a full-scale interview with yourself to assess every angle of your decision to put pen to paper, the problem your book will solve and for whom, and how your book has selling potential that goes *far* beyond its retail price. (Appendix D: Book-Planning Scorecard and appendix C: Interview Yourself: Ten Questions to Ask before You Start Your Book are great places to start to ensure that you're being strategic from the start. In fact, stop right now and work through the scorecard. Then, when you're finished with this book, do it again and see how your score has changed as a result of everything you learned inside these pages.)

2. You are not strategic about your book's title.

How to avoid it: Identify the words people most commonly use to search for information on the topic your book covers and strategically incorporate them into your title.

3. You are not serious about the editor you choose for your book, instead trusting a friend or a colleague with a "strong" background in grammar and punctuation to do the work for you.

How to avoid it: Understand the different types of editors and the specific kind of editing they do, and hire professionals.

4. You cut corners with the goal of saving money.

How to avoid it: Do your research to understand what it costs to produce a quality book and the consequences of paying less with the hopes of just getting it done. Be realistic with your budget.

5. You think your book will make you rich or that it will make a lot of money with little to no effort on your part.

How to avoid it: Make a plan for marketing your book, know what the numbers are when it comes to royalty payments and how many books you truly can expect to sell in your book's lifetime, and recognize what's required of you to make your book known and get it sold.

This concludes your welcome tour to the publishing world. We hope you'll enjoy your stay.

Joking aside, we trust that you have a better entry point into this multifaceted and ever-changing landscape that is publishing. To immediately begin by sitting down to write your book when you aren't sure what happens later would be like boarding a plane without knowing your final destination. That's not the best way to travel; though, there may be some level of excitement in not knowing where you're going.

We want you to know where you'll land so you can best prepare for and enjoy the journey. Now that we've given you the view from the skies, let's land this plane with your first set of takeaways and to-dos. When you're ready, turn the page to begin embracing your book as a business, with you at the helm as the author and CEO.

TAKEAWAYS AND TO-DOS

Takeaways

- Adopt an ABCD mindset to writing a high-quality book—**A**pproach your **B**ook with a **C**ommitment to **D**oing it right—and commit to making your book your business.
- Ensure that you have a good handle on, or at least a relatively good understanding of, the publishing industry to include, at a minimum, the different publishing models, publisher goals, the people with whom you will interface, and what getting paid looks like as a published author.

- There is no perfect moment or perfect sign that it's time to write your book, but you will have indicators all around you that scream that it's time for you to start writing. Listen to and follow them.
- Avoid pitfalls such as . . .
  - not having a strategy for writing your book or titling your book;
  - trusting friends and colleagues to edit instead of hiring a professional editor;
  - cutting corners in the name of saving money; or
  - misunderstanding how to make money off your book.

To-Dos

- Assess your mindset before you commit to writing a book. Be honest with yourself, and confirm that you are indeed in it to win it, meaning that you're going to do it right, or you're not going to do it at all (or at least not until you're ready to give it your all).
- Review the primer on the publishing industry and write down any questions you have. Get answers to them before you move forward with your book.
- Look through your social media posts, articles, blogs, and other content you've produced to ascertain its quality and impact. If people are responding favorably and on a regular basis or if they are reaching out to you for more, then it's time for you to get published.
- Make note of the pitfalls to avoid and keep them in clear view as you work through your book project.

NOTES

_____

_____

_____

_____

_____

_____

_____

_____

_____

_____

_____

_____

_____

_____

_____

_____

_____

_____

_____

CHAPTER 2

YOU'RE THE CEO, AND YOUR BOOK *IS* YOUR BUSINESS

Something that often surprises first-time authors is how authoring a book far exceeds the writing part. Many begin with the notion "I'm going to write a book," and the focus is on only two things: the writing and the book. There's little understanding of what bridges the gap from point A (the writing) to point B (the book) and, much of the time, no awareness that there is a point C, which is everything that occurs *after* the author has the book. There's even less understanding that a lot of what happens at point C actually needs to be established while points A and B are occurring. This first part of the book essentially discusses point C, which are all of the not-so-glamorous-but-downright-necessary things an author should consider and understand *before* they simply decide "I'm going to write a book."

Too often, authors pen their work and think that's where the work stops, and that is far from the truth if you want your book to be a success. Treat your book like a business and take up your position at the helm. Don't assume that when you're done writing your book, *that* was the heavy lifting. Many think that when the manuscript is done, they've completed the hardest part—cranking out that manuscript, editing, and revising it. It's true that they have gotten a large part of the project done and are to be commended for that accomplishment, *but* if they want to do more with their book than simply revel in the glow of having completed it, they must treat it as if it's a business—which makes them the CEO. This applies whether you are a business owner looking to write a book, if you're retired and have decided to sit down and write your memoir, or if you have been holding onto an idea or a stack of writings and have finally gotten a fire under you to take the next step of publishing it. You must be the CEO of your book.

Did You Catch That?

Too often, authors pen their work and think that's where the work stops, and that is far from the truth if you want your book to be a success. Treat your book like a business.

Now, if simply completing it is enough for you—you've checked off "become a published author" on your bucket list or have reached one more accomplishment that you've been striving for—then carry on! You'll hear no argument here. However, we're led to believe that that's not exactly the case or you would not be reading this book. *Are we right?*

YOUR BOOK IS A SMALL BUSINESS, AND YOU'RE THE CEO

Mainly, what we want authors to recognize is that authoring a book is like starting a small business. When a person starts a small business, they should have a general understanding what they want their business to do for them and their clients. Similarly, as an author, you want to know before you begin what your book can do for you and your readers. And when a person starts a business, that makes them the boss or CEO or founder or some other word you'd like to use. That means you're in charge. You're the CEO of this operation.

Did You Catch That?

Authoring a book is like starting a small business, and you must understand what you want your book to do for you and/or your business.

As an author, you're the owner/founder/CEO of your book. And as that CEO, it's your responsibility to hold, nurture, and promote the mission and vision for the company. You need to be invested in the success and long-term sustainability of your book business so you're not walking into it blindly. This book is yours. It's forever. (Yes, just like diamonds.) So, you need to care for and deeply understand what your motivations, mission, and vision look like.

As the author/CEO, you're the one with the most intimate knowledge of your ideal customer—the person you're trying to reach with your product. Or, in book terms, you know who your ideal reader is and how your book serves them. What does all of this mean? You. Call. The. Shots.

Did You Catch That?

As an author, you're the owner/founder/CEO of your book. You. Call. The. Shots.

For those of you who are writing a book *and* who are also running your own business, we hope this won't be too far of a leap to make. Certainly, if your book directly aligns with the business or field you're in, we're hoping it feels seamless to integrate your book activities with your business ones.

But for those of you who are not entrepreneurial or side-hustlers or who haven't started a business, we hope you find this part of the book beneficial in providing you the big picture of becoming an author. This chapter lays the groundwork, and chapter 3 goes into more details.

THE CEO MINDSET (AND, YES, IT'S IMPORTANT)

Your mindset, belief system, internal dialogue, confidence, self-esteem, attitude—whatever term you want to go with—are critical to your success in nearly anything you set out to achieve. Writing a book and setting that book up like a small business is no exception. You need to know that it's possible and that you have skills to help you be successful; what you don't know you can either find the answers to or the right people to guide you. So, first and foremost, believe that you can do this. Kick self-doubt to the curb; you've got work to do.

A lot of the CEO mindset is confidence. You have to feel confident about your mission and vision to help with the self-doubt that might creep in. You have to feel confident about making decisions to delegate the parts and pieces you don't want to do or have no business doing.

Perhaps where confidence is going to be needed the most is in your marketing and selling. You need to be confident in being the face of your "company" and willing to stand in front of the product you've created (your book) and claim it (and all you say inside it) as yours. If you hide behind the book, putting it out into the world but not letting anyone know it's yours or that it's there, all of your hard work will have been done in vain. Confidence is key and king. Without it, you'll have a less successful book. So, get confident in yourself, and get confident in marketing and selling.

As the CEO of your book, you also need to be committed to the process and progress over perfection and urgency. Don't rush a good thing. Take your time. Do your due diligence. We like to tell our clients that if the world has waited this long for your book, it can wait a little longer. We're not promoting loafing around or procrastinating or making excuses for not doing the work, but skipping steps, taking shortcuts, or skimping on the budget for the sake of getting the book out there quickly and cheaply will not get you your best book or a successful one.

Successful CEOs have strategies; implementation plans; advisors; and clear, specific, intentional goals. They're not just showing up to the office each day, making it up as they go—at least not purposely. They've got their endgame in mind. They're in it to win it. We encourage you to have this hat on when you're working on your book—not just as you begin to write but *before*. Remember, this whole chapter (and the next) is all about what has to be in place *ahead* of the actual writing.

Additionally, CEOs have a general understanding of numbers, finances, ROI, and business investment. We know—boring. We agree; we're book people. But they're necessary.

EVERY BUSINESS REQUIRES A START-UP INVESTMENT

As such, now's the time to start thinking about the fact that you'll be spending money on this book before you make any money off of it. Now is also the time to begin working on your abundance mindset and/or your relationship to money because here's the thing—starting a small business requires an up-front investment. Guess what else requires an up-front investment? A book.

Your book is going to require a little cash advance from you (or a Kickstarter fund or a rich uncle or a financially supportive spouse). No matter how you choose to publish—and there are several options we'll explore with you in chapter 9 and appendix A: The Pros and Cons of Each Publishing Route—you're going to have to lay down some money somewhere along the way. How much and for what depends on a variety of factors. (See appendix E: The Cost to Self-Publish.) But an informed and determined CEO with a clear understanding of what they're doing knows this and is prepared for it.

The only thing you need to know in this very moment is to expect to invest in your book. Whether that's time, energy, or monetary resources, starting anything new will require an up-front cost. Be prepared to INVEST in your book to do it well. Hire great editors, typesetters, cover designers, or a publisher that has all those "greats" already on the team.

If you're not sure who all these people are at this point, don't worry. We'll identify some of these key players in part 4: Calling in the Pros and have also provided appendix F: People on the Publishing Path. Again, if you're not sure what to expect for an up-front investment, check out chapter 10 for the costs to publish and/or appendix E: The Cost to Self-Publish.

And because we're talking about investing, we might as well take a moment to address a question we hear *a lot*: "What ROI can I expect from my book?" We dive deeply into that answer in chapter 10, but what we want to state here is this: what you receive as a return is directly linked to what you do. ROI does not happen with no action by the author.

Pro Tip

You have gotta spend money to make money. This is no less true for producing a dynamite book with your name on it that will be around forever and that you want to be proud of. Do you feel us?

SHOWING UP AS THE FACE OF YOUR "COMPANY"

We already primed the pump here when we talked about confidence earlier in this chapter, but this part is so important that we need to include a little more here. The short version is you MUST get comfortable with promoting and selling your book. Commit this to memory: your book will not sell itself.

Did You Catch That?

Your book will not sell itself.

Truth: no one is going to care as much about your book as you do. Just like no one is going to care about their company as much as the CEO/founder does. You are the face of your book.

Did You Catch That?

Truth: no one is going to care as much about your book as you do.

Your headshot is going to be on the back cover. Your headshot is going to be associated with any event where you're the speaker, and that's because you're the author of [insert your book title here]. Your face is the one on the other side of the computer screen doing a podcast interview or a virtual summit where you talk about your book and maybe even wave it around for everyone to see. Your professional bio now has "author" and your book title listed as a part of your credentials and credibility. You are your book's representative.

Did You Catch That?

You are your book's representative.

As such, you are your book's main spokesperson. This will always be the case even if you choose a publisher who does a little bit of marketing and PR on your behalf or if you eventually pay a PR company, work with a marketing agency, or hire a virtual author's assistant to support your book marketing efforts. (More on book marketing in chapter 8.) You're still the CEO. The book still belongs to you, which means you're the one responsible not only for paying these people but also for ensuring they do a great job promoting your book and therefore you. The buck starts and stops with you.

Now, if you don't work with anyone on promotion, then guess what? It's all you, friend. Be prepared to promote and SELL. The only way your book is going to be known is if you tell people about it. A rookie mistake is thinking that once it's published—and therefore searchable online via web retailers—people will just stumble upon it and you'll passively make money on book sales. This is one of the most common misconceptions about publishing that new authors have.

> ### IN OUR EXPERT OPINION—YOUR BOOK WON'T SELL ITSELF
>
> *STOP! READ THIS. WRITE IT DOWN. MEMORIZE IT.*
>
> *Be prepared to promote and SELL. Get comfortable with talking about your book and talking about it some more. No one will know you have a book unless you tell the world you do. If you want people to read it, they have to know it exists. If you want people to know if it's for them, you need to help them understand if it is. Your book won't sell itself. It has words but not a mouth. You must speak for it—and you have to do so more than just once or twice if you want it to sell.*
>
> *Thank you for your time and for listening to our TED Talk.*
> *You may proceed.*

There are two issues with this mindset (see, there's that good ole mindset again). One, your book won't sell itself. (We know we just said this, but it's *sooo* important to understand.) It doesn't matter how good the keywords or metadata are that make your book pop up in search results. Your book appearing in search results doesn't guarantee sales. (Don't worry about not knowing the terms *keywords* or *metadata*, we cover that in chapter 3.)

Two, you don't want to be relying on book sales alone to make money off your book, and you shouldn't expect that book sales are going to bring you your full ROI. Again, we cover this whole idea of ROI in chapter 10, and we also spend all of part 3 on how to make money from your book.

So, what does being the face of your book and being comfortable with promoting and selling look like? It looks like putting yourself out there on social media and talking about your book via text-, video-, or image-based posts. It looks like emailing friends, family, and professional contacts, letting them know that you just published. It looks like adding a footer to your email that features your book or changing your profile photos or banners on your social media accounts.

▶ What Does That Mean? ▶▶

TEXT-, VIDEO-, OR IMAGE-BASED POSTS

When you post about your book on social media, use text, videos, and images to promote your book. For text-based posts, you can offer an enticing brief synopsis of your book, a provocative direct quote from your book, or a big question that your book answers. If you post a video, it can be a snippet from an interview of you discussing your book, a recording of you sharing some of your favorite lines from your book, or a testimonial from someone who read your book. Finally, in an image-based post, you might have a picture of someone reading your book, a collage of your book as a paperback and as an e-book on a monitor and smartphone, or a picture of yourself at one of your book signings. The options are endless! Regardless of whether you use a text-, video-, or image-based post, aim to promote, inform, or entertain your followers, and always include a link for where people can purchase your book online.

Talk about your book and talk about it some more. Bring it up in conversation. Bring it up in interviews. Bring it up over family dinner at the annual reunion when your second and third cousins ask you what you've been up to this past year. There are all kinds of ways to promote your book (covered thoroughly in chapter 8), but you've got to be willing and ready to do so in order to get the results you want: sales of some kind. When you become an author, it's not the time to be bashful or feel ashamed about self-promotion. It's time to shine, to be proud of what you've produced, and to make sure people know it exists. You're the gosh darn, rootin' tootin' CEO, so step up, speak up, and stand out for your book. (Just so you all know, that "rootin' tootin'" was all Ally right there. All Ally.)

HOW ELSE IS YOUR BOOK LIKE A BUSINESS?

All right, so now that you've got your CEO hat on and you're ready to invest, promote, and sell, let's talk about the other elements of a business that translate to having a book. A business usually sells a product or service. As an author, you're selling your book, which, technically speaking, is both. It's an actual product or, to use the Internal Revenue Service's language, "a good" for which you pay sales and use tax. The service is what your book provides to the reader. That's the material or content you're sharing with them that solves one of their problems by offering them knowledge, inspiration, motivation, and/or transformation.

Additionally, a business operates with an understanding of expenses, operating budgets, revenue streams, cash flow, and sales and marketing plans—just to name a few. Your book business will require an investment up front to handle the expenses to produce the book. You'll need to know what these are in advance so you can create an operating budget. When the book is ready for sale, you'll track revenue and watch cash flow. And, if you're a strategic author/CEO, you'll look for revenue streams outside of just direct book sales and you'll have a marketing plan (or strategy) to help boost sales. From that perspective, you'll want to really pay attention to part 3.

That's not all.

A business has multiple departments or business activities, including administration, financial, marketing/sales, product/service development (which is the actual writing of your book and covered in part 2), and distribution. A book has all of the same. Truly. A book couldn't be any more like a business.

THE DEPARTMENTS OF YOUR BOOK BUSINESS

Administrative tasks may look like email responses to your publisher, editors, and cover designer. They may include setting up tracking sheets or reports. Or perhaps you need to do the research to find these people you'll be working with.

Your financial "department" handles all of the things we mentioned previously: the operating budget, revenue streams, expenses, book sales, and taxes (such as sales and use tax). This department also needs to decide which bank account will receive book monies, and it's in charge of any tax filings that are required in your state as pertaining to the sale of goods. If your state requires sales tax, you might need to apply for a certificate or number in order to sell goods and pay the sales tax you owe. (More on these types of particulars in chapter 10.)

With your marketing/sales hat on, you'll strategize where to promote your book, what to say about your book, who you're trying to reach with your book, and why they should buy your book. (Remember that people will buy something if it meets a basic need, provides a convenience, gives peace of mind, improves their image, bolsters their ego, is fun or entertaining, or saves or makes them money.) You might run social media campaigns, be a guest on podcasts for interviews, or speak live and in person to folks and spread the message that you have a book for sale. You look for opportunities to get your book in front of your ideal reader and watch sales numbers as you go. There are hundreds of ways to market and sell your book. Part 3 offers several avenues.

The makings of a good book include what you're focusing on when it comes to product/service development. This is how you ensure that your product comes to market "hot." You want it to look and sound *gooood*. In other words, don't skimp when it comes to developing your manuscript.

Distribution is both about who you work with as a publisher/press and what they're going to do for you by way of getting your book into stores—both online and off. But . . . it's also about what your own plan is regarding when you are able to sell directly to consumers. If you're not just going direct to Amazon and you are working with a publisher/press that you can order your books from at cost, you have the chance to order copies of your book and then sell them yourself at retail price (or some other price of your choosing).

> **What Does That Mean?** »»
>
> ### COST VERSUS RETAIL PRICE
>
> *Cost: the amount it takes for a publisher, printer, or distributor to produce your book before it's sold*
> *Retail price: the amount your reader will pay for your produced book once it's available for purchase*

The thing about this is when you sell directly to the consumer, you're the one on the hook for distribution, which means shipping that puppy out (more on this in chapter 11).

BEGIN WITH THE END IN MIND (KNOWING THAT THERE IS NO END)

What we want for you as a first-time author (or as an author about to do this again and wanting to do it differently) is to have in mind that your book is a business and you're at the helm. Going into your author journey with this understanding will make you more successful in the long run. When you understand that on the other side of writing and publishing a book is a product you must market, sell, distribute, and continue to market, sell, and distribute, you'll understand that the endgame of having a book is that there is no endgame. The idea that once you have written and published the book the journey has somehow come to its end, or that you've done all the hard work and it's now on the publisher to keep the book alive, relevant, and in front of folks, is misguided and inaccurate. The publication of your book is just the beginning—the beginning of a lifetime of promotion.

Did You Catch That?

The idea that once you have written and published the book the journey has somehow come to its end, or that you've done all the hard work and it's now on the publisher to keep the book alive, relevant, and in front of folks, is misguided and inaccurate. Getting published is only the beginning—the beginning of a lifetime of promotion.

Remember, your book is forever. If you want to be a successful author and you want your book to do well in the marketplace, you must see your book as a small business and you as its owner. Of course, you get to decide what success means to you and how much time, energy, and investment you put in.

We won't tell you that your book has to sell thousands of copies to be successful. However, if your measure of success is even one hundred copies, you'll still need to work for them. If your measure of success is more podcast interviews, you'll still have to determine how you use your book to do that, which means creating a strategy. Define your goals, metrics, and level of success on your terms, but know that to best achieve them, you'll want to look at your book as a business and have your CEO hat on at all times. Getting published is only the beginning.

TAKEAWAYS AND TO-DOS

Takeaways

- Authoring a book is like starting a small business, and as the author, you're the owner/founder/CEO of your book.
- There is an up-front investment to starting any business. Be prepared to INVEST in your book to do it well.
- A business has multiple departments, including administration, financial, marketing/sales, product/service development, and distribution. A book has all of the same.
- Be prepared to promote and SELL. Get comfortable with talking about your book and talking about it some more.
- The idea that once you have written and published the book the journey has somehow come to its end is misguided and inaccurate. The publication of your book is just the beginning of a lifetime of promotion.

To-Dos

- Check in with yourself about your mindset. Are you feeling confident about doing this or doubtful?
- Begin thinking about investing in your book.
- Define what your goals, metrics, and levels of success look like so you can build your book business plan around achieving those goals.

NOTES

_____

_____

_____

_____

_____

_____

_____

_____

_____

_____

_____

_____

_____

_____

_____

_____

_____

_____

_____

_____

_____

_____

_____

_____

_____

_____

_____

_____

_____

_____

_____

_____

_____

_____

_____

_____

_____

_____

_____

_____

_____

_____

_____

_____

SETTING UP YOUR BOOK AND BOOK BUSINESS FOR SUCCESS

If the idea of treating your book like a business sounds too intimidating, think in terms of giving it the attention it deserves after you have decided to bring it to life. Think of how you would care for a baby, pet, or new automobile—you don't just come home from the hospital, pet store, or car lot, then do nothing else. You nurture and support, you feed and walk, you change the oil and rotate the tires. The same goes for your book. Treat it like a business, or if that sounds too intense, take care of it.

To make this more manageable, we're focusing this entire chapter on the nitty-gritty details you need to know in order to best care for your book business. These are the things that are going to set you up for success and help you put on that fancy-schmancy and oh-so-very-important CEO hat.

Inside this chapter, we cover everything from which distributors to use, product identifiers, and pricing to the best times to publish, open bank accounts, and more. Not only have we examined the nuts and bolts of your book business, but we've also included a ridiculous amount of additional information in the appendices: checklists, budgets, tip sheets, and more. This chapter is your 101, and the additional material in the back of the book is your graduate-level stuff, so don't forget to spend time back there.

DISTRIBUTORS

At the time of this writing, the two distributors that lead the industry are Amazon KDP and IngramSpark. Without them, the only person who will sell your book is you. Both platforms allow you to self-publish your e-books, paperbacks, and hardcover books, and both platforms allow you to publish and upload revisions for free (that is, as of the time of this writing. This can totally change). The mistake authors frequently make is publishing only on Amazon KDP because it's slightly easier than publishing on IngramSpark. However, when you publish only on Amazon KDP's platform, the only place your book is available for purchase is on Amazon's sites. Yes, Amazon KDP indicates that through its platform, you have the option to make your book available on a global scale, but that availability extends only throughout Amazon's global scale, meaning your book is available not only on amazon.com but also, for example, on amazon.ca or amazon.in, Amazon's sites for buyers based in Canada and India, respectively. When you publish on IngramSpark, though, your book is positioned to get picked up by other online retailers, such as Barnes & Noble, Books-A-Million, Porchlight Book Company, Walmart, and several others. Publishing only on Amazon KDP cannot get your book on Barnes & Noble's site. The bottom line is you need to publish your book on both Amazon KDP and IngramSpark, not just Amazon KDP.

🎤 **Did You Catch That?**

You need to publish your book on both Amazon KDP and IngramSpark.

METADATA AND PRODUCT IDENTIFIERS

This section is all about the importance of your book's discoverability. Get used to seeing that word or some form of it because the business side of your book relies on your making your book as discoverable as possible, and that starts with your book's metadata—any and all data that describe your book—and product identifiers. This involves choosing the right genre, categories, and subject code(s), plus selecting the best keywords and key phrases. It also includes making smart choices about your book's title, subtitle, pricing, publication date, International Standard Book Number (ISBN), search-engine-optimized long description and short description, and any other relevant information that prospective readers will use to locate your book. We will get to keywords and key phrases later in this chapter. For now, let's get into genres, categories, and subject codes.

What Does That Mean?

YOUR BOOK'S IDENTIFIERS AND METADATA

Your book's identifiers are exactly what they sound like: the specific information that identifies your book and that people use to locate (and buy!) your book.

Genre: a classification system that identifies your book's type of content (e.g., fiction, nonfiction, historical fiction, poetry, or autobiography); it's essentially the larger umbrella under which your book falls.

Category: a division within a genre that identifies your book's topical content; after the broader genre is identified, its category is its subsection that informs where your book is placed in relation to other books that are in the same genre.

BISAC Subject Code: a nine-character alphanumeric code from the Book Industry Standards and Communications (BISAC) Subject Codes List that corresponds to your book's category and that tells book retailers, distributors, and librarians where your book belongs on their shelves. They are not going to read the book's description to figure this out.

Title: the name of your book, usually chosen by the author, that should be focused on what would hook their ideal audience's interest.

> **What Does That Mean?** — *(continued)* —
>
> **Subtitle:** *a phrase following the title of your book that gives the title more context, sometimes conveying the promise of the book and usually rich with keywords for better discoverability.*
>
> **Pricing:** *the retail cost for someone to purchase your book.*
>
> **Publication date:** *the date associated with the official release of your book to the public.*
>
> **ISBN:** *a ten- or thirteen-digit unique product identifier used by publishers, booksellers, libraries, and online retailers for ordering, listing, stocking, and tracking sales of your book.*

Let's return to our baby analogy: at a minimum, you confirm for everyone the gender—for those of us who are fine with categorizing people as such—so everyone knows what pronouns to use (category), you give the baby a name (title), and you apply for a Social Security number (ISBN) and birth certificate (publication date). It's outstanding metadata that will lead readers to your book; that's what they depend on to find their next great read. But if you are working with a publisher, then you do not have to concern yourself with much, if any, of this because your publisher takes care of all these details for you.

Genre Information, Categories, and Codes

In order for shoppers to find your book, booksellers need to stock it, or, in other words, they need to know what area and shelf to put it on in the store. If booksellers don't know where on their shelves your book belongs, then they can't or won't bother to stock it. If booksellers can't or won't stock it, then people can't find it. If people can't find it, then they can't buy it. If they can't buy it, then you can't make money. And if you can't make money, then you don't have a book business. And what's the name of this chapter again? Okay. Let's keep going.

Genre information is encapsulated in the Book Industry Standards and Communications (BISAC) Subject Codes that you enter when you submit your book to IngramSpark or Amazon KDP for distribution. These genre codes, or BISAC Subject Codes, are what libraries and book-sellers use to categorize your book so they quickly and easily know where to put it on their bookshelves because, as you can imagine, it's not enough to have your book simply listed as nonfiction. What *kind* of nonfiction is it? That's where choosing the right genre and BISAC Subject Code gets your book to the right location. Just as a box of Frosted Flakes isn't randomly stocked on the cereal aisle of the grocery store, your book doesn't get randomly stocked on a retailer's book aisle. Frosted Flakes are placed alongside other sugary, crunchy grains of "goodness" as opposed to next to the flavorless, fiber-packed chunks of wheat. There's a method to the madness. And you need to ensure that your book gets placed alongside those books that are similar to it so that when people look for "that thing" your book does, your book is one of the options that automatically pops up in the search results next to other reads that make similar promises.

What Does That Mean? ⟩⟩

BISAC SUBJECT CODES

Developed and maintained by the Book Industry Study Group, BISAC Subject Codes are used by all publishers everywhere and are the industry standard for categorizing books. As interests grow, as our lives evolve, and as more content and different subject matters make it into the marketplace, more book categories will develop, and these codes obviously will expand. As a side note, keep in mind that Amazon uses the BISAC codes, slightly altering them for its platform, meaning that the categories you enter and see on the Amazon KDP platform will not perfectly jibe with the categories you see that are associated with the BISAC codes.

When your book is assigned the right categories, which associates it with the right BISAC codes, it supports proper placement in the bookstore (or digital marketplace) and better discoverability. This means that with these identifiers—your categories and codes—you want to get as specific as possible. For instance, your book may fall into the genre of nonfiction, but don't stop there because how many nonfiction books are out there? Right.

When you drill down, you uncover that your nonfiction book is, for example, a self-help book focused on interpersonal communication. As such, one of the categories or subjects for your book becomes "Nonfiction/Self-Help/Communication and Social Skills," along with the corresponding BISAC code of SEL040000. Further brainstorming leads you to decide that your book is also devoted to personal growth and success. Enter the second category or subject of "Nonfiction/Self-Help/Personal Growth/Success," with a BISAC code of SEL027000.

When you publish and you choose categories that make sense for both your book and your reader, this makes it indisputable as to where the bookseller places your book and exceedingly more likely that the right reader will find it. (For information on where to find the list of all the BISAC Subject Codes, as well as guidance for how to select your codes, see appendix G: Writing and Publishing Must-Have Resource List.)

Did You Catch That?

When you choose categories that make sense, it is indisputable as to where the bookseller places your book and exceedingly more likely that the right reader will find it.

Depending on the platform you publish on, you can place your book in two or three categories. Choose wisely; choose a category or categories that match your book, your reader's expectations, and the promise of what your book delivers. And when it comes to the codes, choose the ones that fit your reader the best or that fit who you think your reader is while trying to capture as many readers as possible. Remember, if your book is not set up to be easily discovered by your ideal reader, then what are you doing?

Or if your book ends up in the wrong space, then that makes it hard for your book to end up in shopping carts—much less in the checkout.

Did You Catch That?

Choose a category or categories that match your book, your reader's expectations, and the promise of what your book delivers.

To arrive at the right categories and codes for your book, the most obvious option is to think about what exactly your book covers and the promise it makes. The next option is to look at other books' categories. Examine those books that are most comparable to yours and that are already on the market, identifying the categories they're in, whether your book fits into any of them, and whether there are other category options available to you. This is one step in making your book discoverable.

Pro Tip

To arrive at the right categories and codes, think about what exactly your book covers and the promise it makes and examine other similar books' categories.

Title and Subtitle

The next step in making your book discoverable is being strategic with its title. We are not looking at titling your book from a creative standpoint; we will cover that in chapter 6. For now, it's time to look at the title of your book from the business side of things.

It can be tempting to think that it's sufficient to give your book a title that you absolutely love, that you believe captures the essence of your book, or that you think is cute or cheeky. However, don't stop at a title you've been sharing everywhere and with *everyone* and end there. If the title has meaning for only you and no one else, then what's the point or value in any of that?

Did You Catch That?

There's no point or value in your book's title having meaning for only you and no one else.

Another element to consider is length. Keep your title between one and six words or no more than sixty characters long. The entire title should be no more than 200 characters. We mention this because there's not a lot of word real estate. You have to be intentional because there's not a lot of space to work with and yet the words you choose for your title have a BIG job: identifying what your book is about *and* hooking your buyer's (reader's) interest.

Be comfortable with changing your title or starting your manuscript without a title. (We won't tell you about our journey down this road!) You may start writing and have no idea whatsoever of what to name your book, or you may have a title but then you finish your manuscript and realize it does not quite capture what you've written. Either way, a good practice is to look at your table of contents, then determine if your title corresponds to your contents and vice versa. Ask yourself if your title accurately reflects the contents of the book or if your table of contents delivers on the promise your title makes. It's like a tie and hankie combo; they need to work together.

Making Your Book Discoverable

The first step in making your book discoverable is identifying its categories and codes (go back to the section Genre Information, Categories, and Codes in this chapter). The next step is identifying the words people most commonly use to search for information on the topic your book covers. The goal here is to selectively add those keywords to your book's title.

At the time of this writing, Google has a keyword search tool that helps you discover the exact search words people use and which ones are the most popular. The point is when you know these words—the precise terms people use to go in search of the problems your book solves—and when you use them to build your book's metadata, you better position your book to show up in those Google results. (See appendix G: Writing and Publishing Must-Have Resource List for information on using Google Ads [formerly known as GoogleAdwords] to identify keywords and popular search terms.) Be as specific as possible with your keywords, though, because this is how you find your target reader and how your target reader finds and ultimately buys your book. For example, the word "stress" could relate to stress in the workplace, the stress placed on word syllables, how to engineer a bridge to handle stress, and many more options. So, use not only keywords but also key phrases so you can be as specific as possible.

Pro Tip

Be as specific as possible with your keywords and key phrases because this is how you find your target reader and how your target reader finds and buys your book.

If you want people to find your book, your title needs to contain those keywords and those key phrases—the words people most commonly use to search for information on the topic your book covers. Ideally, the subtitle is where you will include keywords and/or key phrases because the subtitle can be as long as you want. (Remember to keep your title between one and six words or no more than sixty characters long, and the entire title should be no more than 200 characters in length.) At the time of this writing, you have the option to have two to ten keywords and key phrases associated with your book. But all of them cannot go in your title, and your title also must make sense! That's where you rely on other metadata to do its work; that's where your book's description comes in. Include in your book's description any of those keywords and phrases you couldn't squeeze into the subtitle so that your book is still positioned to be among the online search results when those words and phrases are searched by prospective buyers.

Did You Catch That?

If you want people to find your book, your title needs to contain the words people most commonly use to search for the topic your book covers. Plain and simple.

When you identify the best categories for your book, you know which ones to attach to your title, making it easy for people to find your book and for distributors and retailers to know where to put it. And when you identify the keywords people use to find the kind of content you've written, you make it easy for your book to turn up in search results and for it to land in people's shopping carts.

To be clear and transparent, we are simplifying this process quite a bit. Make no mistake about it—this is a time-consuming process when done personally and manually. But there are multiple tools out there that will identify profitable keywords, what shoppers type into Amazon's search bar, and categories for your book, and if you work with a publisher, they will perform this research for you. Again, see appendix G: Writing and Publishing Must-Have Resource List for information on using Google Ads to identify keywords and popular search terms to help you with discovering the winning words to put in your book's title to improve its profitability.

Price

You do not want to have your price so high that you price yourself out of the market. At the same time, you do not want to have it so low that the total cost of production and shipping is more than what a customer actually pays for it. To determine your book's retail price, conduct market research on books similar to yours in genre, topic, and length to gauge how much you should charge.

Then, find out from Amazon KDP or IngramSpark how much it will cost to produce your book, and you are ready to settle on what you will charge for your book. Remember, that at the time of this writing,

Amazon, Barnes & Noble, and other online retailers will retain anywhere from 40 percent to 55 percent of the net profits from the sale of your book. (See chapter 10 for more on the economics of book pricing and royalties.)

Publication Date

There is no such thing as an absolutely perfect time to publish, but there are some times of the year that are better than others. Unless you are an established author or are incredibly well known, it is not recommended that you publish during the holiday season because new books by big names will have everyone's attention. Established authors know this and target the holiday sales periods. The summertime reading season is the top-selling season for books, but that does not mean you should avoid the spring or fall. Depending on your genre and topic, spring or fall may be the perfect season for getting your book on shelves.

According to a combination of sources including Forbes, BookBaby, and Self-Publishing Review, here's what readers crave and the topics they are reading at certain times throughout the year; use this as a guide for when you think is the ideal time to publish your book:

What Readers Crave

TYPES PEOPLE CRAVE	WHEN THEY CRAVE THEM
Romance, self-help, self-improvement, business, cooking/health/diet, finance, and design	January through April
Adventure, fantasy, fiction, children's books, and travel	May through August
Academic, horror, and paranormal	September and October
Children's books, cooking, picture books, quizzes, and novelty	November and December

These are not hard and fast parameters for when you should publish your book depending on your topic. When you're ready to flip the switch, do it! You don't want any excuse to keep putting it off. But, if you want to be strategic, treat your book like a business, add your book to the marketplace just at the time when people are looking for fresh content on a particular topic, then pay attention to the timing of reading interests.

And when identifying the exact date on which to publish, some will choose to publish on a date that has special meaning to them. For instance, you might publish your memoir on your birthday, or you might publish a book that also serves as a marketing tool on your business's anniversary. You can certainly choose any date you like, but keep in mind that books typically release on Tuesdays.

Pro Tip

You can choose any date you like to publish, but books typically release on Tuesdays.

ISBNs

An ISBN is a *must* if you want to sell and make your book available anywhere other than from the trunk of your car. It is tempting to opt for the free ISBN offered through Amazon KDP (if you choose to go that publishing route and that route only), but with *that* ISBN, you can publish your book only on Amazon, precluding you from making your book available at other marketplaces, such as Target, Walmart, Apple Books, Books-A-Million, Barnes & Noble, and many others. (Remember, your mom told you that there was no such thing as a free lunch. With anything that's free, there's usually a catch.)

To be clear, yes, you can use that free ISBN from Amazon KDP, but if you choose to sell your book at any other marketplace, you will need to get an additional ISBN, which costs. With this, you might say, "What's the big deal? I can get the free one for now, then purchase a second one later if I want to broaden my book's reach, right? Sounds easy enough to me."

Yes, it does sound easy enough, but that choice makes things more complicated for your book and your readers, and you don't want that. Ideally, you want one set of identifiers associated with your title. You want people to be able to go anywhere with one title and one ISBN and be able to easily locate your book. When you have multiple ISBNs associated with the same title, it muddies the water and can cause confusion. So, again, do it right from the beginning, and purchase from a legitimate ISBN provider one ISBN that you own and that serves as your book's one and only identifier of that kind. That way, you make your book available everywhere. (See appendix E: The Cost to Self-Publish for where to go to purchase an ISBN and for the cost involved.)

What Does That Mean? ▶▶

DO IT RIGHT FROM THE BEGINNING AND PURCHASE FROM A LEGITIMATE ISBN PROVIDER

Purchase your own ISBN from the beginning and from a reputable ISBN provider, such as Bowker Identifier Services (also known as simply Bowker), so your book is available everywhere. There are other ISBN service providers out there in addition to Bowker that (claim to) offer ISBNs at price points that are lower than Bowker's prices. Be very wary. Although some of their names may sound legit, some of these providers may not be legitimate at all and may take your money and issue you an ISBN that has already been issued/assigned to a title owned by someone else.

In this case, typically, an author obtains the ISBN early in the writing and/or publishing process, then a lot of time passes before the unsuspecting author uploads their book for distribution, and during the distributor's metadata validation process is when the author finds out that the ISBN is already in use. Oftentimes in these scenarios, the bad actor goes incommunicado, and the author is out even more money with having to go to Bowker to purchase a legitimate ISBN.

The moral of the story? Do not get drawn in by an attractive lower price. Do it right from the start and purchase your ISBN from Bowker.

It's important to note that for each and every format in which you publish your book—paperback, hardcover, or e-book—you will need a different ISBN even if it is the same title and the same edition. So, for example, if you plan to publish your book as a paperback and as an e-book, then you will need two different ISBNs: one for each format.

Pro Tip

For each and every format in which you publish your book—paperback, hard-cover, or e-book—you will need a different ISBN even if it is the same title and the same edition.

Library of Congress Control Number

It is optional to get your book's Library of Congress Control Number (LCCN), and at the time of this writing, there is no cost involved with applying for and receiving one. An LCCN is assigned to the catalog record created for each book in the Library of Congress's cataloged collections. The LCCN is key in the event that the Library of Congress decides to add your book to its collection, and having an LCCN to add to your book's copyright page adds a layer of credibility to your work.

Getting an LCCN is a two-step process: (1) you first will need to apply to participate in the Library of Congress's Preassigned Control Number program; (2) then, you apply for the LCCN. Bear in mind that there is a minimum page count required for your book to get accepted into the LCCN program. Books that are too short will not be accepted and therefore will not get an LCCN assigned to them. Check with the Library of Congress to confirm its requirements.

Again, this step of securing an LCCN for your book is optional, but again, an LCCN adds a level of credibility to your book. Unlike ISBNs, you do not need a different LCCN for each format in which you publish your book. When publishing a paperback plus an e-book of your book at the same time, for instance, the same LCCN applies to both formats. But if you publish a new edition of your book, then you will need to submit an application for a new LCCN for the book's new edition.

Did You Catch That?

Securing an LCCN for your book is optional, but it adds a level of credibility to your book.

Copyright Your Book

Once you write or type your manuscript/book, it is automatically protected under US copyright law without your having to formally register. You are not even required to use the registered copyright symbol, and your work is protected. However, still register your book with the US Copyright Office (USCO). Doing so guards against others trying to lay claim to any portion of your work. With that official registration, certifying you as the owner of the contents of the book, you position yourself to have standing in a legal proceeding. Without it, it's only your word against everyone else's, claiming the date you first wrote and had the legal right to claim ownership of the content. With it, you have irrefutable registered evidence and documentation of when you first wrote and had the legal right to claim ownership of the content. At the time of this writing, you are charged a fee when you submit to USCO your claim/copyright application to officially register your work. (If you are located outside of the United States, be sure to check your local copyright laws, as different protocols are likely in place for copyrighting your work.)

So, do it.

Copyright your work.

You don't want some ticked-off former colleague showing up on the scene, trying to say that you stole their idea and maliciously published it under your name. Get a date stamp on your brilliance, and the second you complete your manuscript, apply for your copyright with USCO so that you can protect your intellectual property. And ensure that you include a copyright page in the front matter of your book (this should appear before your table of contents); it puts people on notice that your intellectual property has been protected, and the copyright certificate, once received from USCO, protects you and your book.

> ### Pro Tip
>
> *Do it. Copyright your work, and ensure that you include a copyright page in the front matter of your book.*

Once your book is published, it's important that you remain in control of your work. Officially copyrighting a book with USCO unequivocally ensures that you are the legal owner of the work you've created in case there is ever a need to litigate in the future.

Bear in mind that once you submit your application to USCO, the copyright process can take anywhere from two to four months. If you're already published, you may wonder if you can still copyright your book. Absolutely. A book can be copyrighted after it's been published. The sooner, the better, though. So, if you do submit your application and receive your copyright certificate after the book has already been published, make sure that you return to your copyright page in your book and update it as needed, adding the year of copyright and the registered copyright symbol.

Still confused? Unsure? Need this broken down step by step? We've got you. It's all inside appendix H: The Self-Publishing Checklist.

BANKING, SELLING, AND TRACKING

As you would do with any business—establish a bank account, track your sales, and strategize how you will get your product or service in front of those who need it—you do the same with your book . . . if you are serious about seeing it in the hands of more than just your cousins and close friends, that is. It's not a must, but if you want to make the most of this product you've worked hard to create, then treat it like a business and have a systematic approach to keeping tabs on its performance and how you can improve its reach.

Handling Sales and Overall Finances for Your Book

Before you start spending money on your book business (or as soon as possible thereafter) and before you start accepting money for book sales, you need to open a business bank account. Yes, you can have your royalties sent directly to your personal bank account, but—there's always a "but"—it makes for a much clearer financial picture as it relates to your book if you have a separate bank account dedicated to all monies associated with your book. If you opened a bakery, you would not blur the lines and use your personal checking account to pay salaries, buy supplies, and accept customer payments for your legendary cream puffs. Well, you can, but what a mess that would be to wade through what's what as you work to keep your shop's doors open and your business thriving.

Open a separate account that is dedicated to monetary expenditures and gains relative to your book. When it's time to assess your book's performance, determine your next steps with your book, or file your taxes for the year, you have those numbers in one place, providing a more streamlined experience for running your book business. Visit your preferred banking institution for more information or to get started. The Small Business Administration's website provides great information regarding opening business bank accounts (learn more in appendix G: Writing and Publishing Must-Have Resource List.)

Pro Tip

If you are already a business owner and your book is directly connected to your business, then there's no need to establish yet another business bank account. Simply use it for all expenses and royalties related to your book. But the operative phrase here is "directly connected to your business." If you own a dental office and you write and publish a book about training puppies, then we're not so sure that there's a direct connection between the two; you'll want to establish a separate bank account for your book. But remember, we're authors, not bankers or lawyers, so don't try to haul us into court for anything related to setting up a bank account for your book. Make sure you seek the counsel of the appropriate professionals who can properly advise you.

Now, before you can open that account, you need a federal tax ID number or an employer identification number (EIN). (And if you already own a business and/or have covered this base, then you can totally skip this paragraph. But only this paragraph. Don't go rogue on us!)

What Does That Mean?

EIN

An EIN, which is separate from your Social Security number, is a step to keeping your personal and business finances from intermingling. Obtaining an EIN is free and can be done online. The Internal Revenue Service's site has information on how to apply for an EIN, plus the Small Business Administration's website contains a wealth of information regarding federal and state tax ID numbers.

After you have your EIN, in addition to opening a business checking account, you will need to open one or more merchant services accounts so you can accept payments. You don't want to rely only on others to sell your book. You will want to sell it on your website and at in-person events. A checking account alone does not position you to be able to accept payments from people; it only positions you to be able to deposit money and pay vendors. Yes, there's the cash box you can pack around, but you're better than that. Besides, who carries cash anymore anyway? That means you need to be able to accept credit card payments and payments via merchant accounts, such as PayPal, Square, Venmo, Cash App, Stripe, and others. Just as was the case with setting up your bank account, you need your EIN, which is dedicated solely to your book's finances, to set up any one of these accounts.

Did You Catch That?

You don't want to rely only on others to sell your book. You need to be able to process and accept credit card payments or other forms of payments yourself via merchant accounts like PayPal, Square, Venmo, Stripe, and the like.

Each merchant account operates basically the same in that it allows you to accept payments, transfer those monies to your bank account of choice, issue refunds, and charge transaction fees. There are, of course, slight differences with each one. The most commonly used ones are PayPal and Square. Keep in mind that PayPal, Square, and most, if not all, other merchant account platforms assess a nominal fee with each transaction processed through their platform. (They have to make their money, too, right?) We recommend that you create merchant accounts with all of the most commonly used payment processors and ways that people like to pay for services and goods: PayPal, Square, Venmo, Cash App, and Stripe, at a minimum. That way, you are able to easily accept payments and send payments for anything associated with your book.

Finally, check with your individual state to confirm whether you need to have a state tax ID number and whether you need to charge sales tax when selling your book within your state of residence. If you personally sell your book across state lines, you will need to conduct research with the Internal Revenue Service or consult a tax attorney and/or a tax expert to find out the ID you need and what taxes, if any, you need to charge when selling your book.

Pro Tip

If an entity, such as a conference or a bookstore, sells your book in a state other than the state in which you reside, then that entity is responsible for taking care of attending to matters related to sales tax. If you plan to sell your book only on the websites of online retailers, such as Amazon or Barnes & Noble, then you do not have to worry about collecting taxes and having an ID to entitle you to do so because those retailers handle the appropriate collection of tax on sales of your book. If you will sell your book (either online from your own website or in person) and will personally handle the transaction, then conduct your research with the Internal Revenue Service to take the steps necessary to ensure you are in compliance as it relates to collecting any necessary taxes and having the proper ID to do so.

Know How Your Book Is Performing

Both the Amazon KDP platform and IngramSpark provide sales reporting that you can access at any time to see your sales to date. At the time of this writing, IngramSpark will actually send monthly sales reports directly to the email address you have on file. When you generate and view these reports, though, keep in mind that both platforms allow for returns, so there may be a discrepancy between the sales numbers you see for a period of time through the current date and the sales numbers you see for the same reporting period some thirty days later.

> ### What Does That Mean?
>
> ## DISCREPANCY IN SALES NUMBERS
>
> *We have experienced this more than once. As a case in point, Ally had one expectation for what she would receive in a royalty check one quarter, only to be faced with the reality of finding herself in the red. More than a dozen copies of her book had been returned six months after a store had purchased them, reducing what she anticipated she would get paid. Ally ended up having to remit a payment to the distributor instead of the other way around, where the distributor would have remitted a payment to her.*
>
> *Bridgett had a similar experience. She had received reports of book sales that were looking really solid for the latter part of 2020, but come January 2021, that all turned around for her. She had not one, not two, not three, but four—count them, FOUR!—huge boxes of books placed at her doorstep by UPS due to returns. Conferences Bridgett was slated to speak at in 2020 had ordered them in anticipation of her appearing on their programs, and we all know what happened to in-person events in 2020. Not only did she have to pay the distributor the cost of printing the books, but because the distributor had on file that she wanted returns sent to her instead of having the distributor destroy them, she was also on the hook for the cost associated with the books being shipped to her. (We're talking thousands of dollars here, sports fans.) While she'd been paid a handsome amount of royalties based on the sale of her books to those organizations, Bridgett's profits were handsomely adjusted due to those returns.*

While you can check your sales numbers as often as you'd like, it's our recommendation that you check no more than on a monthly basis. Our preference is to check far less; there's something about checking only once every quarter or once every six months and seeing a bigger number that's so much more satisfying than a daily or monthly check. But regardless of how often you check, just make sure to check. Ensure that you understand where the most accurate sales data come from! Avoid assuming that everything is A-okay, and be prepared for the possibility of returns. That's a part of conducting business.

Pro Tip

Check your sales numbers no more than on a monthly basis.

What Does That Mean? ⟩⟩

THE MOST ACCURATE SALES DATA

If you have an Amazon Author Central account, book sales information is provided from NPD BookScan, and it includes Amazon print book sales plus the sales of your book from more than 10,000 retailers across the United States. However, these data are not accurate. The most accurate data is contained in your Amazon KDP account, not your Amazon Author Central account. Additionally, your IngramSpark account or your publisher-generated reports will contain the most accurate book sales data.

Historical analysis will tell you in what months your book performs really well and in what months there's a slump. This data will inform your marketing efforts, the strategies that are working, and which ones need tweaking. For example, if you go on a podcast blitz, appearing on show after show and discussing your book in a month's time but you see little sales activity, then you will rethink your podcast strategy. Perhaps podcasting is not a good fit for you and your book, or you need to tweak your messaging, or you need to assess how good of a job you did with ensuring that people knew how to purchase your book. A number of variables are at play, but that's another conversation on messaging and positioning. (Check out chapter 8 on marketing strategies.) On the flip side, let's say you speak at a conference, and in that same month of your speaking engagement, you see a spike in sales. Assuming it was your rock-star performance at that event, that is a conference you will want to attend and speak at again and even rally for the opportunity to make an appearance at a book signing at the event! But you know this only because you put in the effort to track your book sales, so you know how it's performing. (More on podcasting is covered later in this chapter, and for more on speaking at events, see chapter 12.)

DISTRIBUTING, WAREHOUSING, AND SHIPPING

The distributing, warehousing, and shipping of your book will look differently depending on whether you work with a publishing company, if you self-publish and work only with online retailers, or if you choose to perform personal fulfillment and have readers order your book directly through you. It is not uncommon for all of these scenarios to apply to an author. Not only do they have their publisher take care of book sales, but they (the author) can also have their book listed on Amazon's site. Plus, they can sell their book on their website (which means having to have books on hand to fulfill orders). This is quite common and is not as complicated as it sounds. Let's see at how warehousing, distribution, and shipping look in all those instances so that you are prepared.

Distributing

When it comes to distribution—the process and logistics of making your book available to consumers—this is where you want to do more than just sell your book on Amazon. Yes, Amazon is a great starting place, but as we already stated, it limits your book's reach. Everyone flocks to Amazon, but you're missing out on additional opportunities if you do not also make your book available elsewhere.

If you work with a publisher, then the publisher will take care of distribution for you, enabling your book to get listed with online retailers, such as Amazon, Barnes & Noble, Books-A-Million, Bookshop, Porchlight Book Company, Walmart, and others. But if you self-publish, listing your book with Amazon KDP and IngramSpark, then you have done the necessary legwork to get your book widely distributed, and there's nothing further you need to do. Bear in mind that there are other distributors, but Amazon KDP and IngramSpark are the most commonly used ones and tend to be the platforms that have the fewest number of hoops to jump through to get distribution for your book.

What Does That Mean? ⟫

GETTING DISTRIBUTION FOR YOUR BOOK

Amazon KDP and IngramSpark are the industry giants in the book distribution world. If you want to do more than sell your book on your own, and you want to make your book widely available, then you will lean heavily on Amazon KDP and IngramSpark.

Amazon KDP and IngramSpark allow you to self-publish your book and make any updates to it for free. When you distribute with Amazon KDP, you are able to make your book available on a global scale, and your book is listed for sale on all Amazon sites.

Like Amazon KDP, IngramSpark makes your book available on a global scale; your book is listed for sale not only on Amazon's websites but also on other online retailers' sites. Your royalties tend to be lower when you distribute with IngramSpark than when you distribute with Amazon KDP, but your book's reach is vaster than if you publish with Amazon KDP alone.

If you sell on your website, you are personally responsible for all the processing and logistics of making it available and getting it to your consumer. This involves marketing, payment processing, and all the steps in fulfillment: packaging, printing shipping labels, physically getting the packaged books to the post office or another shipment service, paying the cost of postage, and providing the customer with tracking details. You can also enlist an order fulfillment service that takes care of all that for you for a flat rate.

Direct Selling, Warehousing, and Shipping Yourself

As you can imagine, when you work with a publisher or when you sell your book at an online retailer's site or at a physical bookstore, you do not have to worry about the warehousing of your book. Those entities have their own process for stocking and storing your book. However, for those sales you personally handle either via sales from your website or sales at in-person events, you will need to take care of obtaining the necessary number of copies of your book to fulfill those orders.

If you work with a publisher, then you will be able to purchase copies of your book at a significantly reduced rate, usually for what it costs to produce your book plus a nominal administrative fee that covers shipping and handling. If you self-publish and do not go through a publisher, you can order author-priced copies from Amazon KDP or IngramSpark or you can use a printer, such as 48 Hour Books (if you need them in a hurry) or Lulu, which offers print-on-demand options (these are all listed in appendix G: Writing and Publishing Must-Have Resource List).

Now, if you buy author copies with the intent to sell them directly, you'll need to warehouse (read: store) them somewhere. Do you have a basement, closet, or storage space to keep them safe and clear of moisture or strong light? Having your books in a damp or heavily lit place could ruin the pages or fade the cover art.

When it comes to shipping, you can take the books to the local post office, UPS, FedEx, or a fulfillment center. Just note that the cheapest option, a media or book rate, is not always available if you do not ship via the US Postal Service. Also, ensure that you have a tracking number corresponding with your shipment to provide to your customer and to administratively track to guarantee your book's arrival. When you make purchasing available on your website, be sure to note the estimated shipping and arrival time for your customer if they order directly from you.

(Pro Tip)

Conduct your research to ensure that you put in place shipping logistics that make the most sense for you and your budget. Shipping your books as media mail through the US Postal Service will typically be the least expensive route; however, you will be responsible for the packing materials, the actual packing, labeling, and getting the books to the post office. A fulfillment center may be more convenient but will be costlier than the US Postal Service. Do your research, and decide on what your budget, time, and energy can afford.

Settling on a shipping method isn't the only shipping concern. How will you package your books? You can choose to put them in a simple, plain bubble mailer, or you can select something on brand from a place like UPrinting or Zazzle. This is all a part of your book business and your book's brand.

As is the case with any business, there are several moving parts, and in order for it to be successful, all those parts must get the right attention. Treating your book like it's a business is no different. As we've covered here, you have to take care of confirming your book's metadata and product identifiers; copyrighting your intellectual property; and distribution, warehousing, and shipping. Additionally, you have to attend to financials, including banking, selling your book, and staying informed on how your book is performing. You can do all or parts of this yourself, or you can totally outsource all or parts of the work. But never feel like you *have* to do it all or figure it out yourself. Think who, not how. To get you thinking along those lines, our coverage in chapter 13 of partners in the publishing industry who can support you will certainly get you there. For now, think of your book as more than just some words. From the start, treat it like a business.

TAKEAWAYS AND TO-DOS

Takeaways

- Your book is not ready to make a public appearance until you have secured all of your product identifiers and you have taken care of protecting your intellectual property.
- Ensure that your monies that are associated with the production and sale of your book do not mingle with your personal money.
- Be ready to position your book to reach as many purchasers as possible.

To-Dos

- Make a list of the identifiers you need for your book and check them off as you obtain them.
- Prepare to sell your book anywhere (in person and online), track your sales, and be ready to accept and deal with the reality of returns.
- Check with local, state, and federal laws and regulations to ensure that you are in compliance with regard to applying for and obtaining tax identifiers as well as charging sales tax.
- Sell your book on more platforms than just your website and Amazon.
- If you sell your book on your website, have a plan for how you will handle the logistics of distribution, warehousing, and shipping.

NOTES

_____

_____

_____

_____

_____

_____

_____

_____

_____

_____

_____

_____

_____

_____

_____

_____

_____

_____

_____

_____

_____

_____

_____

PART 2

THE MAKINGS OF A GOOD BOOK

CHAPTER 4

UNDERSTANDING THE BOOK LIFE CYCLE

So, let's assume that you know it's time to write a book because you've identified with one or more of the seven signs we covered in chapter 1, and you even went ahead and interviewed yourself using appendix C: Interview Yourself: Ten Questions to Ask before You Start Your Book. You've got your CEO hat on, you understand that your book is your business, and you've got some of your endgame in mind. If you've really been working hard, getting serious, and being intentional, you've also completed appendix D: Book Planning Scorecard to evaluate just how ready you are to do this book-writing thing. This means you're ready to write, right?

Yes and no. It depends on how you're thinking of approaching the writing process.

When people think about writing a book, most think about the actual writing. They think about what they'll say, how to begin, the length of the manuscript, titling, and sometimes cover design. It's fun to imagine what the cover of your book will look like. We don't deny that. We loved dreaming up the covers of each of our books. (Shameless author plug: you can read about our titles in the About the Authors section of this book.)

The thing is, there is WAY more to the development of a book than the writing aspect of things; although, there's no denying that writing is a HUGE piece. No writing, no book. That's a simple enough equation to understand. But developing the manuscript is only one piece—one phase, actually—of the puzzle to bring your book through publication.

PACING, TIMING, AND STICKING TO THE PROCESS

Are you thinking about jumping in to pen the first chapter, or are you thinking about starting with an outline? We would argue that one of these is a better way to begin than the other. We bet you know which one it is. But there's one other thing we want to reiterate before we go there.

You may recall what we said in chapter 2 about being a CEO: good CEOs don't take shortcuts, skip steps, or skimp on budgets. We want to talk about the shortcuts and skipped-steps piece. Sometimes we get authors who come to us with an urgency to get the book written and published. Sometimes that urgency has to do with an event coming up where they need a book. Bridgett got her first book cranked out and published in less than a month (NOT ADVISABLE UNDER ANY CIR-CUMSTANCES!) for a conference where she had been confirmed to speak. She did it without knowing anything about publishing her own book, and she was successful. Bridgett was also very familiar with writing, so she at least had that going for her. Bridgett is in the 1 percent in that she got it done quickly and right. That's to say that it's not impossible, but it's not typical, and it's also not something we would recommend (even Bridgett doesn't recommend it, and she did it).

Now, it is possible that with a fully cooked manuscript and the right publisher who knows what they're doing, you can bring a book through publication quickly. But that requires many things needing to be exactly right. The manuscript has to be totally ready. The publisher has to be totally ready. All parties need to work together as a well-oiled machine. And we all know that life rarely lines up this perfectly.

When you get into this book-writing journey, we want you to understand your schedule, your lifestyle, your other responsibilities, and your restrictions and boundaries around time. We also want you to be aware of how well you work and what causes you to be distracted or to procrastinate. All of these things are factors when coming up with a realistic plan for developing your book and bringing it to publication—not to mention what will make you feel more grounded in what you're doing rather than rushing.

There are two things that can help you with planning and pacing, and that's having an up-front understanding of the book's life cycle *and* developing an outline and schedule to work from. Understanding the life cycle, developing an outline, and creating a writing schedule will only be useful if you're committed to the iterative process of book development and to producing a quality book.

IN OUR EXPERT OPINION—FAST DOESN'T MEAN GOOD

We see a lot of sponsored ads for programs that promote getting your book "done" in ten or thirty days, following So-and-So's proven system. While neither of us has participated in one of those ten- or thirty-day programs, we understand the writing process and that it can be a messy and nonlinear kind of thing. We take issue with the idea that anyone can get a good book done in so few days even if they stop the rest of their lives to travel somewhere else and hole up in a room for that amount of time, focusing only on their book.

It may be possible to get a draft of your book done in a short period of time with determination, focus, diligence, and fending off any and all distractions. But then there are all kinds of editing and revision to get that manuscript where it needs to be for publication, and we would never recommend that the author tackle all that on their own. Now, if there are a lot of steps being skipped, and the manuscript is short, and people are hurrying to hit "print" on a self-publishing platform, maybe they are getting it "done," but then we would ask: what's the quality? In short, we say, if you see one of those ads, keep scrolling.

OPERATING WITH A PLAN AND NOT FLYING BY THE SEAT OF YOUR PANTS

In the writing community, there is the idea that you're either a *plotter* or a *pantser* when it comes to sitting down to write your book. These terms are usually used when talking about fiction or narrative nonfiction (like memoirs), where a plot would be central to writing a compelling story that follows the traditional story arc. As far as we're concerned, these terms are equally applicable and relevant to other types of nonfiction, like prescriptive, business, thought leadership—you name it.

What Does That Mean? ▶▶

TRADITIONAL STORY ARC

You may have heard about the story arc in high-school English class. The traditional story arc is the three-act plot structure that we see comprising most fiction books. The book begins by setting up the "normal" for the main character, then introduces a turning point (often called the inciting incident), which sends that character on a journey of some sort. That journey is made up of a series of moments that add tension to the story, culminating in a crisis, then a climax, and then falling tension before a new normal is established. This story arc looks a lot like a bell curve.

In nonfiction books, this arc could be looked at as the reader going on a journey. The beginning of the book sets up the problem for the reader, the middle part of the book offers transformation or change that helps the reader see a different way forward, and the final act of the book ties it all together to solve the reader's problem and provide next steps.

In our view, to be a *plotter* is to know where you're taking your book before you sit down to write. You're determining the plot before you pen a single word.

A *pantser* is a person who writes "by the seat of their pants"; they have no plan, no outline. We find that this approach is rarely successful in producing a well-written and, eventually, a well-read book. Given everything we've said to you up until now, you can guess which of these approaches we would promote.

We want you to be intentional about the book you write. Be purposeful about what you want to offer and to whom. And take the time necessary—whatever duration that is for you—to go through all the steps and not cut any corners. You're the CEO of this operation, after all, and your book is ultimately your final product—one you have to be confident about and proud to call yours. If you want to produce a fine final product that fabulously represents you and what you have to offer, do not merely wing it (or *pants it*).

Promise yourself right now that you'll take this book thing seriously. Promise us that you'll bust out all the stops. Take your time. Don't rush. And begin with a plan or an outline. We want you to know where you're heading with your book's material before you sit down to write. We also want you to know where you're heading in terms of the writing process or the book's life cycle. Having an understanding of each of the steps along the path to publication (and beyond) will help you best understand the step you're on and how to prepare for the next one up ahead.

THE BOOK LIFE CYCLE

We like to think of the book as having a life cycle because we like to think of the book as though it were a baby (which you probably already knew since we compared the product identifiers in the same way). This means that you, as the author, are its parent. Congratulations! You're both a parent *and* a CEO.

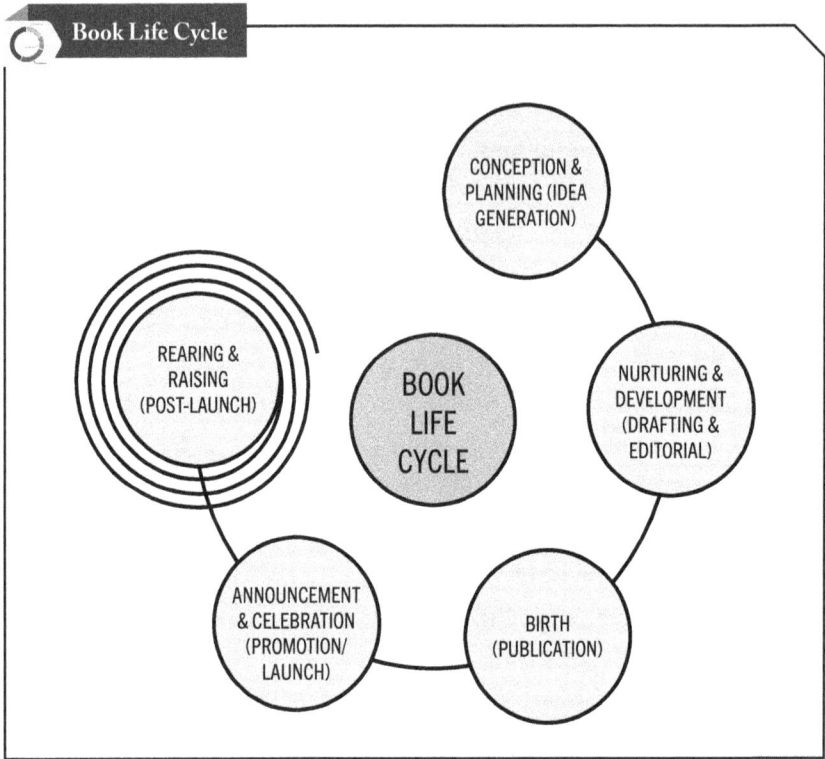

Book Life Cycle

CONCEPTION &
PLANNING (IDEA
GENERATION)

REARING &
RAISING
(POST-LAUNCH)

BOOK
LIFE
CYCLE

NURTURING &
DEVELOPMENT
(DRAFTING &
EDITORIAL)

ANNOUNCEMENT
& CELEBRATION
(PROMOTION/
LAUNCH)

BIRTH
(PUBLICATION)

Phase One: Idea Generation

Consider this, if you will. When you first come up with the idea of writing and publishing a book, you're *conceiving* the idea. This may happen immediately, meaning that the idea comes to you clear and fully cooked, and you're ready to move into writing. Or you may just get vague inklings of the idea and need more time for it to crystallize. Either way, there's a period of time in the very beginning when you have the seed of an idea and need some time to wrap your mind around what it will become and how you want to approach it. This is when having an outline and plan comes into play.

It's like that time during pregnancy when you start thinking about matters like which hospital, which doctors, and how you might change your diet. You might keep the pregnancy to yourself while you secretly search for baby names, pediatricians, and daycare providers. You create your birth plan and wishes.

This phase of the book life cycle is a good time to create a mind map, make an outline, and conduct research or gather resources. You plan, document, and envision your book. You get geared up to actually write the book with direction and clarity.

So, what goes in a book plan or an outline? You should include the following at a minimum: an overview or synopsis of your book, your reader profile, a working table of contents, and chapter abstracts. Let's break down each of these.

Consider your synopsis as an initial crack at what your back-cover blurb might be. It's a paragraph that summarizes your book, identifying who it's for, what it's about, and what it will offer the reader. By writing this (even if it evolves), you have something to work towards. It's like having your North Star. As you draft your manuscript, ask yourself, "Am I meeting my own objectives that I laid out in my synopsis?"

Your reader profile is a summary or bulleted list of psychographics, characteristics, or qualities of your reader that relate to why they would be interested in your book and what your book could offer them. You might choose to give your reader avatar a name and picture in addition to their profile description. Having your reader in mind can be helpful as you draft because you check in with that reader. We know it may sound weird, but have a conversation with your ideal reader. Ask them what they would need to know. Does a certain passage make sense? What else might they need to feel like their problem has been solved? Remember, your book is here to solve some kind of problem for your reader. So, talk with them as you write.

A working table of contents is what it sounds like. It's the at-a-glance list of parts and pieces to your book in order of how you intend for them to appear. The reason why it's a "working" table of contents is that titles and chapter placement are bound to change as you actually write the material. (Trust us. We know.) For a comprehensive list of what you should include in your table of contents and what's optional, see appendix H: The Self-Publishing Checklist.

Chapter abstracts are summaries of what happens in each chapter. Some authors write these out in paragraph style, while others create a bulleted list. They are your CliffsNotes version of what you intend for that chapter—its focus and main points.

If you want to go deeper with your outline, you can also do your own work around thinking about categories, BISAC Subject Codes, keywords, and a book comparison analysis. A book comparison analysis involves looking at recently published books (as in, the last two years) that are similar to yours, as well as the negative reviews of those books, to identify how your book fills a different gap in the market that these comparable books create. See what readers say is missing in those books or what is inadequately covered. This is good to know for positioning your book and your messaging—both of which are marketing items that will benefit you later.

Some outlines can even include ideas for your cover design, who you intend to work with down the road, what publishing path you're considering (which we discuss in chapter 9), the budget you have in mind, and more. How far you take your outline is up to you, but we say, at a minimum, start with the basics (a synopsis of your book, your reader profile, a working table of contents, and chapter abstracts.). With an outline on hand, you'll always know where you are, what you're trying to say, where you're heading next, and, ultimately, what your final destination is.

Now, there is a very formal kind of outline that some publishing paths require for nonfiction books and that is requested before the manuscript is written. This kind of outline is called a book proposal, and traditional publishers require these for most of their nonfiction books. Traditional publishing houses may offer a contract for a book based on the proposal alone and without any piece of the manuscript yet written.

There are several book proposal templates that can be found online that all identify the same types of things being included: synopsis, author bio, market analysis (targeted audience, relevancy, and comparable book titles), table of contents, chapter abstracts, and a sample chapter or two. Even if you don't intend on working with a traditional publisher, using a proposal template as your outline is more than sufficient for getting you in shape for manuscript development.

Phase Two: Drafting and Editorial

So, what's manuscript development? This is the part where you actually put pen to paper (or fingers to the keyboard), and words start to land on the page. Phase Two is when the manuscript is drafted (or written), reviewed, edited, and revised, which we cover extensively in chapter 5.

Returning to our pregnancy analogy . . . a full-term pregnancy is forty weeks. During that time, the woman's body is nurturing the growing life inside her. She eats and drinks certain foods or takes certain supplements. She gets plenty of rest, does yoga, and attends birthing classes—whatever it is that she thinks she needs to do to be in optimal laboring condition to deliver a healthy baby to this world. She might also work with midwives or doulas, depending on her birthing goals.

The development phase of writing a book is also multifaceted and can take several weeks to months (and even years) depending on your work style, schedule, deadline, and other factors. Each person approaches their book differently. Some write fast and furiously until the draft is done, not stopping to read what they last wrote. Others have difficulty moving ahead because they keep reviewing and rewriting the last section, aiming for perfection before they move on. Some write with only a couple of personal contacts (friends or family) to hold them accountable. Others join a writers' group, and some hire a writing or book coach (more on people who can help you in chapter 13 and in appendix F: People on the Publishing Path.)

There are several ways to approach writing the manuscript, and their effectiveness is based on the person and the execution. There is no one-size-fits-all approach to how you get the writing done. Really, there isn't.

A lot of clients come to us with stereotypical tropes about the writers who get up every morning at 5:00 a.m. and who won't quit until they've penned their daily word quota, all before they have breakfast or shower to get ready for work. While the 5:00 a.m. writers' club is a thing, it doesn't mean you have to be part of it.

Others will mention the writing schedules of some of the greats (like Hemingway) or famous writers everyone knows (like Stephen King) and think that that is the template. But they forget that these folks' livelihoods were/are writing. It was their job. We encourage you to realistically think about your schedule and your life, consider how you best work and produce, and come up with your own plan that fits you. To help you out, we've included appendix I: Developing Your Writing Plan, which asks a series of questions for you to consider while putting together a writing schedule and plan for working on your manuscript that best suits you and your life.

But regardless of the writing schedule you choose, there is a sure way to guarantee that your manuscript won't be as strong as it can be, and that is if you think this is going to be a "one and done" kind of thing. In other words, if you believe that you'll write one draft that's going to be pure gold and that one draft will be the final draft, your book will suffer. (Again, trust us on this one.)

Did You Catch That?

If your first draft is your final draft, your book will suffer.

The development phase of the book life cycle is all about taking the right actions and investing the right amount of time to truly create a wonderfully written and polished manuscript. We address manuscript development and more about this phase in chapter 5.

Phase Three: Publication

Congrats! It's delivery day! Push . . . push . . .

Phase Three, the publication phase, is the equivalent of labor starting and ending with bringing that baby into the world. Any number of things can happen during this phase depending on how you are publishing (self/ DIY, indie, hybrid, and traditional).

There is a wealth of information to cover on the various avenues of publishing, their advantages and disadvantages, and the processes that each avenue requires. We won't cover it all here because we'll quickly go down the rabbit hole (and we've devoted much of chapter 9 to explaining this topic). For now, we'll pare it down to two main things:

One, the publication phase includes your handing your manuscript over to the care and attention of a professional who will usher your manuscript through the final editorial stages, production (think cover design and interior layout/typesetting), printing, and then, finally, publication.

Two, do not wait to think about publishing until you're ready to publish unless you know when you get started that you intend to do everything *yourself*. When we're talking about doing everything yourself, we don't mean paying for everything yourself. Paying for everything yourself can be true with several publishing avenues (self/DIY, indie, and hybrid), but the person responsible for the actual work won't necessarily be you. What we're talking about is that you'll be the one responsible for making decisions and implementing those decisions even if that means you're not the one rolling your sleeves up, and instead you're hiring contractors to take on certain pieces for you. And for clarity's sake, when we say "do everything," we mean soup to nuts—drafting, editing, revising, cover design and layout, file creation, account setup, and so on.

Any time that someone else is involved in publishing your book, it means that they may have a different timeline than you have in mind. So, if you're determined to have a book out by a certain date or for a previously committed engagement, consider that date way back during the conception phase. Some presses have a six-month minimum window and can't produce and publish your book without that amount of time. The idea generation phase (Phase One) can also be a good time to consider publishing avenues and presses and to start making inquiries. (Appendices that you will find helpful include appendix F: People on the Publishing Path and appendix J: How to Determine If a Publishing Company Is Reputable.) You can continue to do this kind of work while you write the manuscript as well.

Pro Tip

The idea generation phase is a good time to consider your publishing avenues and start making inquiries.

What Does That Mean?

SIX-MONTH PUBLISHING WINDOW

So much is happening during this time; it's akin to the duck swimming in the water, gracefully gliding along while its little legs and webbed feet are frenetically moving underwater, trying to get from point A to point B. During this six-month window, everything involved with getting your book to market is taking place. Editors, depending on the type of editing your manuscript receives, are dotting all the i's and crossing all the t's. Designers are creating your cover, typesetting the interior to make it gorgeous, and creating social media graphics for your book. Proofers are making sure that all errors have been caught and corrected. Administrative professionals are securing identifiers for your book, such as its ISBN and LCCN. Other staff members are researching categories and codes for your book, submitting your copyright application to USCO, and submitting your book's details to distributors in preparation for your book to enter the marketplace.

And all the while, you, the author, are being called upon to review the work that's being completed, make decisions, request changes, or give the green light, approving each step in the process so that the publisher can commence with the next step. There is far more behind-the-scenes work taking place during these six months, and much of the timeline is dependent upon the author's responsiveness, but you get the idea. There's a lot going on! As a case in point, at Press 49, we have a minimum of seventy steps that must be completed by our team members to take writing from a manuscript to a published book. Seventy steps. We don't dare to bore you with listing them all here. The point is that those six months are a must!

Bottom line: research and understand your publishing options and have an idea of which you'd like to pursue before your manuscript is ready to hand over. Otherwise, there won't necessarily be anyone to hand it to just because you say "it's ready!"

Phase Four: Promotion/Launch

The promotion/launch phase is the equivalent of posting the birth announcement on Facebook with the baby's name, weight, and birthday and letting everyone know that the mother is fine. This is when your book is officially out there in the world or at least available for preorder. It's the fanfare and celebration of "I did it! I wrote a book!" It's driving people over to the book in those early days and trying to bump up those initial sales figures. This is the phase where you have the virtual Zoom party and invite all your friends or plan an in-person launch party at the local bookstore.

While the job of promoting your book is *never* done, when the book has first come out is the hottest and most successful time to do so—just like that baby is on top of everyone's mind for the first couple of weeks until they become old news and just another member of the family like poor Uncle Melvin. In other words, this phase is the shortest phase of the book's life cycle. Do you want to know which is the longest? It's the last one.

Phase Five: Post-Launch

Just like our babies are always our babies and we never stop parenting them even when they've started having children of their own, your book requires the same lifelong love and attention. You're never not rearing your kids, and you're never not promoting your book.

Did You Catch That?

You're never not promoting your book.

There's a common misconception that once the book is written and published, it's "over." The truth is that the real work is just beginning. Your book will never be known to other people if you don't tell other people about it. Your book may have your name and photo attached to it in all places. When people read it, they'll hear you speaking to them. But your book has no voice but yours, which means that no one will hear your book whispering their name.

So, get weird. Get creepy. Shout out that your book has arrived so that everyone can hear you. Talk about it before it's even been born (just like the pregnant ladies do). Then, talk about it some more. Post photos of you working on your book. Find a way to connect it to what you've got going on in life that you write about on social media. We know we sound exaggerative; we just want to make sure that you get the point: don't be silent.

IN OUR EXPERT OPINION—YOU ARE YOUR BOOK'S VOICE

We're not kidding when we say that your book has no voice but yours. The harsh reality is that your publisher is likely going to talk about your book only during its initial publication and initial launch stage. Some publishers may consider you on their front list for a year and help promote your book for that duration, but that's uncommon. Most will promote your book for the first one or two months and then they're moving on because they've got other projects. It's not personal. It's just the nature of the business. They may truly love you and love your book, but the reality is that they have a lot of other books in the pipeline that also require their attention.

The caveat to this, of course, is if you have a contract with a publisher that includes a certain amount of marketing and publicity that extends beyond the initial publication and launch period. Otherwise (and in any instance), you must constantly be your book's voice.

You have to tell people you have a book in order for them to go searching for it, see you, and then read (or hear) you. This is a lifelong activity. Promoting and marketing your book also happens to be the activity that will inevitably bring the bucks you invested in your book back to your pocketbook (more on that in chapter 11).

Why Knowing the Book Life Cycle is Helpful

When you know these five phases before you start writing, you can make a master plan for your book that isn't just about the writing or the content. You can consider things in advance that you otherwise wouldn't know you should be thinking about, like publishing. If you want to ABCD (**A**pproach your **B**ook with a **C**ommitment to **D**oing it right), then leverage the knowledge of these five phases to prepare you to enter into each phase well-informed. You'll be able to anticipate what you need to do next each step of the way because you understand that writing a book is way more than just writing. (For a succinct recap of the book life cycle, see appendix K: The Book's Life Cycle [the Recap].)

YOUR ENDGAME AND HOW IT INFORMS DECISION-MAKING

Now, the other thing you want to have in mind before writing is your endgame. What are your long-term goals for this work? Maybe your goals hinge on a particular event where you want to have the book available for sale. So, that's a deadline-driven goal. Maybe your goals are more related to the season of your business. Your coach or mentor is telling you that it's time to publish a book on your methodology or signature system and turn that book into a customer funnel.

What Does That Mean?

CUSTOMER FUNNEL

The customer funnel (or purchase funnel) is a model used in business that illustrates the journey someone takes from being a prospect to becoming a client or a customer, and it's applicable to your book business as well. The widest part of the funnel is where prospects become aware of a product or a service, then the funnel is at its narrowest once prospects convert and finally buy.

The widest part of your book business funnel looks the same; it's where the largest number of people become aware of your book. Maybe they are at a conference and hear about it, you appear as a guest on a podcast and they hear about it, you post on social media about the upcoming release, and so on. Next, the customer goes from knowing about a product or service to developing an interest in it. Then, they evaluate whether it's a fit for them and may even engage in negotiation with the seller before finally completing the purchase.

With your book, they hear about it, develop an interest, then go to Amazon (or wherever), read about it to see if it solves a problem they have, and decide if they want to make the ultimate decision to buy. As you can imagine, with each step in the model, the funnel gets more and more narrow as there are fewer and fewer people who move from awareness to interest to evaluation to negotiation, then to a purchase. With your book's customer funnel, you might start with thousands of people who are aware of your book, but as they move through the funnel, only a fraction of those thousands ultimately purchase your book.

Perhaps your goals are more intrinsic. You wrote on your bucket list ten years ago to publish a book by your fiftieth birthday because you always dreamed that you'd one day get to say you were an author. Knowing these types of goals can inform your writing schedule or help you weed out publishing options based on timing.

Goals can also be unrelated to personal or professional motivations. For example, if one goal you have for your book is to retain full creative control over the book (title, design, categorization), this might inform in which publishing direction you want to go. If one of your goals is to have an entire website dedicated to the book's main message or content, but you have no interest in maintaining it, this may help you recognize who else you might need to contract in order to reach that book-related goal.

No matter what, we recommend beginning with the end in mind. Knowing what you hope to achieve with your book will inform your process and your approach from the start and come into play through each phase of the book's life cycle. We've included some reflection questions at the end of this chapter to help you better understand your motivations and objectives in writing your book.

(Pro Tip)

Knowing what you hope to achieve with your book informs your process and approach throughout the duration of your book's development.

CUTTING CORNERS IS ANOTHER WAY OF SAYING "SKIPPING VITAL STEPS"

The one thing we want to urge you to consider is to abandon any idea of cutting corners. Ally is a book coach and ghostwriter, and she's often asked why writing a book can take so long or how one can cut corners to either fast-track the process or make it more economical. The thing is that cutting corners leads to skipping vital steps and ending up with a lower-quality final product.

People don't think they need all the editing (which we cover in chapters 13 and 14). Or they decide to get cheaper editing or cover design through Fiverr or Upwork, and the lower cost and faster turnaround time end up more important than the quality of that person's work. We are not suggesting there are not talented people on either of those sites. That's not the point.

The point is that you often get what you pay for. We see this all the time.

What you pay for a bite to eat at a truck stop is one price point, what you pay for a meal at [insert the name of your favorite fine-dining establishment] is another, and the quality of their food correlates with the price you pay. Truck-stop options are typically fast and cheap, and while they may seem tasty to some, they're terribly unhealthy for you. Or what about the handwritten sign stuck in the ground at the end of the street that says "will do odd jobs": are you going to trust that person to do your plumbing just because they said they could when you called the number written in permanent marker on the cardboard sign? No. You want a certified plumber. You want the premium rate because you want the premium service and the leak in your faucet fixed for good.

There will always be different price points and levels of expertise and experience when it comes to who you need to help you produce a fine, professional-looking (and feeling) book. You don't need the Bugatti of services, but please don't choose the beat-up car in the back of the lot with 400,000 miles on it.

Pro Tip

- *Hire professionals with experience.*
- *Pay professional rates.*
- *Don't skimp on a beautiful cover design or industry-standard typesetting.*
- *Don't skip over levels of editing or rely on family and friends.*
- *Never say things like "meh, it's fine."*

This is *your* book. Your final product. Your name, your face, your content, your intellectual property, your legacy. Bust out all the stops.

Repeat after us: *I will approach my book with the commitment to doing it right.*

🎯 Did You Catch That?

Repeat after us: I will approach my book with the commitment to doing it right.

TAKEAWAYS AND TO-DOS

Takeaways

- Understand the book's life cycle so that you always know which stage you're in and what to focus on while also knowing what's up ahead.
- Take the time to outline your book and plan your endgame before you begin.
- Once the book is written and published, it's not over. The hard work of promoting your book continues after it's published; promotion is required, otherwise no one will know you have a book and therefore no one will buy it.
- Don't cut costs or corners. You'll just end up paying more in the long run to fix mistakes that could have been avoided.

To-Dos

- Consider your endgame. Knowing where you're trying to go will inform your process and approach through each phase of the book's life cycle.
- Reflect on and answer these questions:
  - What do I want this book to help me accomplish in the world?
  - Who do I want to reach with this work?
  - What is the main argument I want to make in this work? Or what is the main takeaway for my ideal reader?

NOTES

CHAPTER 5

DRAFT, EDIT, REVISE, REPEAT

What makes a great book is great writing that is intentionally crafted to address something specific to someone specific. As readers, we aren't usually consciously aware of everything that was considered in order for us to have the book we are holding in our hands. And when we read a great book, there's a reason we lose ourselves inside its pages and any sense of time in the process. That loss of time we feel as readers is an indicator that the author did their job and did it well.

When a reader can sit back and enjoy a book without a lot of heavy lifting, it's a good sign. But when a reader has to try way too hard to understand what the author is trying to say or has to constantly overlook the typos scattered across the page, the reader thinks one thing: "I paid money for this?" You can have the most epic idea or most brilliant perspective on your subject matter, but if it's not written well, it'll be for nothing. What makes a great book? Great writing, great editing, and a clear focus on what and who.

Did You Catch That?

You can have the most epic idea or most brilliant perspective on your subject matter inside that book, but if it's not written well, it'll be for nothing.

A great book knows what's at stake or what its main objective is and who it's trying to reach. This means that an author doesn't just sit down and crank out the book, writing on a whim. That's why it is so important not to skip the idea generation phase. This phase allows time for the author to really clarify what they're promising to their reader and who their reader is. Both of these guide their writing.

Pro Tip

If the promise and the reader guide the writing, you have to know the promise and the reader first. So, take the time to plan and outline. Get clear and specific.

In knowing who you're speaking to, you can tailor your position, argument, tone, evidence, and even your sense of humor, or use anecdotes, analogies, comparisons, or metaphors, to make your point or state your case in a way that your ideal reader can understand. Knowing your "who" serves as one compass to guide what you're writing. Then, knowing exactly what you hope to convey to the reader and the result you want your reader to receive serves as the other. Together, they help you to filter and sort what content gets included and how to deliver it.

IDENTIFYING YOUR READER AND THEIR PROBLEM

So, if great writing, editing, and a clear focus on what and who makes a great book, what makes a great nonfiction book, specifically? A book that knows the promise it's making, is as fluff-free as possible, is provocative or goes against the traditional thinking, *and* is actionable. More or less, you've got to have a book that solves a problem. That's the book that will sell. If there's no point, there's no point of sale.

Did You Catch That?

> *A great nonfiction book knows the promise it's making, is as fluff-free as possible, is provocative or goes against the traditional thinking, and is actionable. If there's no point, there's no point of sale.*

People don't want to waste their time and don't want to have their time wasted. With all the audio and video content out there where they can get knowledge in half the time, it's a pretty big deal that a reader wants to spend time reading your book. So, don't squander the precious gift and opportunity of having their full attention to make your case, share your theory, or change their life—whatever you're aiming to do. Clearly define your "what" and "who."

Now, if you're writing a book that showcases your twenty-plus years in your field or your experience delivering a particular product or service to hundreds of people, knowing your ideal reader shouldn't be a challenge. They're likely the same person to whom you're marketing your experience and expertise the rest of the time for your business. Now, you're putting it into book form.

That said, consider how you'll address your ideal reader in your written work. Will you speak directly to them with the use of "you," or will you never utter an instance of "you"? Will you write with contractions and keep the text conversational and informal, or will you use formal, longhand text, keeping everything buttoned up tight? Understanding who your audience is and how you plan to address them is good to know before you start writing.

More importantly, intimately know what your reader needs and what they're struggling with. What's keeping them up at night? What's the thing you always hear your clients or leads say is a constant struggle? Is there something in your industry or field that people keep getting wrong or that you have a different approach or perspective on? Have you come up with your own framework or methodology that has gotten great results for your clientele, and you now want to reach even more people with it? The answers to any one of these questions *might be* the problems you address in your book.

We say "might be" because there are millions of books out there. In your field or industry, there may be books that have already covered the topic (or problem) you're considering tackling. You'll need to have considered what those other titles are and how yours compares and contrasts to ensure that it's new and different enough to have a place in the market. And sometimes it's not necessarily that all of the ideas need to be new, but that the way you convey, explain, and/or illustrate them is. Again, this kind of comparable book title research is great to do as a part of your idea generation phase. Know your problem and if it's already been solved in a book (that you didn't write) before you begin writing your own.

Something else to consider is how much of the problem you will address. If you're using your book to funnel people back to your main business, you might not want to give the whole house away inside your book. You want to acknowledge their problem, suggest new ways of looking at that problem, then invite them to fix that problem. But you don't want to give them every iota of your expertise, making for an incredibly dense and confusing book that scares them off to the point that they won't even give your recommendations a try. Or worst yet, what if they won't even get in touch with you for additional support or services? If you are using your book as a lead generation tool, you want to lead your readers back to your business, not drive them away by fire-hosing them with info.

CREATE AN OUTLINE AND UNDERSTAND THE THREE-ACT STRUCTURE OF A BOOK

Before you sit down to write, take the time to have a solid outline. (Remember, we discussed this in the chapter 2.) Your outline then serves as your writing guide. It helps you stay focused on what you'll address inside your book without creeping over your own scope. An outline may seem like a waste of time to some, but it truly serves as your map, or your GPS, helping you navigate to where you're going. You use your outline to check in with yourself as you develop the manuscript.

Just remember, of course, that just like a GPS can make a course correction as unpredicted circumstances arise, your book outline likely will also have to be adjusted as you work on the manuscript. (Trust us on this one. This book has experienced more than one or two or fifty adjustments.)

A part of your outline can identify who your reader is, what their main problem is, and the primary promise (or objectives) of your book. It's also helpful if your outline includes a working (meaning, it's open to change) table of contents (list of chapters) and chapter abstracts (summaries of chapter content). How do you go about organizing this kind of content into your outline? We suggest that you have a general understanding of the three-act structure of a book.

Every book, regardless of length or genre, has at least three acts: a beginning, a middle, and an end. What occurs in each of these sections is different by genre, but the main principle is the same. The beginning, or opening, act establishes the baseline. The closing, or ending, act wraps everything up. The middle act in between connects the two. We call it the meaty middle. It's where the journey or transformation happens. Several resources, including the well-known online education platform Master-Class, explain how each act comprises a certain percentage of the book: the opening act is 25 percent, the middle act is 50 percent, and the closing act is the other 25 percent.

In nonfiction, you can look at it this way. In act one (the beginning), you spend time introducing yourself to the reader and why you're the right person to deliver this content, the main argument or point of the book and why it's relevant to them, and the result you're promising. This first act is about 25 percent of your book, if you want to use that as a guide.

The second act (the meaty middle) is where you'll dive into the details of the topics; your steps, methods, or perspectives; and other data and supporting evidence that contribute to delivering on your promise and getting your reader the results. What you've set up in act one is now coming to fruition in act two. The transformation is happening.

In the third act, you're summarizing material, reiterating the main takeaways, and inviting the reader to keep going. You're bridging the gap from whatever you set up in act one over to act three, and the reader is walking away better than when they started the book.

So, if you know the problem you want to solve, you'll identify it in the first few chapters of your outline. If you know the results you want your reader to get, you're summarizing those in the last few chapters. The chapters in between (in the second act) are working to connect the two. With this kind of strategic and intentional thinking *before* you start drafting, you're likely to have a more successful first draft and feel more confident about what you're writing when you get started.

GETTING TO THE DRAFTING, REVISING, AND EDITING

After you identify your reader and the problem for which they are in search of answers, it's time for the critical work: drafting your manuscript. This is where you'll actually put pen to paper and write about the solution your reader is looking for. Drafting, revising, and editing make up a majority of the manuscript development phase.

This phase of the book life cycle is critical to the long-term success and quality of your final product. While you very well could fly through outlining and planning, manuscript development is a part of the process you don't want to speed through. Now, that's not to say that you can't write a draft quickly, but drafting and development aren't the same things. One can be quick and dirty (drafting), while the other is focused and intentional (development). Knowing the difference is important and can help you understand even more so that neither is "one and done."

What Does That Mean?

DRAFTING VERSUS DEVELOPMENT

Drafting *is the act of putting words to paper and getting ideas out of your head and onto the page.* Development *is all of the parts of the writing process—drafting, editing, and revising—that ensure that the manuscript's content and ideas are organized, cohesive, clear, and specific and that the writing itself is strong, including using active language, having pristine word choice, and implementing accurate grammar, spelling, punctuation, and mechanics. In other words, drafting is one part of development, but development isn't only drafting.*

You might recall that in the last chapter, we stated that the development phase of writing a book is multifaceted and can take several weeks to months (and even years) depending on your work style, schedule, deadline, and other life factors. There are several ways to approach writing the manuscript, and their effectiveness is based on the person and the execution. There is no one-size-fits-all approach to how you get the writing done. But there is one significant way to ensure that you'll end up with a poorly written manuscript and that is to write one draft and call the book done. (Yes, we know we already said this, but it's an important point that deserves repeating. You know, in case you didn't believe us the first time.)

Let's return to what we said about the difference between drafting and development. Drafting is one part of the development process, but it is not the entirety of the development process. When artists and illustrators draft something, using pencil or doing a line sketch in pen, it's because they assume that there will be mistakes and the original form isn't the final form. It's playing, it's discovering, it's getting initial ideas onto the page where they can become something else.

In writing, *drafting* is the act of getting your words down onto paper, knowing they'll require editing and revision. Now, with the first draft (the first time through), you may find that your words are messy, unruly, unorganized, unspecific, unclear, and far from perfect. That's okay. The point of the first draft is to just get it all down. Editing and revision come after the first draft, and these are both acts of refining what has been drafted.

Did You Catch That?

> Drafting *is the act of getting your words down onto paper, knowing they'll require editing and revision.*

Editing, generally speaking, is reviewing what's been written and looking for how it can be improved. Some people edit right on the computer, others print out the hard copy and use red pen the way a teacher in grade school did, circling words that aren't quite right, or highlighting sentences that need to be fixed, or leaving notes in the margins about missing information or a lack of clarity. Editing is notating what needs to be changed.

Did You Catch That?

> Editing *is reviewing what's been written and looking to improve it. Editing is notating what needs to be changed.*

Revising is the act of implementing the edits. If you've marked that a word isn't the right one, you replace it with a better one. If you've left yourself a note that a sentence doesn't make sense or a particular idea isn't fleshed out enough, you adjust it. By actually writing new words and phrases (and replacing old ones), you're essentially creating a new version of the document, or a new draft.

Did You Catch That?

> Revising *is the act of implementing the edits and creating a new version of the document (or a new draft) as a result of the changes.*

These three actions together create a three-act circuit: draft, edit, revise. You do this multiple times, not just once.

We'll say that again: you do this multiple times, not just once.

Let's think about painting a room. After you've primed it (we'll think of priming as planning your book), you put on one coat of your chosen color. That first coat is the draft. Once it's dried, you can see how thin certain sections are, revealing the primer underneath and making the room look unpolished. You can tell that it's not finished because you haven't gotten the paint to go on evenly everywhere. This assessment of the room after it's dried from the first coat is the equivalent of editing. You're noting which areas you need to go back over. When you're done evaluating, you take another crack at it and put on a second coat (revising). Again, you give the walls time to dry, come back and take another look at it, assessing it again. And if there's still room for improvement, you're putting on a third coat (more revising).

For any of us who have painted a room before, we know that, depending on the original walls, the type of primer or paint, the color, and the finish (matte or glossy) all factor into how many coats of paint you'll need. Likewise, the number of drafts or times you'll edit and revise the same writing is based on a variety of factors. Some people's first drafts are more like bulleted lists and not complete sentences and paragraphs. Others write such full, clean first drafts that they do a lot of heavy lifting up front, which might ("might" being an operative word here) shorten the number of drafts needed to bring a manuscript from start to finish.

If someone is an experienced writer, they may need fewer drafts than a less experienced writer. If someone takes off for four days, and holes up in a cabin in the woods, and only writes, and they're working on a short manuscript, and they've got a detailed outline and absolutely no interruptions . . . and, and, and . . . You can see where we are going with this. It's also possible that the more complex the book project and the longer the manuscript, the more time will be required for drafting, editing, and revising.

One thing we know to be true, however, is that no matter the size and scope of the project or how experienced or inexperienced the writer, one draft, one edit, and one revision won't cut it. Conducting these phases one time through will guarantee that there are holes or gaps in the manuscript—these are macro items that leave the manuscript feeling uncooked. There may be pieces of information missing, ideas that are not fully developed, arguments that lack evidence, disorganized paragraphs needing rearrangements, and more areas in need of improvement.

Did You Catch That?

No matter the size and scope of the project or how experienced or inexperienced the writer, one draft, one edit, and one revision won't cut it.

If you do this "one and done" style, you won't just have macro-level problems, however. You'll also have micro-level problems. It's likely that your manuscript will be lacking strong sentences; precise word choice; or correct grammar, spelling, and punctuation. None of this is because you're unintelligent or incapable or a poor writer.

Macro and micro manuscript problems are the result of rushing a process that takes time, energy, organization, strategy, and attention to detail—not to mention a certain mysterious or organic evolution that is difficult to explain but can be described as "the book has a way of telling you what it wants." Writing is an art form. There's a reason people describe it as "the art and craft of writing." With study, practice, and application, you get better at it—just like painting, sculpting, playing a musical instrument, or dancing. When we first begin any new piece (art, music, or routine), we need time to familiarize, make an attempt, adjust, and do it again and again until we call it ready. You don't have just one dance practice and then host a recital. You don't just write one draft and then publish.

WHEN THE WRITING IS READY

Now notice how we said "ready," not "perfect" or "finished" or "done." The thing with writing (and any art form, really) is that it's never truly any of these things. You're probably familiar with the adage, "A writer's job is never truly done." That's because every time you step away from a piece, you can return to it and find something new you'd like to change. Why is that? Because, as people, we constantly evolve, and as we evolve, so do our opinions, perspectives, knowledge, experience, and the way we would express any of these in written form. What you say in your book reflects where you are in a particular moment in time. You walk away from that book, and later on, it's a new moment in time and you see the world differently, which includes what you've written.

Of course, let's also not forget that you're writing nonfiction, which means that the subject matter you're focusing on may also shift or change over time. Business, psychology, sociology, finance, technology, and even history evolve as humans and experts learn more. Business models change and new leadership principles emerge. Psychological and sociological studies are conducted that lead to new findings about human emotions and interactions. You get the gist. It's likely that what you write about today won't be 100 percent guaranteed tomorrow. You have to be comfortable with that.

Your job is not to get it "perfect" or to even believe that it will always be evergreen. Your job is to know what you're aiming to achieve with your book, who you're aiming to reach, and to deliver the finest possible manuscript (and final product) that achieves those aims and keeps its promises to the reader. Just know that your reader will have a hard time seeing if you've achieved what you've set out to if your book is riddled with macro- and micro-level issues that pull the reader's attention away from the point you're trying to make and, instead, keep them focused on how sloppy the writing seems. Remember, what makes a great book is great writing and editing plus clarity, specificity, and intention around the "who" (your reader) and the "what" (your main point).

SELF-EDITING TIPS AND TRICKS

We've made it clear that after each draft, you're editing it in order to revise it. Eventually, when you feel that your manuscript is as clean as it can be, you'll call in the expert editors to do their thing. Think of this like how you tidy up your hotel room before room service comes in to do the deep clean. (If you don't like the hotel analogy, think instead about how you brush and floss your teeth before you go to a dental cleaning. You're freshening up those pearly whites and your breath as a courtesy to the people who are about to make your smile really shine.) We'll be talking about editors (your "room service" or "dental hygienist") and how they help you later in this chapter.

Before we get to that discussion, we're providing you with self-editing tips and tricks for you to employ as you work on your manuscript independently. There's also a self-editing checklist in appendix L, which you should totally use when it's time to edit your work. (In fact, stop reading and go put a Post-it® note there with a note to yourself . . . We'll wait.)

During the early drafts when your manuscript is still young, your editing rounds should focus on the macro-level items (that's the BIG stuff holding everything together kind of like a belt) that include the following:

- Organization and structure of the whole manuscript (chapter by chapter) and of the material within each chapter
- Clarity and specificity of ideas
- Living up to the promise/objective you've stated
- Plot holes or gaps in the narrative or argument

Here are some methods you can employ that go beyond just the standard red-pen-markup you're familiar with from grade school. These are not exclusive by any means.

You can physically cut and rearrange portions when you think something is out of order by printing a hard copy, cutting the sections (or sometimes individual paragraphs), and rearranging them to see how they could flow differently. There's a different way of seeing your chapter when you have a physical copy to play with than just having the one-dimensional scroll of a document on the computer. Think of this like doing a puzzle on the floor.

Another method is to highlight/color-code your manuscript. Look for the pieces at the beginning of a chapter that identify the focus of that chapter and that set up the premise (also known as a thesis) for that section. Underline or highlight that thesis. Then, highlight or color-code any piece that helps support it to ensure that you've not missed the main point altogether. If, for example, you find that you stated three points and only address two, then you've identified a gap. Leave yourself a note inside the chapter, identifying your need to go back and fill in that gap.

A third method you can use, specifically when it comes to using stories inside your book to illustrate points, is to do a sensory audit. When reviewing a personal anecdote/story or perhaps a client case study, look for what sensory details you have provided to help place the reader in the moment. Can you taste, hear, smell, see, or feel what's happening? You don't always need all of the senses to be present, but having some enriches the writing and makes the scene/anecdote more powerful and impactful. If you want to make your reader *feel* something, use the senses. It just makes sense (pun intended).

Now, as you get into the middle to late drafts when your content is organized, clear, and specific, you'll want to look at micro-level (or sentence-level) items, which may include the following:

- Sentence structure
- Grammar
- Punctuation
- Word choice
- Active and passive voice
- Repetition of words and phrases

To look for these things, we have a number of useful tips to try.

First, look at the first words. Go through the document, only looking at the first word of each paragraph, then each sentence. Circle any repeated words when they appear in a row. You want to avoid three or more sentences that all begin with the same word unless the repetition is stylistic and purposeful. For example, you don't want a paragraph where every sentence begins with "I." Just say out loud to yourself, "I, I, I, I . . ." What do you sound like? Either a celebrity diva on an ego trip or a seal performing for fish. I think we agree that neither is great.

Second, read your manuscript aloud. You can hear the way a sentence sounds when you read it out loud. If it doesn't sound right, you'll want to fix it because it's probably going to trip up someone when they read it even if they're reading silently.

Third, consult a style guide. When you're in doubt about how something should be grammatically structured or punctuated, consult a style guide. A style guide helps you determine how a manuscript should be formatted, how quotation marks should be used, the accurate way to cite or reference information that isn't yours, which numbers should be spelled out, and which should be written as numerals, just to name a few. *The Chicago Manual of Style* is the one used for publishing in the United States. You can buy the full manual, subscribe online, or buy the laminated tri-fold quick guide, but either way, follow the latest edition of *The Chicago Manual of Style*. It's your yellow brick road to the Emerald City where everything shimmers and shines, just the way you want your book to read.

Fourth, replace vague, unspecific words with better ones. Search for words like *mad*, *bad*, *sad*, and *good*. These are not specific or sensory-driven words that truly illustrate what's happening or how someone is feeling. Look for vague words with the purpose of replacing them with strong, active, illustrative words. Grab the thesaurus if you need to. Similarly, look for filler words and replace or eliminate them. *That*, *this*, and *like* are often overused, not needed, or don't specify what they're actually referring to.

Then, when you really believe you're closing in on a "ready" manuscript, it's time for proofreading. This is the editing round where you're just looking for remaining errors that somehow got overlooked. Common items to look for are extra periods, extra spaces, lowercased words when they should be capitalized (or vice versa), the wrong use of a word even though the spelling is accurate (think *their, there, they're*), the wrong plu-ralization, or the inaccurate possession of a word.

At this level, you can read backward to help spot the errors. Start at the last word of the document and read backward right to left and from the bottom sentence to the top. You'll more easily spot these types of minute errors because you're not familiar with the manuscript from this direction. These types of errors are easy to overlook when you've already read your book umpteen times the normal way (top to bottom, left to right). And if you pair reading it aloud with going backward, you're really likely to find the errors you otherwise might not see.

Also, search for words with more than one spelling or meaning. Use the search/find feature in your digital document for words that have more than one spelling and more than one meaning or similarly pronounced words with distinct meanings. Ensure that you're using the right version or right word (for example, *except* or *accept* and *effect* or *affect*).

Pro Tip

FOR EDITING

1. *Review a hard copy.*
2. *Remove all unnecessary information.*
3. *Reorganize.*
4. *Check construction.*
5. *Check for missing information.*
6. *Check transitions.*
7. *Read your document aloud.*
8. *Review each of your sentences.*
9. *Check your word choices.*
10. *Check for spelling and punctuation.*

For details and further suggestions, see appendix L: Self-Editing Checklist

THREE TYPES OF EDITORS AND WHY YOU NEED THEM ALL

Though a lot of the content is up to you to get down on the page, *and* a lot of the drafting, editing, and revising can be up to you, too, you don't have to be the lone wolf here. In fact, we highly recommend that you're not. Once we've worked on something for a while—and in isolation—it can be difficult to see the manuscript objectively. This would be no different than a doctor trying to diagnose their own symptoms or a lawyer who represents themselves; both the doctor and the lawyer have a fool for a patient/client. It's not impossible, but it's not recommended.

Assuming you've done as much drafting, editing, and revising as you can and you're beginning to recognize that you now need a different set of eyes, there are three levels of editing we would recommend: developmental editing; line, copy, or mechanical editing; and proofreading. These are all separate levels of editing that focus on different aspects of writing. Lucky for you, you're now already familiar with these because they go in the same order, looking at the same elements that we just covered in the self-editing section. And yes, we still suggest that you go through each level yourself *and* that you use three different people as your editors even if you did all that self-editing already.

🎙️ **Did You Catch That?**

Even if you did a bunch of self-editing, you should still use professional editors to look at your manuscript at each level of developmental edits, line/copy/mechanical edits, and proofreading edits. You need an objective perspective.

Having three different people better establishes objectivity, as it can be difficult for the same person who reviewed the manuscript from a development perspective to then turn around and look at the work at a line level. We also recommend that you have editors perform these editing levels in a certain order and that you don't move on from one until you feel you've fully addressed any of the issues that have already come up.

We want you to consider this analogy: think of the three levels of editing like taking a pair of shoes to the cobbler. The cobbler will first look at the structural integrity of the shoe (like a developmental editor) before they restring, adjust, or tighten the laces (a line/copy/mechanical edit) and most certainly before they polish the shoe (a proofread). Each editor has a distinct role in ensuring the soundness and overall quality of your manuscript. Use them and also choose them wisely. For more on the different types of editors and what they do, see chapter 13.

Pro Tip

Put your work through three levels of editing at a minimum—developmental editing; line, copy, or mechanical editing; and proofreading—and as many times as you feel necessary to produce a quality book.

Developmental Editing and Editors

Begin with developmental editing; this is the macro level of editing. Developmental editors look at the manuscript first as a whole, assessing it for cohesion, organization, meaning, and clarity—the big things. They have their eyes on how the manuscript sounds as a whole. A developmental editor asks questions such as the following:

- Is this the right number of chapters?
- Are the chapters and paragraphs in the right order?
- Are there any places in the manuscript where the pacing lags?
- Is there a hole in the information presented?

Developmental editing considers all the aspects of a manuscript that make the book readable and enjoyable. These editors make recommendations for strengthening your manuscript. Because of the extensive nature of this type of editing, it is more time intensive and the most costly of all the different types of editing.

When you receive feedback from the developmental editor, revise the manuscript accordingly. Once you feel like the manuscript holds together respective of the feedback and that there are no more big pieces of content to add or revise, you'll be ready for the next level of editing.

Line/Copy/Mechanical Editing and Editors

The next level is a mid-level edit. At this stage, you're employing a line editor, copy editor, or mechanical editor (which are not entirely the same things) to look at things like the structure of the sentences, consistent use of a tense, word choice, accurate application of grammar (the structure of written language that refers to the parts of speech and how they come together), and mechanics (the rules of the style guide, such as capitalization and punctuation). This is not an exclusive list by any means.

What Does That Mean? ⟫⟫

HOW THE LINE EDITOR, COPY EDITOR, AND MECHANICAL EDITORS ARE DIFFERENT

A line editor, copy editor, and mechanical editor perform similar work but are not one and the same. A line editor reviews for creative content, writing style, and language use (at both the sentence and paragraph levels). They focus on the way you use language to communicate to the reader, which might include pointing out run-on sentences, redundancies in repeating the same info but in different ways, unnatural phrasing, confusing digressions, and more. In contrast, a copy editor looks for flaws on a technical level. They correct spelling, grammar, punctuation, and syntax; search for inconsistency in spelling, hyphenation, capitalization, and numerals; and even note ambiguity or inaccuracies in the material (which is pretty darn important for nonfiction books). Last, but not least, mechanical editing is actually the technical and consistent application of a particular style (such as The Chicago Manual of Style*). Mechanical editing can be a part of copy editing.*

When reviewing at the sentence level, an editor asks questions such as the following:

- Is this comma in the correct place?
- Does the subject agree with the verb?
- Are there any misplaced modifiers?
- Is this the right tense?
- Is that the accurate pluralization of this noun?

Editors at the sentence level should also be well versed in the most current edition of *The Chicago Manual of Style*, the guide that is the standard for US style in book publishing.

Line/copy/mechanical editors are less expensive than developmental editors, but as you can see, they offer a different level of service with a different level of skill. Note that some editors at this stage will track changes on your manuscript inside the digital file but will not approve the changes for you, while others will show you a marked-up version and a cleaned-up version. Whether you're making the final changes or the editor is, only once these revisions have been performed do you move on to the final level: proofreading.

Proofreaders and Proofreading

Proofreading is your last crack at catching anything that remains undone. These editing professionals read the manuscript to look for and catch any lingering mistakes that were missed from the previous sentence-level revision. They give the manuscript a final once-over to make sure that it's ready to go to market. A proofreader looks for the stray typo, the missing period, the non-capitalized word. They buff the manuscript.

Proofreaders tend to be the least expensive of all the different types of editors but are the ones you call upon only when you know your manuscript has gotten the fine-tooth-comb treatment and it's just about ready for publication. They will check to ensure that all errors have been identified and corrected.

IN OUR EXPERT OPINION—KNOW WHAT YOU MEAN WHEN YOU SAY "I NEED EDITING"

It's inadequate to call up someone and say, "I need editing." You need to understand the different types of editing and the fact that, because each one calls upon a different skill set, each one requires a different price point. It's like saying "I need maintenance done on my car," but in one instance, you need your tires inflated, in another you need the oil changed, and in another you need compounding to restore damaged paintwork and to prevent rusting. They are all aspects of maintenance, but each one requires a different skill set, different tools, and different investments. (Can you tell that this is a thorn in our sides?)

Someone once reached out to Bridgett's company asking for editing. Once her team determined that this person needed developmental editing, and Bridgett told him the cost was $0.15 per word, he wrote back that $900.00 sounded steep for the editing of only one 600-word chapter that was part of a twelve- to thirteen-chapter manuscript. You could tell that he assumed that editing is just editing, which in many people's minds is making no distinction among the different types of editing, simply lumping them all together and having one person conduct the work of making a manuscript sound great. Know the different types of editing, what type you're looking for, and understand the associated costs beforehand so that there are no surprises. (Learn more about costs in chapter 13 and appendix E: The Cost to Self-Publish.)

IF YOU WANT TO MAKE YOUR BOOK SING, GET A CHOIR

Not so fast! Editors are not the only people you will need during the development of your manuscript, and they are certainly not the only people you'll need to produce a great book. For those who have a fountain of knowledge upstairs but who don't have the writing chops to relay it all well or don't have the time or desire to write it themselves, a ghostwriter might be the ticket.

For those who are coachable and committed to writing their own book and believe they can be taught, they may do well with a book coach. Even then, once the manuscript is drafted, there are still additional folks you'll need, such as a cover and interior book designer, typesetter, and publisher, just to name a few. These are all pieces (or people, rather) to the publishing puzzle, and we discuss each one in due course throughout these pages (both in chapter 13 and appendix F: People on the Publishing Path).

The moral of this very short section is this: writing a manuscript might be a solo act, but developing a great and publishable book takes a choir. Even those of us inside the industry require the professional services of others to help us produce high-quality books; we rarely—if ever!—do all the parts and pieces on our own.

Did You Catch That?

Writing a manuscript might be a solo act, but developing a great and publishable book takes a choir.

AUTHORING THE BOOK: FLYING SOLO OR CO-PILOTING THE SHIP

Given that we are cowriting this book (and we just talked about the fact that writing a book isn't actually a solo performance), we thought we would be remiss to not mention the possibilities of partnerships in authoring a book. While coauthoring can come with the challenges of being consistent in tone, voice, and style and project managing two people on one project, there are also a lot of advantages to working with another author.

If you and your copilot have parallel interests, businesses, target clients, or expertise, and you have similar problems to solve for your reader, this may make for a great partnership. If you're both invested in the project and committed to sharing the load equally, you might find that this is the perfect way to approach a book. Plus, working with someone else comes with a little bit of built-in accountability.

We came together on this project in late July 2022. Ally was doing an interview series with publishing professionals, and Bridgett was invited to be her guest. After the interview was over and we were debriefing, we ended up on a mutual soapbox about what we wished authors knew before they got started. Our conversation was all about the common and frequent things we educate our clients on as we work with them in each of our own capacities.

We realized that there were three main points we wanted authors to know: (1) to treat their book like a business; (2) to commit to doing it well; and (3) to not focus on book sales as their primary goal and as their only revenue stream. At the time, we called it the trifecta. Before we knew it, one of us suggested that this would make a great book, and the other agreed. Bada bing bada boom. Less than a month later, we started.

Neither of us has cowritten a book like this before. But this has been a truly tremendous experience, and we couldn't be happier about having another book each to our own name while having shared the load of the work. And, honestly, the number of things we have agreed on since we got started has been uncanny. It's been like we were meant to write this book together; we've been so in sync.

Of course, having the right copilot to steer the plane is critical to success. We aren't suggesting that it would work with just anyone. Both parties have to be communicative, collaborative, and active partners. Both parties have to share the vision and perspective being offered in the book. And, certainly, both have to agree on the problem the book solves and how the book addresses that problem and its solution. We guess what we are saying is it's not impossible to develop a great manuscript with a coauthor.

IN OUR EXPERT OPINION—MULTIAUTHORED VOLUMES, COMPILATIONS, AND THE LIKE

And because we've discussed coauthorship, we might as well speak briefly on compilations, collections, or anthologies, which are books with multiple authors. Typically, each contributor gets their own chapter. A multiauthored volume can be a wonderful way to ease into getting a publication credit and become familiar with the publishing process. However, there are a lot of multiauthored schemes out there. We've seen some volumes with super unspecific focuses that bring a bunch of people together with a promise of bestseller status but with weak ideas on who the target audience is or how to market it because the creator has put together a book about everything for everybody (which means it's a book about nothing for no one).

If you're invited to be a part of a compilation, be sure that the creator has a tightly focused idea for the book, that they know who they're trying to reach, and that they're clear on what problem they're trying to solve. Most importantly, if they are asking you for thousands of dollars to contribute, understand where that money is going and what you get out of it. Look at it this way: if you can spend thousands of dollars to have your own book with only your name on the cover and only your ideas included, why would you spend thousands to share a space with several other voices?

TAKEAWAYS AND TO-DOS

Takeaways

- The promise the book makes and who the book is for (the reader) guides the writing, which means that these need to be known before the writing begins.
- Finalizing a manuscript isn't a "one and done" (draft) kind of thing.
- Don't skimp on or skip editing your manuscript.
- Writing a manuscript might be a solo act, but developing a great and publishable book takes a choir. Work with professionals to produce your book.
- Don't rule out the option of coauthoring a book, especially if you feel relatively confident that you can find a copilot who's the right fit.

To-Dos

- If you haven't already, identify the main promise your book makes to the reader.
- Develop or refine your ideal reader profile and consider what they need from your book and whether the promise of your book will serve them.
- Create a plan for drafting, editing, and revising.
- Check your network for potential coauthors, people who share much of the same vision, mission, and philosophy that you already embrace.

NOTES

_____

_____

_____

_____

_____

_____

_____

_____

_____

_____

_____

_____

_____

_____

_____

_____

_____

_____

_____

_____

_____

_____

_____

_____

CHAPTER 6

WE DO JUDGE A BOOK BY ITS COVER

Truth bomb: that old adage "don't judge a book by its cover" is a load of crock. We all judge a book by its cover. And when we say "cover," we are talking about all its sides (both front and back) and their individual parts: the design, the title, the font choice, the subtitle. We take in all of that sometimes before we even know who the author is. A good front cover is what draws us in as readers and makes us take the extra time to flip it over and take in the information on the back cover: the description, the author bio, the endorsements. If we are sold on the whole package as it's presented to us via the covers, we often don't care how much the book costs at that point. We are going to buy the book because someone did their job correctly—they made us want that book.

Terrific covers are like terrific packaging of your favorite products. Ever pick up a new shampoo or cologne based on the label to decide if you'll give its scent a sniff? Or do you ever get more excited receiving a gift from someone when it's all wrapped up with ribbons and bows and looking like they spent a million bucks on it? This is great, effective packaging of whatever is concealed inside. It gets us thinking, "This thing is going to be fancy" or "beautiful" or "just what I'm looking for." Great packaging creates an expectation of an incredible product, service, or experience. It makes us anticipate something amazing. This is what a great cover does for your book.

So, imagine if you don't have a great cover. People are probably going to glaze right over it. If they glaze over it, they're not going to stop and spend time getting to know what the book is about and whether it's for them. You might have written some brilliant stuff and the writing might be clean as a whistle—totally polished and precise. But you have to have a great cover if you're going to grab your reader's attention.

One caveat: you can have a brilliant cover but then a sloppy interior. If people flip through the inside of your book and see that the inside isn't as well designed as the outside, they might stop taking the book seriously or wonder what the deal is. Again, you may have written something fantastic, but they do not believe that by how the inside presents. Looks can be deceiving, but it's the way people are *perceiving* that matters because people's perceptions are their reality. You don't want people to perceive that your book isn't worth their time or money.

Did You Catch That?

People's perceptions are their reality. You don't want people to perceive that your book isn't worth their time or money.

Bottom line: having a great cover (and a great interior design) is the third piece of what makes a great book. First comes the commitment to doing it well. Second comes sound manuscript development. Third is all about the packaging.

Did You Catch That?

Having a great cover (and a great interior design) is the third piece of what makes a great book. First comes the commitment to doing it well. Second comes sound manuscript development. Third is all about the packaging.

THE MOST IMPORTANT ASSET TO YOUR "PACKAGING": A GREAT TITLE

Your title is the most important asset to your packaging (and your marketing). When your book sits on a shelf and doesn't get to face out, it's the spine that will appear to the customer first. Your title makes up 99 percent of your book's spine, so it had better capture someone's attention before they blow on by it.

When your book isn't available to be seen in stores but can be ordered online, your title needs to include keywords for the sake of searchability and, therefore, findability. When a reader reads your book and wants to recommend it to a friend, you want them to be able to easily recall the title and not have to fumble trying to get it right.

Did You Catch That?

Your title is the most important part of your packaging and marketing.

Here is a perfect example, using the 2022 Netflix series *The Woman Across the Street from the Girl in the Window*, starring Kristen Bell. This was a terrific series (so Ally believes because Bridgett is pop-culture clueless). Yet, it wasn't a title easily recalled. How many times did we all get the order of "woman" and "girl" messed up or did we say "door" instead of "window"? Most people just deferred to saying, "You know, the new series with Kristen Bell . . . the woman in the house." Because of Bell's celebritydom, that was enough to give people what they needed to go find the series. We believe you'll agree that most of us don't have the luxury of being a TV personality or having such a high profile that it will make everyone's job of finding our book easy by our name alone.

A title needs to be compelling enough to the reader that they take the time to pull the book out from the lineup, look at the cover, become interested in the design and/or subtitle (if there is one), then flip to the back cover. If shopping online, we want our buyers to be hooked enough by the tiny thumbnail image accompanying the search result that they click for the full description or a larger image. The title needs to be easily readable and easily recalled.

Pro Tip

Create a title that is easily readable and easily recalled. Make it short (one to six words) and use your subtitle to evoke the nature or promise of the book.

Main Titles

With those things in mind, we are in favor of shorter main titles, with subtitles that evoke the nature or promise of the book. A shorter main title is good for that easily readable and easily recalled factor. We're talking one to six words, with a preference for four or fewer. You want people to be able to easily remember it and rattle off the title of your book. (Okay. We're going to address the elephant in the room. Yes, our title kinda breaks this rule, but when people go search for our book, they are looking for "Do Not Write a Book," which is only five words. And it's memorable. And oxymoronic. So, yeah. There you have it.)

Shorter titles are also good when it comes to them appearing in a small online thumbnail of the book cover or if you want to purchase a URL to create a website for your book. (And for that, we highly recommend that you purchase a URL that mirrors your book title.) That said, you don't want a short title that is so vague (like *Illusion*) that no one understands what the book is actually about or so broad that it could be about anything within that arena (like *Cooking*). So, go for short and specific, or, like we said earlier, create that punchy, shorter main title, then pair it up with a subtitle.

Subtitles

When you pair your book's main title with a subtitle, it adds specificity and context. The subtitle gives the prospective reader a better idea of the book's topic and the angle you will take with it. Subtitles are typical within nonfiction genres, and they're good for addressing the promise of the book. With novels, short stories, and other works of fiction, you see a mix; sometimes the abstract, quirky, short, and vague, or even a long and complicated main title, can work to create the effect the author is going for. There might be something about that title used in fiction that truly evokes what the novel is about and does just the thing to hook the reader's interest—no subtitle required. However, when it comes to nonfiction (business, prescriptive, biographical, theory, or historical) books, abstract, quirky, vague, and complicated main titles often don't work *unless* they've got subtitles to make sense of them.

The one nonfiction genre that might be able to get away with something a little more like a novel title is memoir. A memoir is considered nonfiction because it's based on a person's life, but it's told in a way that reads like a novel. A memoir does promise something to the reader but not in the same way a business book or a self-help book might.

Bottom line: use that subtitle to convey exactly what you're offering to the reader. Your subtitle tells why people should get your book and read it.

The Job of Your Title and Subtitle

With the title and subtitle of your book, you want people to decide that out of all of the available books in their target interest, they should pick yours. The title needs to cause your ideal reader to be attracted to your book as opposed to somebody else's. It instantly communicates that you know their fears, you know their frustrations, you know their aspirations. Your title creates curiosity, and it creates interest. Use these details to help you brainstorm your title and subtitle, so it's clear to people that they *have* to have your book.

You don't want to create a title for your book that just hooks the reader's interest but then doesn't deliver. That is the equivalent of clickbait titles in emails or blog posts; their sole purpose is to get someone to click on them regardless of if the content inside matches the subject of the original title. Ultimately, your title, regardless of length and specificity, needs to reflect the contents of your book. Your main title and subtitle need to illustrate the tone, promise, or premise of the work that lies within. In some ways, because you're aiming to elevate the main idea of your book, keywords associated with your book's content should naturally come up when you're brainstorming titles.

Did You Catch That?

Your title needs to reflect the contents of your book regardless of length or specificity.

And brainstorming is one of our suggestions for how to go about coming up with a good title. Write down all kinds of ideas you have. Study the titles of other books in your category and see what they're doing. If you notice a pattern or a trend in the titles, imitate that pattern while applying your book's content focus. Search your book for phrases or key ideas you return to repeatedly. Run your ideas by your mastermind or networking group, best friend, spouse, or online community. See what lands with them and why. Specifically, ask them to tell you what they think your book is about based on the title suggestions. If they are able to get an accurate idea, then you're on the right track or maybe have even hit the nail on the head. If they are totally out in left field, you may need to rework your ideas.

Either before or after (but preferably before) you settle on what you believe is the perfect title, conduct a search to ensure the title is not already in use. At a minimum, check Amazon's and Barnes & Noble's sites to confirm that there is not already a book with that title or one incredibly similar to it. If there is, then you need to go back to the drawing board. And for extra measure, check domain registrars, such as GoDaddy, to ensure that your book title's URL is available, and if it is available, purchase it! Having the URL is not a must, but it's highly recommended. You do not have to build the site right then and there; it's about laying claim to it for when you *are* ready to build the book's website or webpage. (We talk more about your book's website or webpage, its marketing hub, in chapter 8.)

Don't be alarmed if you workshop half a dozen (or more) titles, trying to get it right. We tried on and played around with thirty-six ideas before we finally landed on the one you see on the cover of this book. We had been working on the manuscript for eight months before we finally nailed it. When you're trying to get your main title to be snappy and memorable and your subtitle to convey the book's promise, and you want to match both the tone and personality of your book, all while the title and subtitle do the job of hooking your reader's interest—that's a lot to consider with the number of words you have to work with.

Admittedly, we were growing a little frustrated that the title just didn't seem to want to come, but we knew better than to settle for one of our ideas just to call it "done." We were committed to waiting it out until we finally manipulated enough of our key ideas and words into the right mash-up. And just like we've found ourselves in mutual agreement with so many other decisions with this book when we got to this iteration, we both knew we had found it—the perfect title for this book (and for us). It was worth the wait, and we know how critical it will be to the book's success.

THE MAKINGS OF A GREAT COVER

When you pick apart the pieces of a full cover (front and back), there are several elements that go into it, and precision is required to fit it all inside the trim size of the book. The cover design isn't just about the main image on the front, whether it's photography, an illustration, or an abstract design. The design is the placement of your title, subtitle, and name on the front and your description, endorsements, bio, and other data (pricing, category, barcode, and ISBN) on the back.

Front Cover Design and Hiring a Professional

Now, we know you can do a lot of wonderful things with stock photos, copyright- or royalty-free photos, or free platforms like Canva, but we beg you—please don't use them. Hire a professional cover designer, or a graphic designer at the very least, to design your cover. They know things about photo choice and placement, light, shadow, contrast, tone, sizing, layering, font choice, and the list goes on. They know the role a cover plays in book sales and will be intentional with how the whole cover comes together, understanding how both imagery and wording integrate to make an eye-catching design that matches the spirit and promise of your book and captures the essence of your book's message.

A great cover designer will also know how to take some of your ideas (if you have some) and make them come to life in ways that you would never imagine if you used free online templates. Plus, when authors use stock images and free templates, their covers are usually pretty easy to spot. And in those instances, you know what readers think? "Isn't that cute." Or worse: "Isn't that amateurish?"

(Pro Tip)

Hire a professional cover designer, or a graphic designer at the very least, to design your cover.

IN OUR EXPERT OPINION—BE OPEN TO EXPERTS' RECOMMENDATIONS

We can appreciate an author who has a specific vision in mind for their cover. We want authors to have a vested interest in their final product and to love how their book looks at the end of the line. However, authors aren't typically cover designers or graphic designers or any kind of designer. They don't have a trained eye to understand the balance of color, or dimension, or what makes a cover really sing. So, please, we beg you. Have an open mind to experts' recommendations. They know how to design, so let them.

And we know there are some authors who really, really, really want their picture on the front cover, especially if it's their first book, and they will plead their case with graphic designers. We know. We get it. We did it ourselves. But that was before we knew we shouldn't. How does the saying go? "When you know better, you do better." Right!

Here's the deal. If you walk through a bookstore and see a book with a picture of Oprah, Arnold Schwarzenegger, or Taylor Swift on the cover, then there's nothing to write home about. It's expected. It makes sense. Their stardom sells. However, if you see a book with a picture of Aaron Hawkins (Bridgett's husband) on the cover, then you won't give it a second glance (unless he has completely stepped out of his element to write a book and then has consented to take some out-of-this-world, really eye-catching photo).

The point is that unless you're a big name, a celebrity, a well-known politician, an influencer, or the like, then you have no business putting a picture of yourself on the front cover of your book. None. A designer who is a professional cover designer and/or who knows the book industry should know that a picture of yourself on the back works just fine, but the front cover is prime real estate that's reserved for getting folks' attention. Let those graphic designers do their jobs to design a killer cover for you.

The Back Cover Blurb

Beyond the cover designer who pulls it all together, however, you're going to need some damn good people with their marketing hats on to help with that back cover blurb: the marketing description of your book. This is the main paragraph on the back cover that describes what the book is about and what it promises the reader (or what the story is about if you're writing a memoir or narrative nonfiction).

Some authors write that back cover blurb themselves, but if you're working with an established press or publisher and they have some marketing folks on the team, let them have a crack at it. They know how to write copy that's optimized for search engines, and they know how to speak marketing in ways that authors often don't when it comes to promoting their own books. This may seem counterintuitive. Wouldn't the author know their book better than anyone? Yes, but knowing your book intimately doesn't mean you know how to write the marketing copy that will sell your book the best.

Consider how you might fill out your own dating profile online compared to how your best friend might do it. Your friend is probably going to do a better job. They see you objectively, while you see yourself more critically. They're likely to toot your horn way more than you will.

We cannot always do the best by our books when we are as close to them as we are. That said, your input is critical to helping marketing people best come up with that blurb. They'll rely on you to know the key selling points, who you're trying to reach, what you're promising, and how you're trying to solve a problem. You can see how it's a good thing that you did all that up-front work before you began writing so you can answer their questions well.

🧑 Did You Catch That?

Your input is critical to helping marketing people help you sell your book.

Back Cover Endorsements

When it comes to endorsements, get some. Even when a reader isn't familiar with the person who wrote a testimonial that appears on the back cover, that person's name and title (their byline) legitimize the book. For the person who's considering buying the book, it lets them know that someone else read this, thought it was good, and would recommend it to others. A back cover without endorsements looks like someone who hustled to the "print" button too quickly. Sometimes your press or publisher will help you find endorsers, but more likely, you're going to know the people who are in your field, industry, or inner circle that would be most appropriate to ask to review and endorse your book. And just so we are abundantly clear, *inner circle* does not mean calling upon family and friends to write endorsements for your book. Unless they have the expertise, education, and/or background that unequivocally qualifies them to be seen as people whose endorsements add credibility to your book, then their testimonials do not belong on your cover or in your book's front matter.

You won't need more than two to three endorsements, and they don't need to be long. They can't be. There's not as much space back there as you might think. While it's wonderful to have long and gushing endorsements—and if you get them, KEEP THEM!—more often than not, you can't fit all of them on the back cover. Choose the most exquisite excerpt and put the rest of the endorsement elsewhere, like in the accolades in your front-matter section, on your book's website, on your book's sell sheet, or on social media. Don't waste a great, long, praiseworthy endorsement, but know that you might not be able to use the whole thing on the back cover. (For more on endorsements, see appendix M: How to Get Testimonials and Advance Praise.)

ACCOLADES IN THE FRONT MATTER

When someone opens the front cover of your book, the very first thing they see is a page that contains glowing reviews from your endorsers. Typically titled "Advance Praise," these testimonials come before everything. They come before the title page, any dedication, or the table of contents. This is where those lengthy testimonials you had to abbreviate for the back cover are placed in their entirety, so your readers can see the praise and honor your book received in full detail before it even landed on the store shelves.

Font Choice and Legibility as a Part of the Design

How all these words that appear on your cover get presented can be important. What we mean is font choice and point size. You want the font choice of your book cover to complement the imagery that's been selected and evoke the kind of emotional response you're hoping to get from your reader. For example, if your book is comical, you might like something resembling a Comic Sans font. If you're writing a horror novel, perhaps something more like Chiller. If you're going for something more romantic or epistolary, perhaps a handwriting or calligraphy font like Lucida Handwriting. These are exaggerated choices to make a point. These may look awful on a cover, and we are by no means cover designers. What we are suggesting is that your font choices elevate the overall essence of your book.

We also suggest that your font choices be ones that are easily legible. Your readers shouldn't have a difficult time reading your title, your name, or anything else for that matter. So, when choosing between design or clarity, go with clarity, but there are plenty of font choices out there to get the happy medium—something that's both clear to read and evokes a certain tone or personality of your work. However, defer to design and typesetting experts who have all things regarding fonts on lock.

Pro Tip

When choosing between design or clarity, go with clarity.

Did You Catch That?

Your font choices should elevate the overall essence of your book.

Cover Elements Are Brand Elements

The thing people often don't think about when it comes to their cover design is how they leverage the art, fonts, and any other elements well beyond just the book's publication. Your cover designer can make these items available to you for use in a variety of other places. For example, you can use on your website the same fonts that appear on your cover so that your website and book match. Expanding on this idea, consider everything related to your book being in the same colors and fonts and using the same images. Now you've turned your book into a brand because everywhere you talk about your book, it looks the same. Your bookmarks, mugs, tote bags, Post-it® notepads, or any other marketing swag you put together can now be branded the same. (Hint: we are getting you in the frame of mind to begin thinking about your book as the driver of multiple revenue streams, which we discuss in chapter 11.)

You can even show up to speaking events or book signings wearing colors from your book cover's color palette so that you become a part of the brand, too. We mean in a lot of ways that you ARE the brand when it comes to writing nonfiction. This all goes back to that whole idea from chapter 1 about how your book is an extension and a representation of you. It also works in reverse. You are an extension of your book and can also be a part of its representation.

CONSIDERATIONS FOR THE INTERIOR DESIGN AND LAYOUT

Because we are speaking about consistency, we believe that we should also state this: your interior design should complement your cover design. If you've used certain font choices on your cover, your interior designer should pull those into the interior—not everywhere by any means, but in a way that brings it all together. Perhaps you use the primary font for chapter titling, or for the reflective questions you post at the end of the chapters, or for the information in the headers or footers. Another feature we've seen is the cover design or graphic significantly reduced in size and then used to accompany the chapter number at the start of each chapter or to signify a break or shift in thought between paragraphs in the body of a chapter.

When the interior of a book matches its exterior, it's like adding that whipped cream and cherry to the top of your ice cream sundae. Plain ole ice cream in a bowl looks pretty darn yummy by itself, but when you add the fixings, it transforms into a whole new bowl of deliciousness that you just cannot wait to try. In other words, a well-done interior that complements the exterior is going the extra mile to have a professional-looking, well-designed book that people can tell was intentional even if they're not conscious of it.

Did You Catch That?

A well-done interior complements the exterior and makes for a professional-looking, well-designed book that people can tell was intentional.

Now, when it comes to the interior, it's not just about the cleverness of the chapter header design or what to do with available white space. The interior also needs to have the standard front-matter sections: the inside title cover, the copyright page, and a table of contents. These are the minimum requirements.

In the back matter, you want acknowledgements and about the author sections. In the body of the book, sandwiched in between the front and back matter, you should have a header that indicates the book title and/or chapter title (though we have seen books omit these) and a footer with the page number. (For a comprehensive list of the order of the parts of a nonfiction book, see appendix H: The Self-Publishing Checklist.)

The font choice for the body of the book should be clear and clean in at least a twelve-point font, with paragraph spacing at 1.15 to 1.25 and indenting at each paragraph (read: nothing fancy, super tiny, huge, or ridiculously spaced and lacking indents at the start of a paragraph). All of these elements may seem obvious, but we've seen books done without attending to these points, and, unfortunately, they look sloppy. They look like someone who cut corners or who didn't take the time to learn what was standard.

PAY ATTENTION AND ADVOCATE FOR A GREAT-LOOKING BOOK

A lot of the time, we see sloppiness happening with self-published or some indie-published books. Avid readers are aware of what traditional, well-done books look like. So, when that book order from Amazon arrives, you get a close look at it, you flip it open, and you see that things are out of order, missing, or poorly done; in this case, unfortunately, your first thought is "this is a shitty self-published book." While a lot in self-publishing has changed and a ton of self- and indie-published books can look fantastic, a lot of others can look poorly. Those poorly done ones cause the good ones to get a bad rap.

If you're an author eyeing the self-pub or indie-pub route, we aren't knocking it. This book and our individual books are all indie-published, but when people pick them up, they don't scoff at them, remarking on how they were published. They don't even know or care how they were published a lot of the time. Why? Because they look legit. They were professionally done. And we each busted out all the stops on each of our books (including this one) to ensure that no reader missed out on the fabulous stuff in between the covers because they were too distracted by things like bad covers and ugly interior design and layout.

It's amazing that self- and indie-publishing options exist in the publishing industry today. It opens up the world to a lot more great authors and great books. There's less competition to be published with these options available. You can get a book to market more quickly. You have more creative control. You get higher royalties (more on what that means in chapter 10). The advantages of going either of these routes abound. But such benefits, especially speed, don't mean you should skip out on doing right by your book.

More importantly, if you hire an indie press to do most of the heavy lifting for you, you don't just take a backseat and stop paying attention. Yes, you're paying for their professional services and guidance, but don't just be a bobblehead, nodding at everything they suggest. Advocate for yourself and your book. Be an active participant and a business partner. This is YOUR book at the end of the day, so you need to know about and weigh in on all the decisions. Consider their expertise, of course, as they know what they're doing more than you do at this stage in the process, but that doesn't mean you have to give up all creative license and executive decision-making power.

(Pro Tip)

Don't just take a backseat once you've hired a press. Advocate for yourself and your book. Be an active participant.

That said, we want to offer this piece of advice: vet your press before you sign on the dotted line. Truly, you should do this even if you're going to self-publish by hiring separate cover designers or typesetters. Go look at the books they've previously published and evaluate if you think they've done a fine job producing a great-looking book. Always know who you're working with, what their portfolio looks like, what their prior successes are, and what their contract includes. Just like lots of people have the initials MD at the ends of their names and completed the same umpteen years of schooling to become doctors, we all know that some doctors are better than others, that there are some we would trust more than others.

Did You Catch That?

Vet your press before you sign on the dotted line.

Don't assume that every indie press (or private contractor) is an outstanding professional that will deliver an outstanding product and that, therefore, you can just sit back and relax. Do your homework before engaging in services, then stay alert—not in a paranoid, hypervigilant way but in an "I care about my book and what happens between now and publication" kind of way. You don't want to get to the end of the line having a poorly designed and poorly produced book that gets sent to readers looking half-cooked.

All of that said, we are making your detective work easier. You will want to review appendix F: People on the Publishing Path so that you know who you will need, and there's a list in appendix J: How to Determine If a Publishing Company Is Reputable to help you keep a watchful eye for dodgy publishers, with questions to ask to avoid them.

Truly, the most beautiful thing about this part of the book is that by having a better understanding of what makes a great book, you know all the things you need to do to ensure yours qualifies as one. Regardless of which pieces you choose to do and which you choose to hire for help, your own standards will be higher, which means your final product will be better. A better final product means a better chance that someone will want to buy that product—so long as they know it exists, of course, which is where we are heading soon. Part 3 is all about profiting from your brilliant and badass book. But before we get there, we are making a pit stop. We can't talk about the makings of a great book without discussing what some people are doing during this emergence of AI to get their book "done" rather than "done *right*."

TAKEAWAYS AND TO-DOS

Takeaways

- Your title is the most important asset to your packaging and marketing so choose it wisely.
- Above all else, your title needs to reflect the contents of your book.
- Have a professionally designed cover. We don't want people to judge your book harshly and, therefore, not buy it.
- Cover elements are brand (and marketing) elements.

To-Dos

- Start developing a rock-star title, trying these methods:
    - Brainstorming. Write down all kinds of ideas you have.
    - Study the titles of other books in your category and see what they're doing. If you notice a pattern or trend in the titles, imitate that pattern while applying your book's content focus.
    - Search your book for phrases or key ideas you return to repeatedly.
- If you already have a title, give it a test run.
    - Share your ideas with your mastermind or networking group, best friend, spouse, or online community. See what lands with them and why.
    - Specifically ask them to tell you what they think your book is about based on the title suggestions. If they are able to get an accurate idea then you're on the right track. If they are totally out in left field, you may need to rework your ideas.

NOTES

_____

_____

_____

_____

_____

_____

_____

_____

_____

_____

_____

_____

_____

_____

_____

_____

_____

_____

_____

_____

CHAPTER 7

BE SMART ABOUT WRITING YOUR BOOK WITH AI

L oosely translated, artificial intelligence (AI) stands for "fake smarts." So, with that, you have a good idea of our stance on using AI to generate your book. But read on so you can get the full scoop because we are not just penning our personal perspective on the role AI should or should not play in getting your book to market. We also propose some strategic uses of AI while completing your book project, and we give you a glimpse into legal implications concerning the matter that you will definitely want to check out. (All of a sudden, you're sitting up a little straighter, aren't you? We figured you would. Any mention of the law usually gets peeps' attention.)

Now, if we'd written and published this book when no one was talking about AI or freaking out that the bots were about to take over the world, then we could have totally skipped this chapter. ChatGPT, the chatbot we've all grown to know (and love?), entered the scene in late November 2022—just as we were all trying to figure out (for the umpteenth time) clever uses for leftover turkey—and it changed the content creation world. You can tell one of those nifty platforms—and by the time this book comes out, we are sure there will be far more than ChatGPT, Jasper, and Copymatic available—what kind of content you want generated, and in no time, it spits out words that sound impressive; on point; and, where applicable, just like you. A lot of the time, they are even grammatically correct.

(That sounds like a college student's dream when pressed for time to create an essay that's due at 8:00 a.m. the Monday after homecoming weekend, right?) But just so that we are abundantly clear, and before we get all riled up about how incredible it is that technology can assist in writing, take note of what you just read. It can *assist*. That means it should not be used to generate an entire manuscript! If your manuscript is generated entirely by a bot, we would argue that the bot gets the byline. You know, as in "written by [Your Name Here]," except it would read, "Written by The New-And-Improved Artificial Intelligence."

Did You Catch That?

AI can assist, but it should not be used to generate an entire manuscript. If your entire manuscript is generated by a bot, then the bot gets the byline.

Hundreds of tutorials are circulating online demonstrating how to write a book in just a few hours. And at the time of this writing, hundreds of books are available on Amazon that are authored, or more aptly put, coauthored (read: assisted) by AI. There's no doubt that the number of available AI-authored books is on the rise.

For us, this raises a number of philosophical quandaries about integrity, the creative process, ownership, plagiarism, originality, intellectual property, and author rights—to name a few. (By this we mean who gets to claim the ownership, intellectual property, or royalties on the book? The person who merely plugged the book terms into the engine and sat around, waiting for the program to do its thing, but who might not have penned a word or come up with an original thought in the process?)

You can totally use AI tools to assist with generating ideas and ensuring that your content is grammatically correct. Some platforms even incorporate search-engine-optimized features along with plagiarism checking, which as book people, we find extremely important. Platforms such as Grammarly, Chegg, and EasyBib offer plagiarism checkers that can detect similarities in text, including AI-generated text, and can create properly formatted in-text citations and references, aiding you in avoiding plagiarism. There's no doubt that these are useful crutches from time to time. Our lives are busy enough as they are—you don't have to ask us twice to sign up for something that's going to take away some of the legwork. We agree that employing AI as a tool can be helpful, a time-saver, and a great collaborator for brainstorming or maybe even research. In a fraction of the time it would take you to do it on your own, you can use AI to generate a search-engine-optimized book description, an engaging press release announcing the exciting news of your forthcoming title, or even targeted marketing copy that you customize and manually tweak to use in your social media posts and elsewhere. You can use it to identify potential diversity, equity, and inclusion issues in your manuscript; sift through dense legalese that may be present in contracts; or find information on titles that contain content similar to your manuscript so you can gain a competitive edge. We could go on and on.

What Does That Mean?

SEARCH ENGINE OPTIMIZED

In its simplest terms, to make something search engine optimized means that you design or write material in a way that increases the chances of your work appearing in search results. It's the process of improving your text to include the exact words and phrases people typically use to search for answers to the problems your book (or product or service) solves, thereby increasing your book's visibility in places like Google or Microsoft Bing. You optimize your book so that it has a greater chance of appearing on search engines.

AI as a neutral resource that is available to us isn't the problem, really. It's how it's used and for what. Without spending hours discussing the helpful features of AI technology, we want to focus on what it can't do and why we so strongly discourage you from thinking that that is the ultimate route to take with your book.

EVEN THE BEST AI-WRITTEN BOOK CAN'T DUPLICATE YOU

We could stop right there with that sub-header. Nuff said, right? There's only one original. One. Sure, you can access or utilize the best AI program on the market. Then, as you tell it what you want it to produce, pages quickly fill with strategically placed words and sentences from a platform trying to be you. And yes, the amount of content AI produces in a short period of time is delightful. But AI cannot establish you as the expert. It can't reach into your memory bank and pull all the experiences and anecdotes to perfectly place within the manuscript. AI is not you, and it can't tell your story. Nobody (or no electronic thingamajig) can create or tell your story better than you can.

Yes, there are plenty of people out there who *think* they know you and therefore know your story and are happy to share their version of it (but for all the reasons you can think of, we need them to stop, and stop it right now). AI cannot get the real . . . the raw . . . the emotions . . . the experience . . . the "you just had to be there" type of presentation. "A" and "I" are used to spell *authenticity*, but AI cannot *capture* authenticity. Look, the "A" in "AI" stands for "artificial," the antithesis to "authenticity."

> **Did You Catch That?**
>
> *AI cannot capture authenticity.*

Don't get us wrong. It's a great starting point. But that's just it—a starting point. You, my friend, need to finish it. And finishing it means filling in all the details that just are not out there in the world for a platform to capture and use to cook up a piece of writing. Finishing it also means reading every word the AI platform wrote and determining if it at least makes sense or whether it's organized the way you would organize it for your audience. Finishing it means checking it to make sure it's not pulling a direct quote from some other source without proper citation and referencing. The point is that if you're going to use AI content generation, don't just prompt the thing and then hit "print" or publish over on Amazon (or anywhere).

You may shoot back at us with "I'm not a talented writer" or "I don't know where to start a manuscript. I need some kind of help, and AI sounds like just the ticket! Besides, how is using AI any different than working with a writing coach or a ghostwriter but in a more efficient way?!" We certainly believe in working smarter, not harder. And we are not saying to avoid AI-generated content like the plague. What we *are* saying is that AI can be a tool. You can get ideas. You can use it as a starting point. You can give it a try to see what it creates, then use it to develop your ideas. You can use it for certain components of your book business. (Recall the idea of using it to help create your book's description, press release, or social media content. That's what we're talkin' 'bout.) But it should not be the whole enchilada. It should not write your entire book.

The word *write* is a verb, which means that taking action is involved. Writing is actually several actions. It has a process, one we are all taught in school. You brainstorm, you draft, you edit, you revise, then you publish (or you pass it in if you're still thinking in school terms). Remember everything we talked about in the prior chapter? Writing is taking an idea and being the one to work with it, mold it, and shape it until it becomes the final thing you want to put out there. When you sit down to put in a bunch of keywords and terms and ideas into an AI platform, you are *prompting* the tool to produce a result, such as a manuscript. Prompting, not writing. Your best content will be generated by you, not some program. Trust us on this one.

Pro Tip

Use AI to give your creativity a jump start, then add content that exists only in your head.

Think of how the microwave revolutionized cooking. (But let's be real. Is popping a few ingredients into a box, closing the door, punching a few buttons, and watching your food rotate on a glass plate really considered "cooking"?) When the microwave hit the scene, we didn't throw out our cooktops and ovens; it brought convenience to our lives but did not replace us getting in that kitchen and cheffing it up. A microwave could never replicate or replace a real meal. And now that AI is on the scene, it doesn't mean we throw out our pens, pencils, paper, and writing abilities. AI can never replicate or replace you.

CHOCOLATE OR VANILLA? MEH, CLOSE ENOUGH

You are a living human being, and you've been there, done that, and done some more. You've walked the walk, and you have the scars to prove it. No matter what may be out there in the cloud, on the blogs, in the posts, on the web—you get the idea—nobody can tell your story better than you can tell it. Nobody is going to sound more like you or look more like you than you. If you send the bot to be you, you're going to get a pretty stiff, pretty basic, vanilla version of yourself or, if you're lucky, maybe a slight twist of the flavors.

Yes, we will agree that a fully AI-generated manuscript is a pretty good knockoff, like some of those counterfeit luxury goods sold by vendors on the sidewalks of Canal Street in New York City's famous Chinatown. (No shade toward New York. We love The Big Apple, and we know that those vendors exist in plenty of other cities across the country and online.) But we also agree that the real thing is always better than the knockoff. Always. (Think of that awful nacho cheese sauce sold with chips or pretzels at outdoor affairs versus your homemade béchamel. And don't get us started on that stuff in the supermarket's refrigerated seafood section called krab!)

Your book deserves better than a knockoff, and your readers deserve better than a knockoff. Knockoffs can be functional, are usually cost-effective, and even look okay. But what's really happening is people are settling for the knockoff when what they want is the real deal. They deserve the real deal, which is you. You deserve the real deal, which is a book you carefully crafted and wrote. You shouldn't be reading your book, going, "It's okay. It does the job." And you don't want your reader thinking that either.

Plus, when AI strings together words that sound like you, that may have come from you, that may describe you, it's much like that game of telephone you played in elementary school. You start by sharing something with the first person in line. That information then makes its way down the pipeline through many different people, and voilà! The end result either lands completely in left field or is . . . well . . . close enough. And that's your book! *That's your book?!* Your AI-generated book is something that's described as "close enough."

HOW IS WORKING WITH A WRITING COACH OR GHOSTWRITER ANY DIFFERENT?

When it comes to the writing coach and ghostwriting front, we are all about humans helping humans! This means a dedicated and creative business partner right at your fingertips. This means that all of the emotional aspects that make a great story are still present. The techniques that make a genuine connection with your readers are still present. The thought process and analytical details are still present.

BUT WAIT—there's more! What about basic project management and ensuring the book is completed? Or a holistic partnership and guidance? How about story and manuscript development?

Working with a book coach or ghostwriter is working with a dedicated and collaborative creative business partner. They are bringing their writing expertise and understanding of story/book development to the project. This is their creative expertise. Because they are familiar with a book's life cycle (see chapter 4), the publishing process (chapter 9), and in some instances, book marketing (chapter 8), they can also look at your book project through a business lens.

This combination of creative and business acumen makes a book coach or ghostwriter a holistic—and invaluable—partner for the author. They are able to see the book from a variety of perspectives and comprehensively guide their client through the various stages of book development. A book coach or ghostwriter supports and guides the author in the story development or book outline and planning to ensure that the book holds together. They ensure that there is cohesion and a solid organization of ideas and concepts.

Not only will an experienced book coach or ghostwriter lend their deep understanding of a book's development and publishing phases, but they'll also command both project and process management to ensure that the book is brought through planning to completion. They will identify the way they work (process management) and establish the respective tasks and milestones required to write the book by a set deadline (project management). In short, the author has little administrative responsibility to facilitate the project or dictate the next steps.

Bottom line: AI can't offer you a personalized and focused conversation around any of these elements when it comes to your specific book. The search results may give you a wealth of information, but you'll still have to sift through and make determinations for yourself—determinations that might not be great to make on your own, especially if/when you're doing this for the first time. You may also find a lot of bad advice or one-size-fits-all approaches. Just because AI generated the result doesn't make it true.

Knowing what's best for your situation and your book isn't something you're going to be able to just pop into a search bar and receive. Having professional guidance, experience, and expertise when you can afford to have it is always going to be better than the Magic 8 Ball approach AI can offer. It may be efficient to throw out your question, shake things up, and see what pops up on the screen as the answer, but we think we can all agree that the Magic 8 Ball is nothing more than a fun parlor trick. It isn't something to be used as a replacement for free will, personal effort, and informed decision-making.

WHAT READERS WANT FROM YOU

As a professional in your industry, an expert in your field, or the owner of your very personal experiences, your audience wants *your* personal knowledge straight from you. Organizations hire you as their keynote speaker because you bring power, energy, and top-notch expertise. If you're a business coach, you are hired because you have the experience and skills to help other people succeed. You're an entrepreneur, pouring into the success of your ideal audience. And you're a step ahead because it's your expertise people are grabbing ahold of.

Your book is no different. They want you inside the pages as much as they want you inside their organizations and conferences or on their stages and podcasts. They want to know that what they're getting is 100 percent from you and by you, and if there's anything that's not yours, you're professional enough to give them the original source. Are you with us on this one?

You're a professional, and becoming a published author sets you apart. It puts your unique stamp on the world. You educate your audience by sharing what you know—and what you're damn good at because you're killing it out there!

The internet is filled with how-tos and guides that people are latching onto. But you have a unique perspective that's undoubtedly a lot better. You see that there's a simple solution to other people's shortcomings. You can even back it up with proof and statistics. You see the need time and time again. (Sound familiar? Like when we talked about all the signs that show you it's time to write your book in chapter 1? There's a method to our madness here.)

People want to learn from you. If you're successful in your field, people want to know *how*. Google and Amazon are the two most successful search engines. Imagine your expertise popping up as the solution to your ideal audience's challenges! They search for their question, and you return the answer. But how are you sharing the following?

- Insider details
- Obstacles you've overcome
- The how-to method containing your mark
- Secrets that set you apart from your competition

There's no way AI can successfully share that. Your book markets you. It markets your brand. It markets a world of greater opportunity for those who depend on a subject-matter expert like you.

INTELLECTUAL PROPERTY AND OWNERSHIP

We're going to cut to the chase here: when the printing press has stopped and the ink has dried, do you really want to place yourself in a position of having to put up some kind of fight, where you're trying to defend yourself as the right and true author of your book? We don't know how all of this will shake out with intellectual property and ownership boundaries, but at the time of us drafting this book, the courts were just starting to get involved with determining the scope of copyright ownership in the instance of AI-generated material.

One such case that caught our attention was the April 2023 US Supreme Court decision in *Thaler v. Vidal*. The Supreme Court declined to hear a challenge by computer scientist Stephen Thaler who had been denied patents for inventions that his AI system had created. A lower court had ruled in the US Patent and Trademark Office's favor, indicating patents can be issued only to human inventors. The lower court determined that (1) Thaler did not create the inventions for which he was seeking patents—it was his AI system that created them—and (2) Thaler's AI system, an inanimate object, could not receive the patents and be considered the legal creator of those inventions because it is not human. The Supreme Court agreed on all fronts. The owner of any patent—the ability to lay claim to the ownership of any intellectual property—lies with the rightful creator, which, in this instance, was an AI system. But the kicker is that Thaler created the AI system! Let that one sink in for a minute. Thaler wasn't simply trying to formally establish himself as the owner of the intellectual rights to his AI-generated material; he also created the AI system that generated the material. You'd think all bases were covered, but not so fast—he still couldn't claim ownership! Ouch! So, if you think about turning to AI as the answer to creating your manuscript, then also think about the possibility of ending up in the uncomfortable position of having to defend yourself as the outright owner of your book's contents.

Think about this, too: By allowing AI to generate a manuscript for you, you do not know if you are infringing upon someone *else's* copyright! What do you think of that?! With AI snagging and paraphrasing copy here and there from the internet, you do not know the exact sources of that content, and you may inadvertently end up stepping on someone else's toes—someone who has and can *prove* full ownership of their intellectual property and who also has no problem with hauling you into court, claiming you stole their ideas and presented them as your own.

Did You Catch That?

> If you use AI to generate your manuscript, you may inadvertently infringe upon someone else's copyright.

At the time of this writing, USCO does not conduct plagiarism checks or engage in any kind of verification process to authenticate a book's author. But also keep in mind that the USCO is not a court; it can issue a copyright, identifying someone as the owner of intellectual property, but it's not the ultimate determiner of whether a copyright is legally enforceable. It's up to the courts to decide that. A court may decide that if you, the human, are involved in a significant way or made a significant contribution to the writing, then you are indeed the rightful owner of the intellectual property. However, how is "significant" quantified? Is it the number of hours you put into the work? The number of words you actually wrote versus the number of words that came from AI? Suffice it to say that "significant" is subjective.

The Amazon KDP platform has even added a new AI-related question to which authors and publishers must respond during the book upload process. Amazon wants to know if AI tools were used to create any portion of the book, including texts, images, and translations, and if such tools were used, then you are prompted to list the names of those tools and/or platforms that were employed. Why is Amazon collecting this information? For what will they use the data? Will the information get forwarded to other publishing-adjacent entities? Good questions. When you find out the answers, give us a holler.

Again, we don't know all of the implications or where all of the legalities around AI will land. But given the AI-generated musical mash-ups that were breaking the internet during the first half of 2023 and the legal issues that could be brewing as a result (like the *Thaler* case), do you really want to use AI to generate your *entire* manuscript and run the risk of one day not being able to claim full ownership of your book?

Did You Catch That?

Do you really want to use AI to generate your entire *manuscript and run the risk of one day not being able to claim full ownership of your book?*

Writing a book is a big deal. Don't put yourself in a position where you're not sure if it's the best content you could have produced, where you're not sure if your readers get the authentic you, or where you question if a day will come when you are not able to 100 percent lay claim to your "hard work." Have no doubt that it is indeed *your* hard work that went into creating a book that your readers love and that you are proud to hold as your work of art.

Use AI as a tool, not as your ultimate shortcut for producing your book. Remember, you took an oath (figuratively speaking) at the beginning of this book to Approach your Book with a Commitment to Doing it right (ABCD mindset). We're telling you that the right way isn't the AI way.

TAKEAWAYS AND TO-DOS

Takeaways

- AI should not be used to generate an entire manuscript.
- Aside from not being able to fully capture your authentic voice, if you use AI to create a book from cover to cover, it may cause complications with your being able to rightfully lay claim to full ownership of your book.
- Avoid confusing AI as a smarter way to get the same support and service that ghostwriters and writing coaches provide. AI is not a substitute for a whole, live, breathing human writing expert.
- Accept and take advantage of AI as the tool that it is, designed to assist you with getting a start with pulling together your ideas, but do not view it as a clone of your brain.
- Be intelligent with your use of AI. When you do that, you can feel confident in what you have created.

To-Dos

- Learn about the AI tools that are currently on the market. Research them and find out the advantages and drawbacks to each of them.
- Give yourself some credit, and start with your own ideas (you have plenty of them!), then turn to an AI tool you trust only if you find yourself at a point where you simply cannot get any solid thoughts flowing.

- Research the current legal issues and implications surrounding the ownership rights of AI-generated content. The most important question you want answered is this: if there is ever a question as to who created my book and whether I am the rightful owner of its contents, will I prevail in a court of law?
- If you find yourself wanting to rely too heavily on AI to generate your content, then start researching ghostwriters and writing coaches; they are the more legitimate, safe, and supportive route to take.

NOTES

PART 3

PUBLISHING, MARKETING, AND MAKING MONEY FROM YOUR BOOK

CHAPTER 8

MARKETING STARTS BEFORE YOU PUBLISH

B efore you start to market your book, embrace three guiding principles. The first rule of marketing is know exactly what you want your book to accomplish and what you want it to do for you and/or your business. If this is still a little hazy for you and before you read another word, return to chapter 2 to get clear on your author presence and platform and the precise expectations you have for yourself and your book.

> **What Does That Mean?**
>
> ## AUTHOR PRESENCE AND PLATFORM
>
> *When you have an author presence and platform, you know for whom you're writing, and you know how to market your writing and use your overall visibility to reach your target reader wherever they spend time. It's everything you do online, offline, and in person to create and grow awareness of who you are, what you do, and what you believe in, with the goal of boosting your visibility and making it easier for your ideal readers to find and connect with you, your brand, your business, and your book. You make yourself known for the topic that you write on, so when people think of your book topic, they automatically think of you.*

The second rule of marketing your book is do not expect to see returns right away from your marketing efforts; if you do, then great, but we implore that you are realistic with yourself and your book. (We cover all kinds of details on ROI in chapter 10.) View all of your efforts as a long game focused on telling the world about your book and furthering your goals for your book.

And the final rule of book marketing is you are the best marketing tool your book will ever have. Ever. You can hire all the pros, buy all the ads, and get all the fancy schmancy graphics and assets, but you, your essence, your voice, your presence—YOU are the best marketing tool your book will ever have. Hands down. End of story. Without a doubt. Case closed.

We know what you're thinking: "But doesn't a publishing company do the marketing? Won't they market my book?" Not necessarily. As we indicated earlier, a publisher may highlight your book for a short while leading up to your publication date and possibly for a short while after your book is released, but then they turn their attention to other projects and clients. Yes, it is to everyone's advantage if they market your book, but their wheelhouse is publishing, not marketing. Remember, they're *publishers*. They publish books. They are not *book marketers*.

🎙️ **Did You Catch That?**

YOU are the best marketing tool your book will ever have, but don't go this alone.

But while you are the best marketing asset your book will ever have, do not go this alone. You are not a marketing expert, and even if you are, you still need a team to get all the work done. There are so many ways you can approach marketing—so many!—and some will align better with you, your book, your personality, and your goals than others will. For those reasons, rely on the marketing and public relations professionals referenced in chapter 13 to help you get the word out. Take every opportunity to advertise your book's upcoming release because if you don't say anything, no one will know about it.

WHEN SHOULD YOU START MARKETING AND SELLING YOUR BOOK?

It's never too early to start telling people about your book. In fact, you will want to start marketing and preselling your book before it's even published. Seriously. As soon as you have an idea and a title, start telling people about your book that's on the horizon. And once you get your cover design finalized, start including your book's image and information about your book on all your marketing pieces and everywhere you spend time online. This approach has multiple benefits. Aside from the obvious in that it gets your book in front of prospective buyers and readers, it motivates you to get it done! If you know you have put it out into the universe that you are writing a book and you have folks excitedly waiting to see what you create, you feel further compelled to deliver.

Did You Catch That?

It's never too early to start telling people about your book.

Make this prepublication period a win for everyone. Here's what we mean: customers are more willing to buy before a book is printed if they think they can get a deal. Have a special presale price to encourage early purchases. We recommend that you offer at least 20 percent off the list price for presale orders. As long as you make a profit—not that that's always the goal—you might go even lower, keeping in mind what, if anything, you will charge for shipping and handling (think postage, envelopes, tape, and mailing labels) and the time required to address envelopes, stuff them, and take them to the post office (or the fee to use an order fulfillment service).

Wondering about logistics? See appendix N: The Logistics of Book Presales for exactly what to do to organize book sales before your book even publishes.

Pro Tip

After your initial launch, you need to sell your book throughout the year if you want to continue to see sales coming in. Take advantage of holidays and celebrations to breathe life into your book and into marketing it. While established authors will take advantage of the holiday season to get a bump in sales, there's absolutely no reason you cannot do the same. If a holiday or special time of year is on the horizon, then remind your community that your book makes the perfect gift! Encourage the purchase of copies of your book for . . .

- *Mother's Day*
- *Father's Day*
- *Grandparent's Day*
- *High school and college graduations*
- *Retirement gifts*
- *Just-because/thinking-of-you gifts*
- *Get-well/while-you're-recuperating gifts*

WHAT MARKETING ASSETS DO I NEED?

Be selective about your marketing assets, ensuring they align with your brand and the overall image you want for you, your business, and your book. Put in place what makes the most sense, but don't feel the need to impress folks by trying to get all the things to market your book, ostensibly throwing cooked spaghetti against the wall to see what sticks. Know what marketing tools are worthwhile and respectable.

At a minimum, the marketing assets you need are high-quality, high-resolution, professionally designed graphics and images of your book; a webpage for your book; and a sell sheet. This means enlisting experts and not slapping something together on your own (unless that's your area of expertise and you have a killer eye for design). Additionally, while testimonials are not absolute requirements and not having them will not make or break your book, having them is a smart marketing tool.

Pro Tip

Enlist experts to produce high-quality, high-resolution, professionally designed graphics and images of your book, a webpage, and a sell sheet.

IN OUR EXPERT OPINION—BESTSELLER CAMPAIGNS

You may feel the same as a number of our authors, wanting an Amazon bestseller status strategy included in your marketing plan. We have authors who see it as a major goal and a sign of success. At times, it almost feels like it's the only reason they want to get published! We always aim to be of service, but at the same time, we have a different mindset.

The bottom line with earning Amazon bestseller status is to create a 99¢ e-book campaign on Amazon KDP, and as long as you can get as many people as you can to buy your 99¢ e-book during a dedicated hour, temporarily outselling the previous bestseller that's in the same category as your book, then wham-bam, you're a bestseller. To increase your chances of success, you can (and some authors do!) choose a really obscure category, one that has absolutely nothing to do with your book, to accomplish bestseller status.

At the time of this writing, Amazon is working to crack down on this practice by reducing the number of categories you can assign to your book from ten to three. However, let's keep it real; there's absolutely nothing stopping people from putting their book in a

> *strange category for the sake of tricking the system and blowing the last bestseller out of the water, then updating their categories at a later date (not that we are giving you a blueprint so you can go out and do this. Actually, we are begging you not to do this).*
>
> *A more respected bestseller is one that has performed remarkably well across multiple channels and not for just one hour on Amazon. Authors who have their books featured as bestsellers by the likes of The New York Times, The Wall Street Journal, USA Today, or The Washington Post earn that distinction because they sold tens of thousands of copies of their book in a year, and at least 5,000 copies were sold each week after the book's initial release date. These sales are diverse, meaning that they did not come from a preexisting list of the author's followers or the author's personal website or that thousands of them did not originate from only one marketplace, such as Amazon.*
>
> *But back to the Amazon bestseller ambition: Is it a worthwhile marketing pursuit? Will bestseller status increase sales? Will it cause people to have greater respect for you and your book? Will it make a difference in the grand scheme of things? Maybe. Maybe not. It's all a matter of personal preference.*

Again, in the marketing materials department, your book needs great graphics, a website or webpage, a sell sheet and press kit, and testimonials. Let's scratch the surface of what you need.

Graphics

Once your book cover is designed, your designer can generate 3D images that you can use to create social media posts; add to your book's webpage; and put on collateral, such as bookmarks, retractable banners, ads, flyers, merchandise, and such.

Website or Webpage

You have a couple of choices here. If you already have a website, then you can create a page on your existing site that is devoted to your book. However, if you do not have a website, then you can purchase a URL—ideally, the URL is the title of your book—to create a website for your book. (Make it easy on yourself; your book's website can consist of a single landing page that includes all the details about your book.) Or you can do both: use your current website to promote your book plus have an additional one dedicated to your book.

Your book's website is its home base. It's where people land after they Google your book and the first place they go to find out about your book. It is your book's marketing hub.

👤 **Did You Catch That?**

Your book's website is its home base. It's your book's marketing hub.

Regardless of whether you choose to create a page on your current website for your book or if you choose to purchase a URL to create a website solely devoted to marketing your book, keep the most important information clearly visible, and do not overcrowd the site or page with irrelevant content. For a breakdown of what to include in the design of your book's website or webpage, see appendix O: What You Need on Your Book's Website or Webpage.

🎤 **Pro Tip**

Regardless of whether you choose to create a page on your current website for your book or if you choose to purchase a URL to create a website solely devoted to marketing your book, keep the most important information clearly visible, and do not overcrowd your site or page with irrelevant content.

Sell Sheet and Press Kit

Your book's sell sheet is your book's résumé. It is a one-page description of your book that tells a bookseller, a gift shop, or another business everything it needs to know about your book before they decide to purchase and stock it. If you want to get your book into brick-and-mortar establishments, a sell sheet is a must. It gives prospective buyers a clear sense of who you are and what your book is about and is a lot more succinct and cost-effective than mailing out tons of copies of your book, hoping they'll attract a buyer's attention. For guidance on constructing your sell sheet, see appendix P: What You Need on Your Book's Sell Sheet.

Pro Tip

Ensure you create your book's sell sheet: a one-page description that includes everything a potential bookseller needs to know about your book.

In addition to a sell sheet, you may also have a press kit (including an author Q&A) to prepare for interviews. Your press kit is the expanded version of your book's sell sheet that provides more detailed information on your book, your full author bio, and links to download high-resolution images and other ancillary content. An author Q&A includes several pre-written questions and answers about you and your book and will likely get used word for word by interviewers when you appear on shows. (Yes, shows. More on that later in this chapter.)

Did You Catch That?

Your press kit is the expanded version of your book's sell sheet, providing more detailed book information, your full author bio, and links to downloadable high-resolution images of your book.

Testimonials and Advance Praise

Testimonials and advance praise put your book in front of your ideal audience as well as in front of more people than you'd get it in front of if you *didn't* have the testimonials. People who are associated with your book's topic and the people who will read your book are the ones you want to seek out. Known authors in your book's genre or prominent figures in your book's field, those who are respected in your industry or who are well versed in your book's topic, and anyone who influences your ideal audience make great candidates for writing testimonials, providing advance praise, getting more eyes on your book, and adding credibility to your work.

Once you have your testimonials, use the fire out of them! In addition to including your testimonials on your book's front cover, within its front matter, and/or on the back cover, you should show and use your testimonials whenever and wherever you have the chance to do so. That means they should be on your book's website, in your marketing materials, added to your social media posts, and referenced during interviews—wherever you have the chance, leverage them! Your testimonials indirectly tell others, "Look who else thinks my book is all that! You really should read it!" And don't forget that as people purchase your book online, they can leave online testimonials and reviews, too. For more on getting testimonials and advance praise before your book is published so that the reviews will spark interest in your book once it's published, see appendix M: How to Get Testimonials and Advance Praise.

> Pro Tip
>
> *Once you have your testimonials, leverage them any and every chance you get.*

HOW DO YOU GET THE WORD OUT?

After you tell all your family, friends, and close colleagues about your book, what do you do beyond that? Great question. Such a great question that there could easily be an entire book just on answering this one thing. (And there probably is—we just didn't write it.) Allow us to at least give you a surface-scratchin', 30,000-foot view of how you can make more people than just those in your contact list aware of your book. (Note: There is so much more to this. So much more. But this gets you started.) Remember, if you don't talk about your book, no one will know about it.

Blogging and Video Messaging

Many people who already follow you will buy your book because they know and like (or love) you and what you do. People are even more likely to buy the book if they know what it is about. Beyond just a paragraph or two of content, you can post a chapter to your website or blog every few days to build interest in the book. (Bear in mind that if you go the traditional publishing route, you are not necessarily at liberty to do this. Only if you retain the full rights to your book can you get creative with posting content like this.) Additionally, consider a Facebook or LinkedIn Live every so often where you talk about your book, or, if you already have a video presence on social media, include an invitation to preorder your book at special pricing for a limited time.

Email Marketing

Create an email list focused on getting as many readers as possible to sign up. Your email capture form (the thing that takes people's names and email addresses) will need to be visible and connected to your website or webpage. To do this, you'll need to set up an account with an email auto-responder system/email marketing service for this effort and then have your webmaster (or you) embed the email capture form on your website or webpage. Mailchimp, ActiveCampaign, AWeber, GetResponse, Constant Contact, and ConvertKit are a few such email marketing services, and some have free plans for up to a certain number of email list subscribers and/or up to a certain number of sent emails.

Once you create your account and have everything connected between your webpage and the email autoresponder system, you will need a sign-up incentive. Then, you need to set up automated emails that introduce subscribers to your content. Ensure you set up a custom email template so that your branding is consistent. (Does this sound complicated? Enlist marketing, website, and administrative experts who can successfully execute all of this with their eyes closed. This is where skilled and reliable author virtual assistants can come into play if paying book-specific experts isn't in the budget but you need some support. More on who to hire and for what in chapter 14.)

Send out messages to everyone on your list, telling them about the good news of your upcoming book release and how they can preorder their copies. Ensure you include a link that takes them directly to the pre-sale page on your website. Marketing assets, such as images and graphics (which we already covered in this chapter), will come in handy here.

What Does That Mean?

EMAIL AUTORESPONDER SYSTEM

An email autoresponsder system allows you to capture the names and emails of people visiting your site and automatically communicate with them after they've provided that information. For this to work, you need to understand a few of the individual pieces.

- **Email list sign-up:** *Put a sign-up form on your website, add a sign-up link to your email signature, and invite people to sign up via social media.*
- **Sign-up incentive:** *Provide a free PDF, digital download, or coupon code to purchase your book at a special rate; a free fifteen-minute consultation; or some other free content as a hook to encourage people to sign up.*
- **Automated emails:** *A sequence of pre-written emails that are automatically sent from your email service provider as responses to new email/newsletter subscribers.*

Podcasting

Podcasting is a way to reach a different audience who might not use social media as much as they listen to podcasts during their morning commute or an evening bike ride. It is a way to connect with fans who would never hear about you otherwise. You can be a guest on already established podcasts or you can launch your own podcast. Here are options for what you can do if you opt to launch your own show:

- Multimedia: Turn sections of your book content into podcast episodes.
- Series: Produce a short run of an eight- to twelve-week series to get noticed.
- Writer network: Help out fellow writers while also getting the word out about your book by inviting other authors onto your show to be guests.

When going on podcast shows, partner with micro-influencers, anyone with a show who also has 10,000 to 30,000 social media followers. This way, they are not too big and busy to not respond to you, but at the same time, they have a large enough following that you can benefit from. Borrowed ethos is where all the goodwill the public has with the micro-influencer transfers to you just by your being on their show. Search Apple Music and/or Spotify categories for shows with topics that complement your book topic/area of expertise but that do not compete with it, then search social media for the total number of followers these show hosts have to identify if they are micro-influencers. (Unsure of how to get on podcast shows? See appendix Q: Podcast Guest Best Practices for how to become a guest and what to do during the interview and afterward.)

Media Outreach Campaigns

Reach out to media outlets to pitch your book for coverage by them, and make sure you focus not only on pitching your book but also on providing relevant, interesting, and exclusive content that audiences will love. That is what the media are looking for: content that will draw in their audiences. Makes sense, right?

Create several ways to present your book and your expertise by creating several different pitches from different angles to appeal to different media outlets. Shows are always looking for content; producers are constantly working to generate ideas for show segments. Think of the current news cycle and how your book connects to a news story or an issue that is front of mind for audiences or how your book offers a different perspective that may not have been considered, a solution to a big issue that's currently in the news, or interesting strategies for dealing with a news headline.

Create talking points on the topic, have a publicist professionally write a press release, then distribute it to the masses. Essentially, have a ready-built news story so that TV producers and journalists don't have to write the story. Look at it this way: you're doing them a favor and improving your chances of getting a foot in the door and on a show if you deliver both a ready-built news story and a source (your book!) to speak about it.

Book Tours (In-Person or Virtual)

Often the easiest press to get is in your hometown. People love local celebrities, so make sure you have appearances at all of the media and events in your city. While this may be harder if you're in a major market, smaller towns are ripe for facilitating opportunities to connect with local fans. Here are some suggestions for in-person events:

- Bookstores: Show local support for local readers by hosting several events at bookstores, such as signings, Q&As, and readings.
- Newspapers, TV, and radio: Local media outlets love to feature guests and experts from the area.
- Groups, clubs, and associations: Identify local book clubs, reader groups, and/or writing workshops that meet in your area, and take the time to meet with them in person.

- Schools, universities, colleges, and academies: Similar to media outlets, local schools and universities often love to partner with local authors for on-campus events.

Be prepared to answer questions such as "what is your exact release date?" and "how will your book be distributed?" This means that you will need your book's sell sheet, a key marketing asset discussed earlier in this chapter.

Also, venture outside your city and make a list of the cities in which you want to have a book signing. Ideally, you'll want to include those cities where you have a following or members of your personal and/or professional community. Folks are not likely to just show up without knowing you or without knowing someone who's local and connected to you.

Finally, consider virtual events and/or virtual book tours, where you have any combination of the following leading up to your official publication date:

- Guest blog posts
- Interviews
- Podcast, TV, and/or radio appearances
- Social media contests
- Live social media events
- Webinars
- Video content posted by blogs
- Book reviews

Your Already Established Networks

Whether it's a coworker or your second cousin, connect with people who are already in your circle. Now is the time to pull out your contact list and reach out to everyone with whom you have worked in the past to tell them about your book and to ask them to support you by making a purchase or two. (But be careful with private messages on social media or sending mass messages to your network, letting them know about your book. We are not social media experts, but we do know that if you're not careful, are unaware, or you are not following the platform's community rules to a tee, then you can run the risk of ending up in social media jail. Not that either of us is speaking from personal experience or anything . . . Just sayin' . . .)

Additionally, call in favors from family and friends, asking them to provide early reviews of your book and to preorder copies for themselves. Finally, look at additional groups and connections you have. Are you a member of a local wine club, or do you volunteer at a nonprofit organization? Make sure they know about your book! They can't support your book if they do not know about it.

Book Launch Team

Coordinate a team of fans that is hyper-focused on getting the word out about your book prior to its publication date. Put the fans on an email list and look for fun ways to get them involved, such as providing you with early reviews/advance praise of your book on Amazon; brainstorming promotion ideas; posting about your book on social media; and promoting your book on their own blogs, podcasts, and any of their other platforms.

Potential Partners

Seek out nonprofits that could benefit from your book. Ask these potential partners what corporations like to partner with them, then go to those corporations and suggest that they sponsor and subsidize a quantity of your book for their preferred nonprofit partner.

Return to those organizations with which you have conducted business, let them know about your upcoming book, and offer a discount on bulk orders or offer your services in exchange for them purchasing X number of copies of your book.

Remember, know exactly what you want your book to do for you, and view your marketing efforts as an ongoing strategy for keeping your book relevant and on people's radars. Be strategic about the tools you use, and no matter which ones you choose, know that you and your presence are the best marketing tools you will have to promote your book.

Pro Tip

Do not engage in every single marketing strategy. You will run the risk of spreading yourself thin, getting frustrated, or simply not shining in every lane. Identify a select few that resonate with you and that you feel most confident in executing, then commit to those strategies.

TAKEAWAYS AND TO-DOS

Takeaways

- Make sure that you know what you want from your book and that it aligns with your author presence and platform.
- Do not wait for your book to be published before you start to market it. The sooner you get the word out, the more your book will enjoy sales and exposure.
- Even if you choose to self-publish, do not take the DIY corner-cutting approach, especially with the creation of your marketing assets.
- Be selective about how you get the word out, and do not go it alone. Again, rely on the experts in marketing and public relations to create a plan for you.

To-Dos

- Decide with which assets you want to market your book, and hire graphic design experts to create them.
- Identify how you want to get out and market your book and with whom you will partner to do so. Make choices that are most comfortable for you and that do not feel like a drag so that you are able to engage at full capacity.

NOTES

CHAPTER 9

KNOW YOUR PUBLISHING OPTIONS

To understand how to make money from your book, it's imperative to first understand the different routes available to you for getting your book to market; the investment required, where applicable; and the advantages and disadvantages of each of those publishing models because all of them impact the monies you will see as a result of being a published author. In short, there are four models—traditional, hybrid, indie, and self-publishing—and each one comes with its own set of pros and cons.

TRADITIONAL PUBLISHERS

Traditional publishers, such as Simon & Schuster or Penguin Random House, are the ones you often hear about or see in the big-box stores. To play at this level, you often need literary agent representation that plays as a gatekeeper. A literary agent's job is to get you in with the publisher. There's a whole process for getting a literary agent, then a whole other process for them to get your book seen by a traditional publisher.

What Does That Mean?

A WHOLE PROCESS FOR TRADITIONAL PUBLISHING

Many indie and hybrid presses are pay-to-play models, meaning that if you can afford their services, they'll most likely work with you. This doesn't mean they don't have standards for the quality of the books they choose, but there are no gatekeepers between authors and the publishing team.

With traditional publishing, most often than not, an author has to secure representation via a literary agent. They have to first win over the literary agent, then the literary agent goes to bat for them with the publishers. Researching, querying, and landing a literary agent can be a long and competitive process. Plus, there are very specific submission requirements per agent that must be followed to gain their attention, and even then, there's no guarantee that you'll hook their interest or even hear back from them. And there's no promise that if you do hear back, you'll land them as an agent or that they won't ask you to work on the manuscript some more before taking you on as a client and/or "shopping" your project to publishers.

There are some agents who charge a high reading fee before even consid-ering taking you on as a client. Be wary of those. One way to confirm whether an agent is reputable is to check if an agent is a member of the Association of Authors' Representatives. Vetting and securing agent representation can take years and several rejection letters.

The agent then pitches your manuscript to publishers, which can also take an unknown amount of time. And if you are lucky to sign on with an agent, they can take a 15 percent commission on your published book. (This is on top of the high royalties the traditional publisher retains.) A lot of authors don't want to invest an unknown amount of time trying to jump through the first hoop with no guarantee of securing representation and then no guarantee of securing a press.

Perhaps some of the biggest things to know about this publishing model is that it can take a LONG time—a long time as in YEARS—it's highly competitive, you need to have a damn good book or book idea that will sell, and you give up a majority of your rights (if not *all* of your rights!) to the work. The advantage here is that you don't pay the publisher to publish your book.

Did You Catch That?

> With traditional publishing, it can take years, it's highly competitive, you need to have a damn good book or book idea that will sell, and you give up a majority of your rights (if not all of your rights!) to the work.

Traditional Publishing Advantages and Drawbacks

ADVANTAGES	DRAWBACKS	THIS OPTION IS A GOOD FIT FOR YOU IF YOU ...
• The author does not need to pay any money up front. • The publisher takes care of everything; the publisher edits, formats, prints, markets, and distributes your book. • The book will be published properly. • The author may receive an advance against future royalties.	• There is a one-in-a-hundred or a one-in-a-thousand chance that you will get a return call from an agent or that the publishing company will provide any feedback on an author's proposal and manuscript. • It can take a long time, sometimes years, to get published. • The publisher makes all the decisions; the author does not have any say in cover design, marketing, editing, or creative license—all the things that go into making a book successful. • The author sees a royalty rate of 5 percent to 20 percent.	• have written a tremendous book that has a strong likelihood of getting the attention of a traditional publisher. • have a platform; an extremely large following of tens of thousands, if not hundreds of thousands, of followers; or you are a big name with celebrity or influencer status.

Traditional publishing is a route that works well for an author with a BIG platform—think celebrities, well-known politicians, and social media influencers—and/or an author who has already published a book that sold well. In reality, this is not an option for 99 percent of people. However, if you have the motivation, a book that will have wide appeal and the promise of selling tens of thousands (if not hundreds of thousands) of copies, and you can get the eye and ear of a literary agent, then this is the best fit for you.

HYBRID PUBLISHERS

There are hybrid publishers who blend the best of the traditional publishing world with the best of the indie publishing world. They have people on staff to produce an amazing book. They may have an application or submission process to check for quality standards and may still reject some books or force authors to go through a developmental edit/revision the way the big traditional publishers do. But with hybrid publishers, the rights to the work remain with the author. The profit margin for the author is also better with a hybrid model. One of the biggest things to know about this publishing model is you pay to work with them and to receive their services, but hybrid publishers do not accept all manuscripts and may require extensive editing of a manuscript before publishing or may opt to not publish a manuscript at all.

Did You Catch That?

Working with a hybrid publisher does not guarantee that you will get published. Hybrid publishers do not accept all manuscripts and may require extensive editing of a manuscript before publishing or may opt to not publish a manuscript at all.

Hybrid Publishing Advantages and Drawbacks

ADVANTAGES	DRAWBACKS	THIS OPTION IS A GOOD FIT FOR YOU IF YOU . . .
• You can get published quickly—in a matter of months instead of years. • Your book will be of excellent quality. • You'll save a tremendous amount of time. • They will help you market your book. • You own your content to use to generate revenue through other products. • You will get distribution for your book. • Your royalty rate will be higher than if you work with a traditional publisher.	• While your chances of getting published with a hybrid publisher are higher than they are with a traditional publisher, there's still a chance that the hybrid publisher will not accept your book. • If your manuscript is accepted for publication, the publisher may insist on massive changes to the content before your book is published. • There is an up-front investment.	• see the up-front fee as an investment in your future or the future of your business. • already have an incredible manuscript that needs little to no developmental or substantive editing, or you are fine with having to make massive changes to the manuscript at the publisher's request. • do not have the time or interest in managing all the publishing details and would rather leave it all to the professionals. • have the money or are willing to pay for a professional product. • see other avenues for monetizing your book (e.g., speaking engagements, attracting clients for bigger projects, using the book as a basis for leading masterminds or master classes).

INDIE PUBLISHERS

Indie publishers offer authors a full range of services—from cover design, line editing, typesetting, and marketing support to simply offering a few bells and whistles, like getting your account set up with a book distributor and ensuring your Library of Congress registration. Indie presses leave all rights and final decisions to the author. They may not have any specific requirements for the author's manuscript other than that the author pays for the services rendered. Like the hybrid model, the profit margin for the author is better with this kind of press than it is with traditional publishers.

Indie Publishing Advantages and Drawbacks

ADVANTAGES	DRAWBACKS	THIS OPTION IS A GOOD FIT FOR YOU IF YOU …
• You can get published quickly—in a matter of months instead of years. • You'll save a tremendous amount of time. • You own your content to use to generate revenue through other products. • You have major input in your book. • You are guaranteed to get your book published. • Your royalty rate will be higher than if you work with a traditional publisher.	• Because this type of publisher may recommend changes but may not insist on any changes to the content before publishing your book, you may not have the absolute best product possible. • There is an up-front investment.	• see the up-front fee as an investment in your future or the future of your business. • do not have the time or interest in managing all the details and would rather leave it all to the professionals. • have the money or are willing to pay for a professional product. • see other avenues for monetizing your book.

SELF-PUBLISHING

Self-publishing means you're doing it all yourself. That's where the word *self* comes in. Now, it does not mean you actually design your own cover or edit your own work, but it could mean that you're the one finding all of these professionals yourself and are project managing all of the moving parts and pieces. It could also mean you're the one ensuring you're registered with the Library of Congress, choosing your price point, setting up your own online accounts, and uploading your own files to distributors—you are essentially doing all the things, or finding the professionals to do all the things, to get your book to market. See chapter 13 to get a full understanding of the professionals you need to self-publish.

Self-Publishing Advantages and Drawbacks

ADVANTAGES	DRAWBACKS	THIS OPTION IS A GOOD FIT FOR YOU IF YOU . . .
• You are guaranteed to get your book published. • You are in control of the timeline for how long it takes to get your book published. You do not have to wait to get your book published. You publish when you are ready. • You retain creative control. • You do not have to allow other people to determine your success. • You and your readers decide the worth of your words, thoughts, and ideas. • You retain the majority of the royalties. • Successful self-publishing will make it more likely that your next book could be picked up by a literary agent and traditional publisher. • You do not spend a ton of time trying to get an agent's attention. • There is nothing to stop you from using your book content to develop and sell supplemental materials (e.g., courses, updated versions, and an audiobook rerelease).	• You have to pay as you go for services you contract. • You are working with independent contractors with varying standards. • You have to vet and hire people to perform all the services required to get your book ready to market, or you have to figure out how to do it yourself.	• have a lot of time to devote to the book. • want to manage all the details. • want or need to keep costs down.

When you self-publish, you're in charge of it all, which is both an advantage and disadvantage. This can be one of the most cost-effective publishing options, but that doesn't mean it comes without a cost. You'll still be paying someone at some point (a cover designer, an editor, a typesetter) or expending personal time and energy to figure out how to complete the work on parts of the project yourself. For a list of everything you need to do to take care of publishing yourself, see appendix H: The Self-Publishing Checklist.

There are advantages and disadvantages to each publishing model or type, so understanding your goals for your book, your timeline, and your budget is beneficial when making decisions about which publishing route to take. You also have the option to work with a publishing consultant who can guide you through the process. Naturally, that comes at a cost to you. For more support on sorting through how to choose the publishing model that's the best fit for you, see appendix A: The Pros and Cons of Each Publishing Route.

TAKEAWAYS AND TO-DOS

Takeaways

- All publishers are not equal, and each one will impact the control you have over your finished book and the profit margins you see.
- Getting published by a traditional publisher is often regarded as the most ideal route by authors who are just starting out, but it's not the most realistic route for most authors.
- Just as traditionally published authors have realized success, so have self-, indie-, and hybrid-published authors.
- No one publishing route is better than the next.

To-Dos

- Identify your long-term goals, vision, and budget for your book.
- Understand the advantages and drawbacks to each publishing model and how each one aligns with your publishing budget and your book business goals to determine which one resonates with you.
- Be honest with yourself, your proposed book's topic and content, and your budget. Ask yourself which publishing route is truly the right one.
- Conduct further research on your preferred route to confirm that it is the best and most realistic choice for you, your book, and your book business.

NOTES

CHAPTER 10

THE TRUTH ABOUT YOUR SPEND, YOUR ROI, AND YOUR ROYALTIES

"You should NEVER pay to get published!"

"If a publishing company says you have to pay them to publish your book, then it's a scam! Run in the other direction!"

"The publishing company is supposed to pay *you*! You don't pay the publishing company!"

How many times have you read or heard these kinds of statements online and elsewhere from well-meaning people who want to "educate" and steer new authors away from the perils of publishing? It can all be so confusing. But because you read chapter 9, you know how to navigate your way through all of this to find the truth.

The fact is no, you do not *have* to pay to get published, but as we also covered in previous chapters, the likelihood of your book getting picked up by a traditional publishing company, where you do not have to pay to get your book into the marketplace, is next to nil. Getting the attention of a traditional publishing company takes a lot of skill, talent, and patience and is not much of an option for the majority of the population. It is true that in traditional publishing, the author receives an advance in some instances as well as royalty payments. Again, that happens only some of the time, and it's not promised or guaranteed. Therefore, we're back at square one: if you want to get published, then you will have to pay to get it done. (And the last time we checked, no one's working for free.)

With this in mind, we do not include traditional publishing in the conversation around expenses and ROI. What we will tell you is that your royalties from a traditional publisher are far lower than if you publish via one of the other avenues (self, indie, or hybrid).

Did You Catch That?

If the goal is to get published, you will have to pay to do all the work yourself or have others do it for you. Getting the attention of a traditional publisher takes skill, talent, and patience, which a majority of authors do not have.

Now, because there are scammers out there in *every* industry, don't settle for the first publisher you find. Just as you would in any other instance, conduct your research to find reputable publishing partners. (For more on this, see appendix J: How to Determine If a Publishing Company Is Reputable.)

IN OUR EXPERT OPINION—THE TRUTH ABOUT PAYING FOR PUBLISHING

Many people will quickly indicate that reputable publishers do not ask for money. That's simply not completely accurate. According to international research and data analytics group WordsRated, only one to two percent of the population will get published by one of the Big Five traditional publishing giants: Hachette Book Group, HarperCollins Publishers, Macmillan Publishers, Penguin Random House, and Simon & Schuster. So, what are the remaining 99 percent supposed to do?

The Big Five choose to publish only those authors whose books have great promise of selling tens and hundreds of thousands of copies—those books that are going to essentially sell themselves oftentimes simply because of the name of the author that's on the cover. Therefore, the publisher can assume all publishing costs and rely on taking a percentage of the sale of the authors' books to keep their doors open. However, not everyone has the name Oprah Winfrey, Joanna Gaines, Bill Gates, Jennifer Lopez, Barack Obama, or [insert the name of the latest and greatest person who has everyone's attention].

For authors who can't sell thousands and thousands of copies of their books in the blink of an eye, they have to go elsewhere. That's where hybrid and indie publishing companies come in, and if you work with those publishers, you have to pay. While some of them publish amazing books that enjoy all kinds of success, it's typically not at the level of traditional publishing companies. Publishing companies that require you to pay are not scammers, they're not shady, they're not pulling fast ones on you, and they're also not running a charity. They are running a business, and in order to keep the doors open, they have to charge a fee for their services.

SET REALISTIC EXPECTATIONS

While it's true that what you put into your book is what you will get out of it—if you put in the time, effort, and research to make it a quality product, then readers, reviewers, and your industry will recognize, respect, and reward you for your work—this adage is not entirely accurate when it comes to your total financial investment and the ultimate return on that investment. Can you write a book with the expectation that you will yield enough profits to pay your mortgage, with an expectation that you'll be set for life or that you will be able to retire and live off your royalty payments? Sure! However, it's not a *realistic* expectation regardless of whether you publish your book yourself or if you invest in a publisher to do the work for you. Realizing this early on will save you a wealth of disappointment and will set you up to make smart decisions with marketing and positioning your book.

WHAT DRIVES SELF-PUBLISHING COSTS?

The average cost to self-publish a book—doing all the work yourself or finding the experts to take your manuscript from a rough draft to a finalized book that's ready to go to market—ranges from $500 to more than $5,000. Why such a huge variance in investment?

Did You Catch That?

The average cost to self-publish ranges from $500 to more than $5,000.

Imagine purchasing a home that's the same square footage and model as the one that's five houses down from you, but yours has a lawn that was professionally designed by a high-end landscaper, stonework on the facade, and custom garage doors. Plus, on the inside, it has upgrades galore, from the paint on the walls to the doors; faucets; light fixtures; flooring; window treatments; and even the high-efficiency, elongated, comfort-height toilets with accompanying bidets. That house that's five doors down is essentially the base model, and it shows inside and out. Yes, both are the same house, but there are several factors that determine how much you pay.

> ## IN OUR EXPERT OPINION—PAY MORE THAN $500
>
> *If you're paying only $500 in total to publish your book, then that means you are ostensibly doing all the work yourself, which WE DO NOT ADVISE YOU TO DO UNDER ANY CIRCUMSTANCES WHATSO-EVER. If you want to be taken seriously as an author, then you want a book that looks like it should be taken seriously. One that costs you only $500 to produce will likely get more snickers and laughs than it gets serious looks and sales.*

There are several factors that determine if you will pay closer to $500 or $5,000 and upwards to self-publish your book. We discuss those factors here. (And for a specific breakdown of costs down to the penny, see appendix E: The Cost to Self-Publish.)

THE LENGTH OF YOUR MANUSCRIPT

When you reach out to editors and publishers, one of the questions they ask is "what's the length of your manuscript?" They want to know this answer in terms of how many words you have written, not how many pages you have written. That's because in book publishing, length is measured not by the number of pages you have but by the word count, and editing costs are typically calculated by the word (e.g., a 75,000-word manuscript at $0.05/word will cost $3,750.00 for editing). Fonts and font sizes can change the page count; however, regardless of the font you use or any changes you make to the font size, the word count does not change, keeping fee calculations consistent and more predictable for everyone.

Word processing programs, such as Microsoft Word, typically provide the word count for you, but if you need a general guideline, a typical page with one-inch margins typed in twelve-point font, with standard spacing elements between words, and with single-spaced paragraphs contains approximately 500 words. Naturally, the longer your manuscript, the higher the costs you'll incur when it comes to editing and proofreading. And no matter the length of your manuscript, for professional editing services alone, you will definitely spend more than $500.

Did You Catch That?

In book publishing, length is measured not by the number of pages but by word count, and editing costs are calculated by word.

Additionally, the length and complexity of your manuscript will factor into how much you pay for typesetting. After your book's interior is formatted, it can extend beyond the 125 pages you landed on in your word processing program. Typesetters typically charge by the page based on the final formatted page count, not based on the page count of the manuscript you present to them. Some genres require more graphs, charts, and diagrams to illustrate and support points than other genres require. So, if you have such elements, plus you need a designer to create them for you, then that is a charge in excess of the per-page fee. Therefore, the longer and more complex your manuscript, the greater your typesetting/book interior formatting spend.

THE STATE OF YOUR DRAFT

If you hand over an incredibly rough first draft to any editor without bothering to read through it to check for clarity and to correct any errors on your own—you're just glad to be done and are closing your eyes and clicking "send"—then it will require more time for the editor to put the manuscript through heavier editing and therefore may require more money. For instance, while developmental editing may include some level of mechanical editing, the work of a mechanical editor is not what the developmental editor has been hired to perform. As such, if you send off your manuscript to a developmental editor, they may charge an additional fee if heavy mechanical editing is required in order for them to apply developmental edits. Or if you send over your manuscript to a mechanical editor without having applied any developmental edits (possibly with the goal of saving a little moola), your manuscript may get returned to you with the admonition that you first hire a developmental editor before sending it over for line edits.

The hope is that you present an editor with a manuscript that is relatively free of substantive, grammatical, and mechanical errors. (For an explanation of the different types of editors and the different editing services they perform, see appendix E: The Cost to Self-Publish.) They don't expect perfection, but your writing should, for example, indicate that you know the differences between *there*, *their*, and *they're*. Read: Although it's the editor's job to make your manuscript shine, still take a pass through your writing before you send it off to them. It's kind of like doing a little straightening up of your hotel room before housekeeping comes; give your editor the best version of your manuscript in an effort to save yourself avoidable additional expenses. (For a list of what you should do before you hand over your manuscript to any kind of editor, see appendix L: Self-Editing Checklist.)

Pro Tip

Take a pass through your own writing before you send it off to editors.

THE GENRE AND COMPLEXITY OF YOUR MANUSCRIPT

If you write a children's book that is fewer than 1,000 words, then the editing demands are obviously less than they are with a longer work of fiction or nonfiction. (But keep in mind that with a children's book, there will be illustration costs that you would not incur if publishing in a different genre.) If you publish a nonfiction book, a historical fiction book, or an academic publication, then an editor may be responsible for fact-checking, reviewing references, and creating footnotes, necessitating a more in-depth edit and more money.

THE EXPERIENCE OF YOUR CONTRACTORS

You have to assess your budget and determine if you want low-end, mid-range, or top-of-the-line results. You may be willing to lean toward working with a less experienced and less expensive developmental editor if you feel confident in the arrangement of your ideas and the strength of your content. However, because the design is not in your wheelhouse and you really want your book to look amazing, you may decide to splurge on the best of the best among typesetters and book cover designers.

Bear in mind that the experience of your contractors, not only in their industries but also in working specifically in the book publishing space, will drive your spending. A designer may have a brilliant career in creating marketing collateral for a university but has never designed a book cover; they recently became a contractor because they want to get their feet wet in the industry, they came highly recommended by a friend, and they are willing to take on your project at a reduced rate. A typesetter may have decades of experience in magazine design and layout but has never formatted the interior of a book; however, they have been thinking about launching their own side hustle in the book publishing space and are willing to give your design project a shot. Then, there are those who know exactly what you need, how you need it, have been working in the exact area of book publishing that you need, and are ready to roll up their sleeves and provide you with not only a finished product that checks all the boxes but also with an invoice with a price tag to match. You get the idea.

In short, are you hiring folks who know what they're doing, who think they know what they're doing, or who don't have a clue but will bumble and fumble their way through the job for you? And because you're not an expert at this, you may not know if the job has been done well or not. If you want to publish a high-quality book (and the assumption is that you surely do!), then you must hire contractors who are well versed in the book publishing industry, and you already know you will pay more for those professionals who are highly skilled and highly experienced and who are therefore better positioned to create for you a high-quality book.

THE FORMAT(S) IN WHICH YOU PUBLISH YOUR FINISHED BOOK

What you pay is also determined by whether your manuscript's final production is created as a paperback, a hardcover, an e-book, and/or an audiobook. (At a minimum, you will want to publish a physical book and an e-book.) With each of these formats, you need different files, which come with different costs.

> **Pro Tip**
>
> *Publish a physical book and an e-book at a minimum.*

In the final production—regardless of whether you publish as a paperback, a hardcover, an e-book, or an audiobook—you will need a cover file and an interior file, the latter of which is simply the actual pages that contain the contents of your book. Because more work is involved with a hardcover book cover design that may also include a dust jacket that has five parts to the cover (inside left flap, front cover, spine, back cover, and inside right flap), a designer may charge more to generate that type of cover than they would for a paperback cover design that has only three parts (front cover, spine, and back cover).

When it comes to creating the e-book, you can take the front cover that was created for your paperback or hardcover and have it converted to the type of file needed to upload for access via e-reader devices, a conversion that may cost additional money. For your e-book, you also take and use the interior file that was created for your paperback or hardcover; however, there is an additional investment required to convert your interior file from a PDF to an EPUB and/or MOBI file, which makes your e-book accessible via e-reader devices.

For an audiobook, you will need to factor in the cost of a narrator. Even if you attempt to keep costs down and decide to narrate your book yourself, you will need the equipment, time, and editing know-how, or you will need to enlist a professional sound editor unless you're a rock star like that and can read thousands or tens of thousands of words that are mistake-free.

So, while the average cost to do the work yourself can be anywhere from $500 to $5,000, some authors opt to take another publishing route that has them hiring an indie or hybrid publishing company that does all the work for them. That investment can be upwards of $10,000 or more to get their book published. But for that flat investment, an indie publisher takes care of all this for you; you have input on your book project, you know you will be published, and you know that it will be done right.

🎙 **Did You Catch That?**

For a flat investment, an indie publisher can take care of everything for you. You'll still have input, know you'll be published, and know it will be done right.

YOUR SPEND VERSUS YOUR ROYALTIES

Before you balk at the idea of paying a publisher five figures to publish your book, arguing that if you do it yourself, it will cost far less, our response is, of course, it will cost far less. That's the case with any service. Unless you are getting the family and friends rate, a publisher (or any other service provider) will not charge you an at-cost rate. Your hair stylist will not charge you only what the shampoo, conditioner, and color cost them to give you those luscious-looking locks; you're paying for so much more than that to include the cosmetology education they attained, their expertise and time as they also listen to all of your troubles while you sit in their chair, and so on. When you get an oil change, your auto shop will not charge you the wholesale price it paid for the liquid gold. And the dry cleaner will not charge you only what it costs to freshen up your outfit that has you looking oh-so-fly at the company gala or in the club. If any of them did, then they would not be in business for very long. Similarly, there is no way for a publisher to stay in business; engage in professional development; or stay current on industry trends, changes, and regulations—all the things needed to be a reputable business—if you pay them exactly what you (someone who is not a professional publisher) pay to do the work yourself.

And if you pay to get your book done—whether you do it all yourself or invest in an indie publisher—then the proceeds generated from sales do not equate to a 1:1 ratio. The total expenditure to produce your book will not be the same number you see in royalty payouts—at least not within the first year of your book being published. (And quite frankly, given that the Nonfiction Authors Association indicates that the average self-published book sells only 250 copies in its lifetime, you cannot realistically expect that type of payout at any point, either in the first year of publication or over the course of several years.) And if you pay an indie or hybrid publisher to perform the work for you, it's certainly not a 1:1 ratio.

You are paying for a service, and quantifying ROI in such an instance is incredibly difficult and not straightforward.

For instance, when you have a service clean your home, how do you calculate that ROI? Is it based on how happy you feel living in a dust-free environment? What is the return on your investment? When you have a plumbing service unclog your toilet, how do you calculate that ROI? How do you quantify what you got from that investment? How do you quantify, for instance, the peace of mind you get from knowing that your bathroom is fully operable?

Simply put, the fees remitted to attend to all the logistics and services required to get your manuscript to market as a finished and reputable book may far exceed the monies the average self-published author can expect to earn from book sales, and calculating ROI is not necessarily clear-cut. All the more reason why it's abundantly important that you are clear on your real reason for writing and publishing and that you have a mindset around your book that brings you satisfaction.

Did You Catch That?

The average self-published book sells 250 copies in its lifetime.

REAL TALK AROUND RECOUPING YOUR INVESTMENT

To be clear, yes, there are self-published authors who have realized astronomical success with their books. But trust and believe, they busted their chops or hired professionals to first write a killer book and then to market themselves and their book nonstop. Non. Stop.

So, if you plan to make publicizing your book a full-time endeavor, where you are getting the word out on a constant and consistent basis via a multitude of channels, then you stand to be on a trajectory of recouping the bulk, if not all, of your investment and then some. Note that this is not easy, is not done overnight, and requires a lot of work on your part.

> **Did You Catch That?**
>
> *Publicizing your book is not easy; it's not done overnight, and it requires a lot of work on your part.*

A Full-Time Endeavor

This marketing campaign is made possible when you approach your book as a business in and of itself, and the marketing of said business is a full-time endeavor. You talk, post, speak, blog, and advertise your book everywhere. You're on social media, podcasts, and websites. You're at events and in periodicals—putting your book in front of everyone on every medium every hour of every day, with the goal of your messaging reaching enough interested people and banking on a good percentage of them purchasing your book. It's what you do each day; you perform like a business owner—you strategize and then execute those practices that you believe will lead to book sales.

It's a full-time job, and seldom is this manageable or sustainable for the self-published author who oftentimes is already employed full time for a company or is in the throes of running a thriving business. And even if neither of those applies, unless an author is a marketing pro who's ready to engage all around the clock (cue Michael Jackson's "Workin' Day and Night"), then taking on the job of getting the word out about your book every morning, noon, and night is not a workload you'll have the time for.

NUMBERS DO NOT ALWAYS TELL THE FULL STORY

Recall that we indicated that the average self-published book sells 250 copies in its lifetime. That's it. 250 copies. So, we know you're doing the math. If the average cost to self-publish a book ranges from $500 to $5,000, then, on the surface, it would appear that you will need to sell a minimum of 250 copies of your book at $20 per copy—an average retail price of a trade paperback—to earn back your $5,000 investment, and even fewer copies if the total cost to produce your book is on the lower end.

The operative phrases here are "on the surface" and "it would appear." First, there's more math involved with determining what your payout will be from book sales. Second, book sales alone are not where you will make your money as a published author, and this is not the mindset you should have; rather, look at your book as a vehicle for sales. More on that "vehicle" paradigm shift a little later, but first, some numbers . . .

Did You Catch That?

Book sales alone are not where you will make your money as a published author, and this is not the mindset you should have; rather, look at your book as a vehicle for sales.

THE ECONOMICS OF YOUR ROYALTY PAYOUTS

Naturally, when you self-publish as opposed to working with a publisher that does all the work for you, you will retain a higher percentage of profits from the sale of your book. At the same time, you bear the responsibility of ensuring you have taken care of *every single aspect* of publishing.

What Does That Mean?

YOU ARE RESPONSIBLE FOR EVERYTHING

When we write that you are responsible for taking care of everything when you self-publish in an effort to keep your costs down and your royalties a bit higher, that means that it all falls on you to ensure all the work gets done. You will want to examine if it's really worth it to take on all the work. Some of your responsibilities as a self-publisher include, but are not limited to, the following:

- *Decide on your title*
- *Perform developmental and mechanical editing*
- *Review edits and make revisions*
- *Request reviews from advance copy readers*
- *Secure an ISBN, a barcode, and an LCCN*
- *Become versed in the more than 1,100 pages of the most current edition of* The Chicago Manual of Style *to ensure your manuscript conforms to all its rules*
- *Design your front and back covers*
- *Engage in another round of revisions because seeing your words in a new (and gorgeous) format will cause it to read differently, and after the passage of time, you will have additional/different ideas*
- *Engage in a third round of revisions because we 100 percent guarantee that there will be changes you will want to make after seeing the book in print*
- *List your book on online retailers' sites*

You get the idea . . . There's a lot of work involved, and this list is not exhaustive. These are only the main points of what needs to get done. For a comprehensive list of everything you need to do to get your book published, see appendix H: The Self-Publishing Checklist.

Let's examine the economics of how your royalty payouts will look if you take care of all the aspects of publishing yourself versus whether you work with an indie or hybrid publishing company.

When you make your book available through a distributor, such as IngramSpark, that distributor will submit your book to its global distribution channel network, making your book available not only on Amazon's site but also on Barnes & Noble's, Books-A-Million's, Porchlight Book Company's, and other booksellers' sites at a wholesale price of 55 percent off the list price, meaning that booksellers can get copies of your book from the distributor at 55 percent off retail, then sell it at full retail price and retain the difference.

At the time of this writing, that discount of 55 percent is a standard that allows for the widest availability through most resellers and retailers. In essence, it's the industry standard. You are certainly at liberty to offer a lower discount, but doing so will turn away some booksellers. (Everybody's looking to make money, right?) With IngramSpark as your global distributor, after deducting the cost of production (ink, printing, paper, glue, binding, cover materials, and more), you receive a royalty percentage of what remains.

In the upcoming IngramSpark Distribution charts are examples of book royalty payout expectations when distributing with IngramSpark. In the examples, the paperback retails for $19.99 with a hypothetical (but realistic) production cost of $3.97, and the hardcover retails for $29.99 with a hypothetical (but realistic) production cost of $9.66, with a 55 percent royalty retained by the distributor in either instance. (That 55 percent royalty retained by the distributor is that 55 percent discount we talked about that is extended to booksellers.)

Bear in mind that production costs will vary depending on the length of your book and the current cost of book publishing materials and labor. (For instance, a book of 40,000 words will have higher production costs than a book of 25,000 words due to needing more paper and a cover with a larger spine to accommodate those 15,000 additional words.)

Also keep in mind that if you work with a publishing company, expect the company to retain a percentage of your royalties. The examples in the charts depict the author receiving a 70 percent royalty payout and the publisher retaining 30 percent of royalties, which is the industry standard.

After IngramSpark takes its standard 55 percent royalty from the retail price of the book and then deducts the production cost, your take is what remains. If you sign on with a hybrid or indie publishing company, your take is your royalty percentage of what remains.

Sample Royalty Payments with IngramSpark Distribution

DISTRIBUTING VIA INGRAMSPARK FOR A COMPANY-PUBLISHED BOOK	
To calculate royalty payment per copy sold, use this equation: [(retail price − distributor's royalty rate) − production cost] × royalty percentage	
Paperback with a 70 percent royalty rate	$3.52 royalty payment per copy sold
Hardcover with a 70 percent royalty rate	$2.68 royalty payment per copy sold

DISTRIBUTING VIA INGRAMSPARK FOR A SELF-PUBLISHED BOOK	
To calculate royalty payment per copy sold, use this equation: (retail price − distributor's royalty rate) − production cost	
Paperback with a 100 percent royalty rate	$5.03 royalty payment per copy sold
Hardcover with a 100 percent royalty rate	$3.84 royalty payment per copy sold

In the examples in the following Amazon KDP Distribution charts, the paperback retails for $19.99, with a hypothetical (but realistic) production cost of $3.47, and the hardcover retails for $29.99, with a hypothetical (but realistic) production cost of $7.66, with a 40 percent royalty retained by the distributor in either instance. At the time of this writing, Amazon KDP's royalty rate of 40 percent is more favorable to authors, and its production costs are less expensive than IngramSpark's, the leading global distributor. If you opt to distribute your book via Amazon KDP, selling your book only on Amazon, that limits your book's exposure and potential, of course, but it certainly increases your payout-per-book potential. After Amazon KDP takes its standard 40 percent royalty from the retail price of the book and then deducts the production cost, your take is what remains. If you sign on with a hybrid or indie publishing company, your take is your contractual royalty percentage of what remains.

Sample Royalty Payments with Amazon KDP Distribution

DISTRIBUTING VIA AMAZON KDP FOR A COMPANY-PUBLISHED BOOK	
To calculate royalty payment per copy sold, use this equation: [(retail price – distributor's royalty rate) – production cost] × royalty percentage	
Paperback with a 70 percent royalty rate	$5.97 royalty payment per copy sold
Hardcover with a 70 percent royalty rate	$7.23 royalty payment per copy sold

DISTRIBUTING VIA AMAZON KDP FOR A SELF-PUBLISHED BOOK	
To calculate royalty payment per copy sold, use this equation: [(retail price – distributor's royalty rate) – production cost	
Paperback with a 100 percent royalty rate	$8.52 royalty payment per copy sold
Hardcover with a 100 percent royalty rate	$10.33 royalty payment per copy sold

---

So, given the amount you need to spend to produce your book and the fact that the average self-published book sells approximately 250 copies in its lifetime and unless you plan to beat the pavement, selling the hell out of your book and doing little else, you will not make all your money back from book sales. Quite frankly, only one group of people has to be hyper-focused on the number of copies of the book they sell, and that group is the people who are *only* writing and selling books and nothing else. This is a group of people who aren't attaching their book to a business they already own. So, it's an absolute *must* that they concern themselves with book sales numbers because they don't have anything else to sell but their books; that's their only way to pay the bills! But for you, that is not the case. You are in a better position. By not being a professional writer, you are able to take your book and use it to do so much more with it.

> 🔦 **Did You Catch That?**
>
> *Only one group of people has to be hyper-focused on their sales numbers and that is professional writers, the people who make their money by writing and selling books and nothing else.*

BOOK SALES ARE NOT WHERE YOU MAKE YOUR MONEY

Yes, the investment you make in covering all the logistics involved with creating your finished book can easily surpass the total royalty payments the average self-published author can expect to earn from book sales no matter how well written and how well marketed the book is. (And if you are in the 1 percent of the population that gets a contract with a traditional publishing company, then instead of a royalty payout that can be as high as 70 percent if you self-publish or use an indie or hybrid publisher, your royalty payout is more like 5–20 percent. And we're not even being hyperbolic here. That's real talk.) But book sales alone are not where you will make your money as a published author, and this is not the mindset you should have.

We said earlier that you use your book as a "vehicle" for sales, and what we mean is that your book opens up doors that may have been previously closed. And those doors might lead to new revenue-generating opportunities. For example, maybe there's a conference you really want to speak at, but it requires all of its speakers to have a published book. Those speakers are allowed to host a number of copies (maybe hundreds) in the conference bookstore. More importantly, because your book is also aligned with the services you provide in your business, your ideal customer is at the conference. What does this mean?

In this best-case, hypothetical scenario, your book opens the door to the conference because you can now apply with a book to your name. You get accepted. The conference organizers invite you to send one hundred copies of your book to sell at the conference. You go to the conference, and your talk is amazing. More than fifty people show up at your session. That's fifty people who now know about you, your business, and your book. A handful of those people book a call with you to learn more about your services. The rest purchase your book in the bookstore (and after reading it, they tell others about it, setting off a ripple effect). The conference organizers hear fabulous things about your talk and see how well your book did in the store. You get glowing conference evaluation reviews and feedback from conference-goers that you can now use for future speaking opportunities, and the conference organizers may even offer to introduce you to other groups and organizations that will need speakers like you. Not only have you made money from speaking, but you made money on book sales, and you might make money if you close with any of the people who scheduled a call with you or if you get another paid speaking gig.

There are a lot of "if/and" pieces to the scenario above, but we are making the case that your book channels revenue possibilities beyond just straight-up sales. When you trace the aforementioned scenario backward, it began with you having a book that got you into the conference. So, when you think about selling your book, think bigger than just getting the individual book into the reader's hands. Your book is a vehicle for so much more.

What Does That Mean?

TRADITIONAL PUBLISHING COMPANIES' LOW ROYALTY PERCENTAGE RATE

Actually, instead of this being a "What Does That Mean?" it's more of a "Why Is That SO?!" Here's the deal. Authors enjoy much lower royalty rates of 5–20 percent and receive much lower royalty payments from traditional publishers because by not charging the author a fee to publish, the company is assuming all the risk associated with getting a book to market. The same types of costs associated with self-publishing or working with a hybrid or indie publisher are the same costs a traditional publisher also faces with publishing a book. Paying an author lower royalty rates is a means for the company to recoup those monies spent on producing an author's book.

Remember, you are to look at your book as a vehicle for sales; your book is your starting point and not the end point. By not being a professional writer, you have more options at your disposal with your published book because your book is so much greater than just a book. It's not just the book itself that will create a supplemental cash flow; it's seeing your book as a vehicle and an investment into other revenue-generating avenues and understanding that it's what being a published author can lead to that will prime the pump for monies to come rolling in. More on that in chapters 11 and 12.

Did You Catch That?

Look at your book as a vehicle for sales; your book is your starting point and not the end point.

TAKEAWAYS AND TO-DOS

Takeaways

*   There are several factors that determine how much it will cost to get your book to market.
*   The number associated with the investment you made in producing your book may not be the same number you see when it comes to book sales. You can put all your energy and focus into marketing your book to see that ROI, but it starts with your being very clear on your goal for getting published so the amount of the royalty payments do not blindside you.
*   The price of your book and royalty payments are the numbers to watch and be clear on.
*   Your royalty payments are only a fraction of the retail price of your book. The check you receive in the mail is what's left over after everyone has gotten a cut.
*   Book printers, distributors, and online retailers are not in the business of volunteer work; they have to get paid, too, for the work they perform to get your book out to the masses.
*   Your book is not a stand-alone product; it is just the start to, and is, an investment into future revenue generation.

To-Dos

*   Sit down and do the math. Establish your budget for getting your book done. At a minimum, you'll want to start with $5,000. If you spend less, then great, but also know that cheap comes out expensive. Be prepared for the possibility of having to spend more to create the book you really want to represent you and your brand.
*   Start calculating how much it will cost to produce your book based on whether it's a paperback or a hardcover and depending on the number of pages it has. You can find out the production cost by entering your

book's binding type, dimensions, and page count in the cover template generator on IngramSpark's site. To get a production cost on Amazon KDP's site, you have to upload your book's interior and cover files.

- Do your research to identify the retail cost of your book, then subtract from it the cost to produce your book and the royalties that either IngramSpark or Amazon KDP will retain to get an idea of the royalties you are projected to earn.

- Start creating a mindset of where you will take your readers with your book as opposed to where your book will take you. Avoid getting consumed with the idea of your book doing all the work; rather, develop the understanding that your book is only the start—an exciting start–of what's to come.

NOTES

CHAPTER 11

KNOW *HOW* TO MAKE MONEY FROM YOUR BOOK

Now that you have an understanding of the economics of your book's royalties from reading chapter 10 and, most importantly, the fact that your book is not the entire wheel but is the hub of the wheel, it's time to examine your wheel's spokes: the additional avenues your book has now created for you as multiple means for making money.

Some authors will argue that they simply want to sell their book and make money that way, envisioning thousands of copies getting purchased on a monthly basis, yielding hefty royalty payments. The reality of that happening is next to nil. It's not *selling* your book that will make you money. It's what *having* a book means that will make you money. Music artists do not make the majority of their money from selling their music. It's all the other avenues and doors that have been opened to them—concerts, merchandise, endorsements, paid appearances, and so on—as a result of being an artist that will net them large profits.

Did You Catch That?

> *It's not* selling *your book that will make you money. It's what* having *a book means that will make you money.*

Note that no one revenue stream is better than the next, and it is not advisable that you engage all the streams or avenues—at least not all at once. Now that you are published, your options for making money off your book include, but are not limited to, speaking engagements (both those you or your company hosts and those created by organizations); masterminds (a small group of people coming together to discuss a specifically defined topic), workshops, and courses designed for both in-person and virtual audiences; and even merchandise that all stem from your book, its title, or the topic it addresses.

We will cover all those options and more in greater depth in the pages to come, but for now, it's important that you do not get overwhelmed by the idea of taking your book and doing more with it. Let's be honest here; it was enough work just trying to write, edit, publish, and market it, so we know you're thinking, "The ink is barely dry on the pages from where my book was printed. Now you're saying I have to think about doing even more with it?!"

In a word, yes.

But don't get overwhelmed. Stay with us, okay?

Remember WAY back in the beginning of the book (chapter 2) when we asked you to consider your endgame and what do you want your book to do for you? Well, we've come full circle.

The answer to that question has to go beyond "make me money." (Although that's not a bad answer. That *is* what this chapter is all about, isn't it?) But we want you to go deeper. Do you want it to . . .

- demonstrate you as a thought leader?
- put you in front of your ideal client?
- boost your visibility?
- establish your credibility?
- position you to have more opportunities?
- grow your current business?
- teach others what you've worked and fought hard to learn over the years and decades?

Once you figure out what you want your book to do for you, look at the avenues for achieving that. To assess which ones (even if it's just one for now) are the best fit for you or the best starting point, ask yourself the following questions:

- Which would I enjoy?
- Which do I already engage in and love (or like)?
- Which is currently a part of my personal and/or professional development plan?
- How do I prefer to invest my money to further engage with a message that resonates with me?

Your answers to these questions will help you determine which avenue you should seriously pursue as a viable and enjoyable means for making money off your book.

Let us be abundantly clear here: whatever you choose, you do not want it to be a chore or drudgery. If speaking terrifies you or if you'd rather be the one who's getting eulogized as opposed to the one who's giving the eulogy, then you do not want to drag yourself onto stages, knowing you hate the idea of giving a presentation. If it does not bring you joy or does not light you up, then you have to wonder why in the world you're doing it. Settle on what energizes you and make that your focus for extending your book's reach and its earning potential.

Did You Catch That?

> *If it does not bring you joy or light you up, then you have to wonder why in the world you're doing it.*

And if doubt is creeping into your mind, making you wonder whether people will want more from you after reading your book, trust us on this one—they will. It starts with what we covered in part 1: crafting a book with a message that solves a problem, makes a goal more achievable, and is one that others enjoy. When you have a book that contains a message that others enjoy, they will want other ways to engage with your message. We guarantee it. (Now, don't get carried away. When we write "we guarantee it," we mean that people will want to engage with your content. There is no way we—nor anyone else—can guarantee how your book sales will look. And while we're on the topic, if you *do* encounter someone who guarantees you a certain number of book sales, you will want to look at them with a discerning eye. For realz.)

But if you are satisfied with getting your book written and published, and you have no interest in taking it any further, then there is absolutely nothing wrong with that. Many authors take that route, wanting to leave a legacy, tell their personal story, add "published author" to their already impressive list of accomplishments, give their followers another way to connect with and learn from them, or make an impact, and that's it. If any of those sound like you, then selling your book will suffice meeting your goals.

So, before you read on, decide what you want your book to do for you. If you want it to make you known in a certain arena, establish you as an expert, start a movement, or grow your community of followers, then you will want to do more with your book, using the content as a foundation to generate additional revenue. If you want to be seen as the obvious answer to your target market's greatest challenges, establish yourself as an authority on a topic, have a book that serves as an elevated business card, provide added value to your clients, support and expand your brand, or grow your business, then you will certainly want more options.

Did You Catch That?

If you want your book to make you known in a certain arena, establish you as an expert, start a movement, or grow your community of followers, then you will want to do more with your book.

AVENUES FOR MAKING MONEY

The options or avenues for making money from your book tend to fall into two categories: active streams and passive streams. Active streams are those avenues that require your active input, either as needed or on an ongoing basis, while passive streams require relatively little active input on your part after the initial launch.

Here are several options for extending your book's reach and revenue-generating capabilities. In addition to regularly marketing your book (because, remember, if you don't talk about it, then people will forget about it), these are the activities you should add to your plan for making money off your book.

Active Streams

Speaking Engagements

The beauty of this option is you do not have to worry about creating the content, which can be the most daunting first step to speaking—figuring out your topic. Take the content in your book, and you are ready to craft keynotes, workshops, breakout sessions, webinars, and more. You are at liberty to host these events yourself, speak at events that have already been established by large organizations and that will be marketed and hosted by those organizations, or reach out to organizations to pitch your speaking (and/or other) services. More on the specific types of speaking engagements you can engage in is covered in Chapter 12: Using Your Book as a Speaking Launchpad.

Coaching

Coaching provides your followers with one-on-one direct access to you as an expert on your book's topic, and you help those followers pursue their goals. Based on your expertise/your book topic, these goals can be professional or personal in nature. With coaching, you are guiding people to put in place what you discuss and teach in your book. You can charge by the hour or offer packages of one-month, three-month, one-year, or lengthier access. Or you can be a contractor and have an established coaching platform to do all the heavy lifting with prospecting, marketing, and onboarding new clients while you simply show up to facilitate coaching sessions. Keep in mind that if you contract with an organization to provide coaching, your profit will be lower than it would be if you sought out clients on your own under your own company name. But at the same time, when engaging with a firm as an independent contractor, you do not have to invest in all that goes into securing coaching clients.

And once again, do not assume it was your book that led people to you. Reference your book in sessions, as applicable, and even suggest that the audience buy a copy if you know a coachee will benefit from its contents. (And they will because it'll be more of your voice in their library. It has the answers to the problems that coachees are coming to you for.) If they already have a copy, great! If not, then someone say "cha-ching! You've made a sale!"

Consulting

This is where you show up as the expert, and companies pay you for that expertise—those years or decades of everything you've learned and experienced that makes you so knowledgeable in your field. Companies will hire you to work with their teams to develop processes and systems. You make yourself available to answer questions and to provide guidance, advice, analysis, and recommendations based on your expertise, as demonstrated in your book and/or your business. You serve as an objective troubleshooter who supports an organization by providing strategies designed to support it in preventing problems and/or improving performance. You can charge a fee that grants your client up to a year of access to you, and when you do, you are almost an employee of that company that's hired you. Yes, you can be a consultant without having a book, but being an author makes it a whole lot easier to sell yourself; you're not just a consultant, but you become a consultant who's also a published expert.

Passive Streams

Online Courses

You can have offerings for as little as $9 to hundreds or thousands of dollars. Your online course might be a self-paced experience for your participants, where you take them from A to Z on a topic and there is very little interaction with you, especially with regard to the offerings that are at lower costs. Naturally, you may opt to have a live, weekly, virtual office hour or check-in with enrollees, but that's up to you. There is no right or wrong way for how you run your online courses (or any other offering you design). Just know that the less involved you are, the more passive the stream.

A giant in the online course creation and delivery space is known as the Millionaire Maker. She is the mastermind behind Course From Scratch, and while she does not have a book at the time of this writing, she takes what she knows to deliver results in an online course, and you can do the very same by taking what you know from your book to deliver your own web-based courses. (And if the Millionaire Maker does *not* secretly have a book in the works, then we would be downright surprised. It's the obvious next step for her, and with her success and her throngs of followers, everyone would eat it up!)

Mini e-Books

With mini e-books, you are taking full advantage of your book. What you do is take each chapter of your book and make it its own e-book, and this works quite nicely for those chapters that are how-tos or personal or professional development in nature. This also works nicely for those who do not want to buy your entire book but who find the brevity of a mini e-book more palatable and perfect because it has a targeted message, addressing a specific question or challenge the reader has. Instead of purchasing an entire book on marketing, for instance, a person may be drawn to the one chapter in the book that focuses on social media marketing and therefore more inclined to purchase the mini e-book of that chapter.

Again, don't be afraid to take full advantage of your book. It's yours to use as you see fit. Imagine that your twelve-chapter paperback retails for $19.99, plus you sell each of those chapters on your website as mini e-books, at $4.99 per download. It costs you virtually nothing to make the mini e-book files, and now your $19.99 book is making you $80.00 per copy!

Video Series

Now that you have the writing out of the way, do you truly prefer talking instead? Do you love the camera and being in front of it? Take parts of your book to create a video series. Sell short recordings that are how-to videos based on your book's content or that expound on what you've written, giving real-life examples or action items for your listeners. Much like the case with mini e-books, there is a segment of the population that will gravitate toward a quick video clip before they engage in a three-hour workshop or a 200-page book. They may not even know you have a book but will devour your videos. It's the same content, just in a different format, and it's what some folks crave. So, give the people what they want!

Subscriptions

With subscriptions, participants pay a recurring price at regular intervals for access to your online content, and there is no interaction with you. You read that right—folks pay you to do nothing. Well. Sorta. You've done the heavy lifting with the book, and with the subscriptions, you extend learning by offering content that is not in your book but that is directly connected to your book's topic. You may offer videos, articles, exercises, or even merchandise on a regular basis. It could be on a monthly or quarterly basis. If you opt to offer online content as the basis of your subscription service, then you, of course, need to keep that content up to date or add new material as necessary.

And while we're on the topic of subscriptions, think about making your book a part of other companies' subscription services, such as subscription boxes. This is where companies curate items that speak to their subscribers' interests, and in exchange for a monthly or annual fee, the company sends each subscriber a box filled with items that the companies just know the subscribers will love. And your book may be just the addition companies are looking for to add to their next shipment of boxes. Research subscription box services that look to include books similar to the kind you have produced, and find out each company's process to have your product considered for inclusion in their boxes.

Merchandise

If your book title is a jazzy one, or if you have a theme, slogan, or catchphrase unique to you and your book or that appears throughout your book, then this becomes really easy to put in place. Think glassware, pens, folios, T-shirts, webcam covers, totes, and reusable water bottles . . . Think of the items you love, the swag you're drawn to at conferences, or those little must-haves you use on a regular basis that you would enjoy seeing emblazoned with your slogan, catchphrase, or book title, then go for it! And don't tell anyone, but this merchandise doubles as additional advertising for your book! Sell it on your website, post about it on social media, have it available at your events, and sport the merchandise yourself.

Picture it: you have an intriguing book title that lends itself well to being on a T-shirt. Wearing it generates curiosity everywhere you go. People either ask you about it, sparking a conversation that can lead to who knows what, or, at a minimum, folks don't ask you about it but are inclined to privately Google what's on your tee, and voila! Up pops your book!

Recall in part 1 that we told you that you are to go into writing a book with the understanding that you are starting a business. With these eight revenue streams, you can see what we mean. You are the owner (author) of your company with a product (your book) available for sale, and that book is a vehicle into other opportunities for people to engage with you and for you to make money from your book—money that comes from more than just book sales.

Your book is just the starting point and the vehicle for creating multiple revenue streams. Just as a restauranteur will take one ingredient and use it as the basis of a variety of recipes—using potatoes for a breakfast hash, a side of beer-battered fries to accompany burgers and sandwiches, and fondant potatoes alongside a dinnertime steak—do the same with your book. It all starts with that one ingredient—for the restaurateur, it's potatoes; for you, it's your book.

Did You Catch That?

Your book is just the starting point and the vehicle for creating multiple revenue streams.

There will be those who want to consume your content in the form of a paperback and are happy to purchase it and tell others about it; however, with only your book for sale, you miss out on all kinds of other communities who need or want your content but who would prefer to consume it in different formats. By seeing your book as a vehicle for monetizing your content, structuring and distributing it so that it appeals to a wide selection of people, you satisfy the masses. If you offer only your book and nothing else—no other way for people to learn from you—then you are selling your book short, and, more notably, you are selling your audience short. Cast a wide net and offer your content in an array of formats to widen your reach and make the most of your book and the work you put into creating it in the first place.

> **Did You Catch That?**
>
> *If you offer only your book and nothing else—no other way for people to learn from you—then you are selling your book short, and, more notably, you are selling your audience short.*

Again, the mindset to have is your book is a vehicle and an investment into other revenue-generating avenues. The book alone is a great accomplishment, but the more powerful frame of reference is how your book positions you to make money in other ways that are far more achievable, that make so much more sense for you now that you are published, and that have you making money without selling one single copy.

TAKEAWAYS AND TO-DOS

Takeaways

- Get comfortable with the idea that once you write a book, people will want more from you and your book.
- Know that no one revenue stream is any better than the next. It's not just about how much money you stand to make from the stream; it's about which stream makes the most sense for you and your personality and how you extend your and your book's reach.
- Realize that you are selling yourself and your book short if you do nothing but publish it. If publishing is the ultimate goal for you and your book, then there's nothing wrong with that, but take time to reflect and decide if you and your book want and deserve more.
- Choose your additional revenue streams wisely so that you end up enjoying what you do and running your book business. Others will feel your energy, so do what you love.

To-Dos

- Get clear on what you want your book to do for you. Return to the list of questions at the start of this chapter, as well as the content in part 1, if you need to gain clarity.
- Decide which revenue-generating activities resonate with you and settle on one or two as the first that you will launch as part of your book business. Do not be afraid to abandon an avenue if it's not a good fit for you, then find one that is.

NOTES

_____

_____

_____

_____

_____

_____

_____

_____

_____

_____

_____

_____

_____

_____

_____

_____

_____

_____

_____

_____

_____

CHAPTER 12

USING YOUR BOOK AS A SPEAKING LAUNCHPAD

Allow us to get you sold on the idea of speaking as quickly as possible with the *Reader's Digest* version of how to use speaking engagements to monetize your book, or vice versa. When you use your book as a speaking launchpad, you put yourself, your book, and your expertise in front of . . .

- your ideal audience when you submit proposals to speak at events where you can position yourself as an expert. (And it's an added bonus if book sales are also allowed and/or if the event will also host a book signing for you!)
- target readers, where you only scratch the surface in your speaking engagements, displaying how well-versed you are in your subject matter and prompting audiences to want more—with "more" being heading over to their favorite bookseller to purchase your book (or heading elsewhere to purchase one of your other offerings).
- your ideal prospective corporate client, promoting yourself as the perfect speaker that they should hire to address their team's challenges as they relate to your subject matter. (Did you pick up on the word *hire*, meaning they're willing to write you a check that is significantly more than $29.99, the price peeps pay for a copy of your book?)

Today, a book is an elevated business card for a speaker; it demonstrates that you are qualified to speak on your topic. Many people start their speaking careers without a book, then write one after having created and amassed a library of talks, keynotes, and workshops based on their core message; however, you would be doing it the other way around, wherein you already have your content for your talks—your book!

When you think of being a speaker, broaden your perspective so you go beyond thinking of only getting on conference stages. Yes, that is one option, but also think of corporate workshops, trainings, intimate focus groups, podcast interviews, panel discussions, masterminds, online courses, one-on-one interviews, live Q&As about your book, and the like. Plus, think of in-person options and virtual sessions. When you speak as a result of having a book, and you monetize that speaking, you make money off your book without even having to sell one copy of it!

We realize that, in the previous chapter, we just discussed eight revenue streams that can be derived from your book, so why single out the revenue stream of speaking and devote a full chapter to it? Why the deep dive on speaking specifically?! Simply put, it's one of the best ways to make money from your book because there are so many options available to you that are incredibly accessible to most people.

We also realize that earlier we indicated that you should do only that which you enjoy when working to extend your book's revenue reach, so in keeping with that admonition, what if speaking is not your thing? We get it. But hear (or read) us out.

Speaking is the most obvious next step for authors. It's the perfect springboard and entryway that will get you to all the other revenue opportunities. Once you have a book, people are more likely to come to you with an interest in hearing you speak simply because you're an author. They aren't as likely to read your book and then ask if you have a video series, an online course, or a T-shirt. But when they know you have a book, they will ask if you will come speak, and a speaking platform positions you to explore the other revenue-generating activities discussed in chapter 11.

Makes sense, right? So, for now, have an open mind, and journey along with us.

PUT YOUR BOOK IN FRONT OF YOUR IDEAL CLIENT

Use your book as an elevated business card. If people find you on their own and then purchase a copy of your book to determine if you really know your stuff, even better. (After checking you out online, people are willing to risk a nominal $20 or $30 to see if you really know what you're talking about. In short, when people look for experts in an area, they want to find the person who literally wrote the book on it.) Now, if a prospective client purchases your book of their own volition, then that's ideal, but there's nothing stopping you from putting your book in front of them first, letting them know that you know their challenges and that you can offer solutions.

This is done by thoughtfully crafting a letter that . . .

- identifies the goals the prospect has or the challenges with which they are currently met;
- succinctly clarifies how your book helps them meet their goals or addresses those challenges;
- requests an invitation to work with their team via a workshop, training, a focus group, coaching, or whatever offering you have that you believe makes the most sense for the prospect; and
- details the results you have gotten for others with a similar engagement.

There's no reason to worry if you do not have quantitative data to present as proof of your effectiveness; qualitative data are equally useful. Provide testimonials from satisfied clients or audience members to demonstrate the value you bring. And that's it! Include an autographed copy of your book along with the letter, then execute a follow-up plan (because trust us—that one touch point is insufficient if you're honestly looking for results).

> **What Does That Mean?** ⟩⟩
>
> ### QUANTITATIVE VERSUS QUALITATIVE DATA IN SPEAKING
>
> *Numbers tell a story. It's impressive if you can say 96 percent of your audiences have rated your presentation as "very good" or "excellent" or if a company's contract close rate increased by 23 percent within six months of bringing you in to conduct a training on how to deliver effective sales presentations. However, when starting out as a speaker, you may not have quantitative data, numbers that demonstrate your effectiveness as a speaker or the results organizations have experienced because they engaged you. Instead, you rely on qualitative data—written words and video testimonials of those who've seen you in action and who would happily recommend you to others.*

PUT YOUR EXPERTISE IN FRONT OF AUDIENCES

Think podcast interviews and panel discussions. These options are great for someone who does not like being center stage and who is more comfortable speaking without having to deliver a formal presentation but who still wants to utilize their voice to promote their expertise. Search for those podcasts that have a listenership composed of the type of people you believe would love your book or who need your book. Make a list of topics that directly relate to your book, as well as topics that tangentially relate, and go into the conversations knowing that you will not necessarily speak about your book the entire time you are being interviewed.

As a matter of fact, it's more impactful if you do *not* spend all your time talking about your book. Be a great interviewee who speaks in sound bites—short phrases that are easy for listeners to follow and remember.

Drop aha moments, give great advice and easy-to-implement action items, and make listeners smile and feel like they can do it. Do that, and listeners will be clamoring for more, going in search of your book.

Also, leave nothing to chance; beforehand, ask the host to do you a favor and mention your book during the interview, or, better yet, ask that *you* be allowed to mention your book and where it can be purchased. Look at it this way: you are doing the host a favor by being a guest on their show; the least the host can do is allow for a plug of your book. (For more guidance on how to pitch yourself to podcast shows, see appendix Q: Podcast Guest Best Practices.)

Bear in mind that the protocol for being on a panel typically includes needing to be invited to participate. You can't necessarily call up an organization and say, "Yo. I want to be on your panel." Well, you can, but we are not too sure of how successful you'll be. And some conferences have panel discussions as options. Look for those opportunities in the conference call for proposals.

Panel discussions work the same as interviews except you are not the only voice. Show up like a light, and give great insights, and as people listen to you, they will be drawn to you and your ideas and will want more. Your contributions to the panel will give merely a taste of your knowledge and passion; give them gems, and they will want more in the form of your book.

PUT YOURSELF IN FRONT OF YOUR IDEAL AUDIENCE

Unless putting on events in your industry is your thing, you love it, and you're able to get people there in droves, then the smartest strategy is to rely on other organizations to draw in the masses, allowing you to only worry about showing up and delivering a value-packed presentation. Conduct a search for organizations that cater to your ideal audience—an audience that's searching for answers to the problems that your book solves—and that host conferences, conventions, annual meetings, and the like. You may have to look no further than your own calendar, especially if you have written a book that is based on your professional industry knowledge. What events are annual can't-miss professional or personal development meetings? Those may be some of the same ones you can look to as you create your list of events to which you should submit proposals to speak. The thought here is instead of being an audience member with a published book on your résumé, it makes absolute sense that you transition from being an attendee to being a speaker.

Ensure that you remain abreast of the call for proposals and pertinent due dates. Create a proposal that meets all the criteria, and if you incorporate the conference theme into your submission, even better. Make your proposal audience-centric; everything about it must explicitly demonstrate how the audience will learn, grow, and advance their knowledge. It must confirm for the proposal reviewer(s) that you understand what attendees need and that your presentation will indeed deliver.

Keep in mind that unless you are a big name, conferences do not typically compensate the speakers who appear on their conference programs, especially breakout session speakers. At most, if your proposal is accepted, as a thank you for presenting, the conference will provide you with full registration to the conference. So, at this point, you are likely thinking, "How is that profitable considering most conferences do not pay their speakers? Plus, I'm having to finance my own way to the conference?!" Trust us on this one. Give a killer presentation, then tell the audience . . .

"If you enjoyed this session and want more, then purchase my book [insert title] at [insert 'Amazon' or 'the conference bookstore' or wherever you want them to go get your book]!"

or

"If you enjoyed this session and want more, then sign up for my boot camp that explores all the session topics in more depth. Sign up at . . ."

or

"If you enjoyed this session and want more, then enroll in my online course by visiting [insert website title]."

You get the idea.

Your initial reaction to this may be, "I don't want to get up and make a sales presentation!" Here's the deal: it's not a sales presentation. At least, that's not how it starts and is not its original intent. It's a presentation that solves a problem for your audience; that's what you make sure you do from start to finish, then take one minute of the sixty minutes you've been given to present—1.7 percent of your allotted time!—to extend an invitation to the audience to learn more from you.

Did You Catch That?

You are not making a sales presentation. You are making a presentation that solves a problem for your audience.

So, you get the point: speaking engagements make it possible for you to put yourself and your expertise in front of your ideal clients and readers. Now, before you turn and take off running in the other direction, again, remember that a speaking engagement is not always the equivalent of getting in front of a ginormous room full of people and waxing poetic for ninety minutes. Speaking engagements can be far more intimate, and some don't even require you to stand on a stage with a microphone in your face. In the previous chapter, we identified speaking engagements as an active revenue stream, and now we give you specifics on those types of engagements that come in all shapes and sizes.

Company-Sponsored Events

You can host your own events yourself or take the pressure off and speak at events that are organized and hosted by others. And an added bonus with the latter is some larger organizations may ask if you also have a book to sell, offering to take care of sales for you, wherein you get to retain some or all of the proceeds. Others may even offer to also host a book signing event for you, where all you have to do is show up with your smile and a pen, ready to schmooze and autograph copies of your book that audience members purchase after hearing you speak. (See chapter 2 for more on book signings.)

Also, reach out to companies that are in the market for the kinds of solutions you offer based on your book and your expertise and that are open to hearing you speak on your topic. Companies regularly host a variety of events, such as lunch and learns, leadership summits, sales conferences, and wellness retreats, as a part of their professional and personal development offerings for their employees. They are looking for experts to get on their stages, and you are definitely one with the publication of your book.

Workshops

These are three-hour-to-full-day events marketed and hosted by you or your business. Take the title of your book and make it a workshop, where you take a deeper dive into your book's topics, answer participants' questions about the content, and have them engage in exercises in the workshop and/or outside of the workshop to extend their learning. Again, you can take care of all the logistics, market this as one of your offerings, or shop it around to organizations that have audience members who will benefit from your message.

For those workshops you plan and host yourself, have extra copies of your book on hand to sell during and after the event; don't assume it was your book that brought them to your workshop and that they already have a copy of it. Even if they already have a copy, they may want to purchase a copy for a friend, family member, or colleague.

For those events where an organization hires you to facilitate a workshop, feel comfortable enough to ask if book sales are allowed afterward. Some will say yes, and others will say "not at this time," but you won't know unless you ask. The same goes for masterminds, seminars, and retreats. Everything keeps coming back to your book—either you use it to get in the room, or once you're in the room, don't be afraid to use it (read: sell it like it's the hottest ticket in town) to get into other rooms.

Masterminds

This is essentially group coaching, conducted virtually or in person, that gives participants an extended experience with you. Right now, we get it: it's hard for you to envision that people will want "an extended experience" from you. Here's the deal: if they love your book, they love your message and will want just about any and everything you have to offer beyond what's between those two covers.

One example of this is a strategic storytelling expert and professional speaker who has taken his amazing storytelling abilities that he uses in his book *Show Up for Your Life: 7 Principles to Living an Extraordinary Life* and in his presentations to deliver masterminds to people who want to learn how to make money off their stories from the stage. And people cannot get enough of him! He offers a free webinar that sparks a light. People who attend it may or may not have bought or read his book. None of that matters, though. He masterfully takes the techniques presented in the book and that he already uses in his speaking engagements to then present a killer webinar. Afterward, he invites happy webinar attendees to participate in a mastermind, where they get to learn from him in an extended experience. It's a thing of beauty!

A mastermind goes beyond what people can get in a three-hour workshop, can command hundreds or thousands of dollars per participant, and can run for weeks or months at a time—there are all kinds of models out there. For instance, you might have a three-day mastermind that meets for several hours a day, culminating with a final project that participants deliver on the final day; a four-week mastermind that meets once a week for an hour at a time, with activities for participants to complete in between meetings; or one that lasts for months. It's up to you how you want to structure it. Again, your book's content is the basis of these activities, and there is no right or wrong way to structure and deliver your mastermind.

Seminars and Retreats

Seminars and retreats come in all shapes and sizes. A seminar can be a one-day event or a multiday event, while retreats tend to almost always be multiday events. Seminars can take place at a hotel or on site at a company location. Retreats, because they are designed to get people away from their usual routines for a number of days, tend to take place along the country-side or at a beach—somewhere luxurious and attractive. In both instances, it's like having your mastermind offered in a concentrated format. The average price for either one can start at thousands of dollars per person, with a seminar being at a lower price point than a retreat, and for a retreat, it's that price plus lodging and travel. Or you can price the retreat so that it's all-inclusive. After performing this in one place, you can create a template for this type of event, then rinse and repeat in another location. Again, your book's content gives you the foundation for the agenda and the content—all you have to do is execute.

Train-the-Trainer/Certification

The originator of the Chicken Soup for the Soul series, the mastermind behind Getting Things Done®, and the creator of the In & Out of the Box process are all examples of companies that have done this. The train-the-trainer or certification avenue is for the author who is an experienced speaker and/or who is already running workshops on their topics—topics for which they are known. With the train-the-trainer or certification route, you certify people on your topic. For instance, a training company pays you thousands of dollars per person to attend your three-day event and get certified in your method/process/strategy, then the company pays you a royalty on an ongoing basis as its trainers go out and deliver your content.

Keep in mind that this is a more advanced revenue stream and is not the first one you will want to implement as a means of making money off your book. Start with your book, then get on stage and become known for that thing your book is all about. Next, offer your own workshops, then advance to other offerings, such as train-the-trainer and certificate programming and the like. Baby steps, my friend. Baby steps. You will get to a point where you're known for your offerings and the transformation they bring about, and people buying your book after the fact is just an added bonus. But . . . it starts with your book.

Virtual Events

Don't shy away from online events. More and more organizations are embracing the virtual environment to deliver content to their communities. They are more cost-effective than in-person events and, in some instances, improve event accessibility. For speakers, virtual events help you to maximize your time and reach more people than you would be able to if you had to physically traverse to and fro on planes, trains, and Ubermobiles. Plus, if your virtual engagement is evergreen, living on and made accessible to audiences (and you) long after the initial conversation, then you extend your reach even more by having used your book to launch your speaking.

A WORD OF CAUTION FOR NOVICE SPEAKERS

Once you confirm a speaking engagement, it's imperative that you make it a smooth experience for yourself, your audience, and your host or point of contact (POC). Ensure that you demonstrate yourself to your POC as an easy-to-work-with person (this is *major*) and have a clear plan for working with the bookstore if your book will be sold at the event.

Don't be a prima donna (or a prima don). That can turn people off. Great message or not, you are still remembered as That Person

Who Worked Folks' Last Nerve. When you come off as a difficult person who's not willing to bend or flex on anything or who has all kinds of requirements and demands, with the expectation that the POC accommodate them (like insisting on a bottle of San Pellegrino chilled to precisely thirty-eight degrees waiting for you backstage post-presentation, along with a dozen of freshly cut pink tulips in a Waterford vase, along with your fuzzy slippers and a silk paisley robe or you'll throw a fit), it's not enough that you have an amazing message and an incredible presence on the stage. In everything you do and say, you want to leave a good impression so that you will get invited back or get referred to others in the event contact's network. Simply put, no matter what you do or how you do it, be easy to work with.

WORKING WITH YOUR POC

When you initiate contact, be straight and to the point. State what you'd like to do and the value you will bring to the contact's audience. If you receive a response indicating interest, follow the contact's lead as to what they want to happen next; they will often tell you that they want to talk, you should respond to the call for proposals, or they want to know your rates. Respond as applicable: set up a time to talk, follow the link to submit the proposal, or send over your rate sheet. And always have a contract in place so everyone knows what's expected of each party and when, especially in the instance of a paid presentation.

After confirming the speaking engagement, remain in contact, assuring your POC that you can be counted on to show up and perform. For large conferences where you do not or are not likely to have direct contact with a POC or event host, the following practice is not necessary, but for all other engagements, a best practice is to send a check-in email message at least one week before your engagement. (See appendix R: Speaker Check-in Email Template for helpful messaging to use when communicating with your POC to further put their mind at ease and make them feel confident in their decision to choose you as a speaker.)

When working with your POC, be easy to work with for all the reasons already stated, and then some. That is the number one rule. Make their life easy. They may be simultaneously working with multiple speakers and vendors, or they may be planning the event on a voluntary basis with no compensation. You want to be the person they remember as being a joy to work with. Follow their instructions to a tee. If you are directed to complete and submit an online proposal form by a set date, then do so. If a request is made of you to upload your slide deck (presentation file) to a portal, then get it uploaded on time. If you are required to check in for your presentation thirty minutes before your session, then show up to the presentation room and check in. Simply put, if any request is made of you—within reason—be accommodating. If the host asks if you will supply a handout, even if you ordinarily do not, do so in this instance. It's not about bending over backward; it's about projecting yourself as someone who's easy to work with and with whom they'd love to refer to others in their network or someone they want to reach out to and schedule to speak again.

Did You Catch That?

> The number one rule when working with your POC or the event host is to be easy to work with.

PREPARING YOUR PRESENTATION

As you prepare your talking points, the most important matter to address is this: ask yourself, "What do I want my audience to know or to be able to do by the time I finish my presentation?" Before you make a presentation, you must ask and answer that question, then your content must deliver.

In short, you reverse engineer your presentation, starting with the end in mind. This means you first think about the end of your session, identifying what your audience needs to have gained by the end of your speech, then you work backward to identify the three to five concepts you need to tell them that will lead to that end result. The simplest way to understand this is as follows:

1. Think about what you know based on your book's contents, your industry knowledge, and your own experience.
2. Think about what your audience wants based on the event's theme and focus, the challenges you know they face, and the questions they likely want answered.
3. Take what you know to give them what they want.

Now that you have figured out the end (what everyone will know or be able to do by the end of your talk), as well as the middle (those three to five concepts you will take from what you know to give them what they want), it's time to figure out how to start your presentation. And you do that by creating rapport and immediately solving a mystery.

(**Pro Tip**)

As you prepare your talking points, ask yourself, "What do I want my audience to know or to be able to do by the time I finish my presentation?"

The primary goal of the first minutes of your talk should be to shed light on why everyone should listen to you. This is the unspoken expectation all audiences have—that you will say something from the start that causes them to lean in. To do so, you draw parallels between your presentation and the work everyone does. Explain how this one puzzle piece (your presentation) fits within the larger picture, which is the reality they're facing that brought them to your session; clearly illustrate how your session will contribute to moving listeners closer to fulfilling their personal or professional goals. Let them know what new knowledge or abilities they will have by the time the presentation comes to an end—knowledge or abilities that they did not have before listening to you speak. That is your starting point. This is where the audience realizes *why* everyone should care.

What Does That Mean?

GIVE YOUR AUDIENCE A REASON TO LISTEN TO YOU

Using a hypothetical, we will explain what it means to give your audience a reason to listen to you.

The author of a real estate investing book is speaking at an event where people want to learn about a variety of revenue streams they can pursue as side hustles. The author starts with the end in mind, deciding that she wants to take what she knows about real estate investing to have her listeners walk away feeling like they are better educated about real estate investing and energized to further investigate, or, better yet, to get involved with making money in this lucrative industry.

Now that the author knows what she wants as the end product, she has to determine what points she will make that will drive her talk in the direction she wants to take her audience. The three pieces of information that she believes will drive home her point and move her audience to action are the following:

1. *The earning potential and how it's calculated*
2. *The pitfalls to avoid*
3. *The first three actions one can immediately take to get started*

Some of the information she shares will be from her book, but much of it will be from her personal experiences and background knowledge. To give her audience what they cannot get in her book is a bonus; doing so incentivizes the audience to come to hear her talk.

What Does That Mean? — *(continued)*

With her audience's takeaway in mind, as well as her three talking points, it's time to create her opening message—one that will draw in everyone, establish a rapport that sends a silent message to the audience that the author understands where they are coming from relative to the presentation topic, and make them say, "This is going to be a good one!"

So, with all this in mind, the opening message the author delivers that gives her audience reason looks like this:

"You've likely seen the house-flipping shows or have friends who have dabbled in real estate, or you may have even looked into it yourself. And you wondered if real estate investing is for you or if it's even profitable. By the time we're done, you will know your earning potential as a real estate investor, the pitfalls to avoid, and the three things you can do right now to successfully get started as a real estate investor."

Constantly focus on why your audience should listen. It is because you know how to help . . . because you understand . . . because you will offer solutions. Always think, "What do I do that makes my audience better?" When you take this approach, this automatically excites the audience and makes them want to hear everything you have to say.

Did You Catch That?

Constantly focus on why your audience should listen to you.

As is the case with everything else we have discussed thus far, know when to call in the pros. If you want to seriously pursue speaking and know you need to sharpen your presentation skills or learn more about how to be impactful on the stage, then do not be afraid to invest in the services of a successful presentation skills expert or a public speaking coach that can get you where you want to be.

WORKING WITH THE BOOKSTORE

When you work with an event bookstore, the same rules apply for when you work with your POC. Follow the bookstore contact's instructions to the letter and meet their deadlines. Different event bookstores will have different protocols. Some will have you sign consignment agreements, while others will simply ask you to send X number of books by a designated date, and there's no formal agreement in place. Some will require you to ship the books to the organization's headquarters; others will allow you to hand deliver the books to the event venue. Some events will not have a bookstore but will allow for sales at the back of your presentation room. Others will have an exhibit hall where you can set up a booth to handle sales and signings. To that end, find out exactly how many copies the bookstore wants, where they want them delivered and by when, how they will be sold, and what your take is after sales are final.

> **Pro Tip**
>
> *When working with an event coordinator (at a bookstore or otherwise), follow your contact's instructions to the letter and meet their deadlines.*

What Does That Mean?

YOUR TAKE AFTER SALES ARE FINAL

Know what percentage of your book sales you will be allowed to retain. An industry standard is the bookseller retains 55 percent of the book's retail price. Considering that a conference bookstore is taking on the responsibility of stocking your book and having staff on hand to handle the sales—tasks you do not have to manage—assume that the bookstore will retain some portion of your book sales. Get in writing what that percentage is, how you will receive your payment after the event concludes, whether they require you to submit an invoice in order for the payment to be processed, and by when you can expect to receive payment.

HOSTING YOUR OWN BOOK SIGNINGS

When hosting your own book signing at your own event, keep the following in mind: if you do not have a massive following already in place in the city where you're planning to have your signing, or if you do not have a team in place that will take care of ensuring there is a crowd that wants to purchase copies of your book, or if you do not have some other plan in place to make the event a meaningful one, then a book signing may not be a wise choice. Confirm only those signings where you know you can draw a crowd or where you can rely upon someone else to draw the crowd. And when you do have a signing—whether it's hosted by you or someone else, such as a conference—always make the focus more about making connections with readers than making sales. We are not saying don't worry about selling your book; we *are* saying see the bigger picture, which is not just the book but all the things that come from being a published author.

Now, can you use your expertise to speak and have all sorts of opportunities extended to you without also being the author of a book?

Absolutely! As a case in point, Bridgett did so without a book for eighteen years! Will the opportunities be greater in number and impact *with* your name on the cover of a book? Quite possibly.

And is there far more to discuss when it comes to being a speaker? Without a doubt. There are speaker fees, collateral, speaker reels, the speaker website, how to find conferences and other events to speak at, proposal submission best practices, how to pitch yourself to companies and corporations, effective presentation skills both in person and online, social media profiles . . . the list goes on and on. This chapter was designed to start the wheels turning and to get you to see that when you have a book establishing you as an expert or as someone with a specialized depth and breadth of knowledge in an area, speaking is the natural next step.

You do not have to plan on giving a speech to a crowd of thousands. (That can sound sort of scary for some anyway!) You can do it in person or virtually, on big stages or in intimate groups, at conferences and summits, or for smaller corporate trainings and lunch and learns. You can be a guest on a show or a podcast. There are all kinds of speaking opportunities that are paid, and some that may not come with financial remuneration but that put you and your book in front of your ideal audience. And don't allow imposter syndrome to creep in. Organizations are always looking for a fresh perspective or new content, and as an author, you're in the perfect position to pitch yourself. Use your book to get in the door, and use your book to send listeners out the door. Find platforms that make sense for your message, make it clear that you want to speak on those platforms, then show up and deliver.

TAKEAWAYS AND TO-DOS

Takeaways

- Your book + speaking opportunities = the sky's the limit. Being a published author grants you better access to the stage.

- Expand your mind beyond formal conference presentations on huge stages and in front of thousands of audience members. Seek out speaking opportunities of all sizes.
- When booking and delivering speaking engagements, be easy to work with. We can't stress this enough.
- Don't wing your presentation. Show up prepared, and give listeners the kind of performance you would want to see if you were in the audience. Don't rule out the idea of getting a presentation coach.
- Whether you sell your books in an event's bookstore, at the back of the presentation room, in an exhibit hall, or elsewhere, know exactly how everything will be handled and what's required on your part for getting the books where they need to be and by when as well as how sales and post-event payments to you are handled.
- Focus more on increasing connections and improving your and your book's visibility than selling your book. Use your book to sell yourself and your ideas via speaking, and the book will sell itself.

To-Dos

- Make a list of organizations, events, and shows that have missions and target audiences that align with your book's content.
- Research those places from your list, find out what's involved in their presentation proposal submission process, and make a plan to get involved by attending their events and/or submitting a proposal.
- Send your book to contacts who have platforms you want to speak on.
- Start designing your signature talk, the one that captures the essence of your book. Start with your book's chapters, then use them to craft a message you love and that you can deliver from the stage.
- Decide if you will host your own events and book signings or if you will rely on other organizations for you to make appearances. In either instance, fully prepare for the logistics involved in making it a great time for everyone involved.

NOTES

PART 4

CALLING IN THE PROS

CHAPTER 13

FINDING THE SUPPORT YOU NEED EXACTLY WHEN YOU NEED IT

We hope you're not feeling discouraged, exhausted, or overwhelmed now that you've made it this far. We know there is a lot to think about and consider, which is why we've taken the time to detail as much of it as possible in this book for you. You can be a successful author—we've seen plenty of examples and worked with them in the flesh—and we want to do everything in our power to prepare you and guide you to be just like them. So, take a deep breath and repeat after us: *I can do this*.

And you can.

Here's the thing to remember, however. You don't have to do it all alone. Quite frankly, we encourage you not to. We all have our strengths and zones of genius. When possible, play to your strengths and stay in your lane, and leave the things that fall outside of those to someone else. Remember, you're thinking about this like a business. In a business, you would hire, delegate, and/or contract out certain tasks that you prefer not to do or shouldn't be doing because you won't get the best results. It's no different when it comes to producing a book.

Did You Catch That?

Play to your strengths, stay in your lane, and leave the things that fall outside of those to someone else.

So, if you've read up to now and your mind is spinning, your heart is racing, and you're thinking, "I've got to do all of this?" please do not abandon ship. You do have to ensure that it all gets done, but you don't have to do it all yourself.

Besides, there is a HUGE number of people within the publishing space to support you during any and all of the phases of the book's life cycle. There are people who can help you as early as when you're outlining your book. There are others who can help you run new campaigns to promote your book years after it's been published to bring new attention to your now "old" title and all kinds of folks in between. This is not and should not be a solo endeavor. (Check out appendix F: People on the Publishing Path.)

WHEN YOU SHOULD GET SUPPORT

Truthfully, only you can identify when you feel that you need to tap into the brilliance and skills of others, but we suggest that you look for additional support when you feel that a part of your book is going to suffer if you don't get professional help. After all, our central message is ABCD (**A**pproach your **B**ook with a **C**ommitment to **D**oing it right). Only you can determine what you don't know how to do well or what you don't know how to do at all. These are both indicators of when to go looking for support as well as *what kind* of support you need to find. If it's something you don't do well, find someone who can do it better or best. If it's something you don't know how to do at all, find someone who can teach you how to do it well or who can do it for you, depending on your preference and budget.

If you feel like your book is going to suffer when it comes to the organization and cohesion of the material, you want to find writing professionals—a writing coach or a developmental editor—who can help you sort and filter your thoughts and clarify your main ideas and arguments. If you feel like you've got the organization and writing parts all handled but know that your spelling and grammar are atrocious and you have no business editing your own work, then you want to employ a terrific mechanical, line, or copy editor. If you're not at all concerned with the manuscript, but you have no clue how to market yourself or your book, you need marketing support, and that support either needs to show you the ropes or take over the ropes.

There's another indicator that you need outside support and that's when your book is going to fail to exist without it. Hire publishing professionals when your book *depends on it*—as in, it'll cease to exist if you don't. Another way to look at this is needing life-saving accountability.

Did You Catch That?

> There's another indicator that you need outside support and that's when your book is going to fail to exist without it.

Many people know when they've got a great idea or know what they want to say but struggle to put their butts in the chair and get to it. Most people these days wear multiple hats in their lives and have priorities constantly competing for their time and attention. When you add in the writing of a book, it's easy for many people to deprioritize this activity, especially when they don't see it as "paying the bills" or "feeding their families." In other words, writing a book can be classified as frivolous or less important in comparison to the other tasks they feel beholden to or the people in their lives that they are responsible for. They may really believe in and care about their book project but struggle to give it the time and energy it deserves. So, enter the need for these authors to have accountability and someone (or something) to whom they can report their progress to keep them on track. If your book is going to fail to exist without outside reinforcement, then this is a great indicator that you need to get outside support.

There's also a very black-and-white way to look at when to get support and that is to get support when you can afford to. If you've got the financial means to hire additional support, do it. It'll be a worthy investment.

Truthfully, there are many things you can do on your own and learn to do on your own for free. Between YouTube videos, blog posts, websites, podcasts, and more, there is an overwhelming amount of information out there on writing, editing, producing, publishing, and marketing books—all at no cost to you. So, if your budget is slim, you can still move forward, or you can prioritize which items you spend your budget on.

Yet, we both know that the people who produce the best books tend to work with professionals. Because despite the abundance of available free resources out there, there are three things that are also true: (1) not every free and available resource is an accurate or helpful one; (2) sometimes even when you read and think you understand, it's not always easy to apply; and (3) none of us holds all of the skills we need to produce a great book even if we understand what's required. For example, you can learn about beautiful cover design and what makes a great cover, but if you have no creative design skills or ability, you'll probably end up with a sloppy-looking final cover or settle for some cheap template cover design you found. Neither of these will serve your book in the long run.

Did You Catch That?

The people who produce the best books tend to be the people who work with professionals.

So, if and when you've got the financial resources, allocate them to professional support. Remember, you're the boss of your book business. All businesses require an investment—you have to spend money to make money. Determine what pieces of the author's journey likely are going to be the most challenging for you based on your own skills or experience (or lack thereof), and start there by looking for outside help.

Finally, you'll need to hire support when it's time to publish. We discussed the types of publishing paths available to you in chapter 9, but regardless of which one you choose, it will come with a requirement of outside support. Even the self-publishing model has room for hiring outside support. So, know that as you approach the publishing stage of your author's journey, you'll need support at this point, if nowhere else.

WAYS AND PLACES TO FIND SUPPORT

There are numerous ways to go about finding the support you need, but the first thing is to really understand what kind of support you're looking for. Understanding your sticking points will help you narrow your search. Simply typing "writing support" or "help with publishing" into any search engine, whether that's Google or LinkedIn, is going to produce a ridiculous number of results. But, if you know you need accountability and guidance in shaping the manuscript and drafting it, "writing coach" or "book coach" will produce more refined results. The point is to be specific with what you're looking for so that your search produces better results and you find the best support for your needs. By the time you're done this chapter, you'll better understand the wealth of people within the industry that can help you pen, publish, and profit from your book.

Pro Tip

Understand your sticking points and be specific with your search terms when searching for the writing and publishing support you need.

That said, where do you search for these people? Google is an obvious choice, but you will end up with a lot of results. LinkedIn, as a social media network of professionals, is our recommendation, especially because you can then see if you have any mutual connections between yourself and that publishing professional. If you do, there is the possibility that your mutual connection has experience with that professional. What better way to vet a possible service provider than to hear from a prior client or someone who knows them? (For guidance on vetting publishing professionals and partners, see appendix J: How to Determine If a Publishing Company Is Reputable and appendix F: People on the Publishing Path.)

To that end, talking with friends and colleagues who have previously written books or posted on your social media channels about what type of support you're looking for can be fruitful. Word-of-mouth references and direct introductions and referrals from people you already know, like, and trust can go a long way. Think about any other time you've hired a contractor or service provider on the great recommendation of someone else versus picked someone blindly.

> **Pro Tip**
>
> *Talk with friends and colleagues who have previously published; direct referrals and references from people you already know, like, and trust go a long way.*

Look within professional organizations that are publishing-adjacent or publishing-focused, such as the Editorial Freelancers Association, Nonfiction Authors Association, or Independent Book Publishers Association. We've identified a list of organizations with freelancers and service providers in appendix G: Writing and Publishing Must-Have Resource List. These reputable organizations have search functionalities for finding service providers in the publishing space.

SERVICE PROVIDERS IN THE PUBLISHING SPACE

We know we've told you to get specific on the kind of support you need, and by this point in the book, we'd like to think we've gotten to know you pretty well and can hear you saying, "But WHO is that? What kind of support is available?" We'd also like to think that you've gotten to know us well enough by now to know that we're not gonna leave you hangin'.

We've put together a list of all kinds of folks for various stages of the publishing path in appendix F: People on the Publishing Path, but here is a handful of groups and categories of professionals within the publishing space to support you during any and all of the phases of your book's life cycle.

Book Coaches

Sometimes you might also see book doctor, writing coach, book doula, and book sherpa used interchangeably even if there are slight variations to the services rendered. These providers can range from "one and done" consultations to help authors get their books outlined and organized to longer-term relationships whereby the provider works with the author on a regular basis through manuscript development, providing accountability and developmental review of the material as it's being drafted.

Ghostwriters

A ghostwriter is someone who works closely with the author and writes the manuscript on their behalf, but the author byline (the name appearing on the front and back covers and inside title page) and full credit goes to the author. One exception is when an author decides to give some credit to the ghostwriter by adding "with" between their names on the front cover. For example, take Olive Pennenpaper with Frank Witherspoon. The "with" indicates that the front-runner author wrote it with someone else, and sometimes the "with" indicates a ghostwriter. Another exception is when the author provides credit to the ghostwriter in the acknowledgments section. It's important for an author that when they are deciding to work with a ghostwriter, they know contractually what is being asked by the ghostwriter when it comes to credit.

That said, there's a reason why the word *ghost* is in the word *ghostwriter*: the person is unnamed and unknown, and the author's name that appears on the front cover is associated with the work whether they penned a word or not. This is also why most ghostwriters' contracts will come with confidentiality clauses or agreements. Most clients using a ghostwriter don't want anyone to know that they used a ghostwriter. The author-client will say they're writing a book, and no one else will be the wiser.

Additionally, ghostwriters are the conduits or vehicles for the words, but they own no rights to the work. A ghostwriter's contract with the client should state that the rights (what the client does with the work) and the ownership of the intellectual property (the content itself) belong to the author (client) and that no royalties will be received by the ghostwriter once the book is made available for sale. There are always exceptions, of course, but typically the obligation of the ghostwriter is to write and provide the manuscript to the author. That is the service they provide. At that point, when the manuscript is finished and handed back to the client, the contractual agreement has been met. What happens after that—how it's published or how it performs—is no longer a part of the original contract. There are some occasions where a ghostwriter might work royalty arrangements into their contract, but this is not a typical practice. Again, ensure that you are very clear on what is being asked by the ghostwriter, if and when you ever decide to enter into such a contract. Like any new arrangement, or when hiring a service provider, ask a lot of questions, do your homework, read the contract diligently, and have a lawyer do the same.

All of this being said, you may wonder if and how a ghostwriter gets paid if they are not getting any of the royalties. The ghostwriter gets paid before the book is published. They get paid by the author as the manuscript is being developed and, just like editors, typically charge a price per word. With that in mind, you can imagine how costly using a ghostwriter can be when you're talking about a manuscript of 25,000 words or more and prices starting anywhere from $0.20 per word to as high as $1.00 (or more) per word. Like any other professional service provider, a ghostwriter is paid for their service, and their service is writing the book the author envisions.

Did You Catch That?

Like any new arrangement, or when hiring any service provider, ask a lot of questions, do your homework, read the contract diligently, and have a lawyer do the same.

Editors

A lot of authors are unfamiliar with the various types of editors, asking generally about needing an editor but not knowing what kind they need or the fact that all editing is not created equal. As we discussed in chapter 5, there are—more or less—three kinds of editors, and they work from the macro level to the micro level—the developmental editor (macro level, the first editor you need), copy editor/line editor/mechanical editor (micro level, the second wave of editing you need), and the proofreader (micro level, the last read-through). For a refresher on the different types of editors and what they do, return to chapter 5. Or, if you need a quick-and-dirty glimpse at the levels of editing and what they each entail, we've hooked you up in appendix B: What Does That Mean? The Greatest Hits.

Book Marketers and Publicists

These professionals are focused on marketing and sales activities after the book has been published. They are the strategists or worker bees whose aim is to promote to your ideal reader you, your book, and its main message. These service providers may focus on an author's social media and online presence (including an author's website), speaking and podcast appearances, book awards, opportunities, and recognitions; getting the book into book fairs; running ads or bestseller campaigns; or pitching to media outlets and publications. Some do all of these things, and some are narrowly focused on only one or two of these specific activities.

> ### IN OUR EXPERT OPINION—THE LOWDOWN ON BOOK AWARDS
>
> *We already got on our soapbox about bestseller campaigns in chapter 8, but we want to address book awards for a moment, too. Our perspective here is similar to our stance on bestseller campaigns. From a marketing perspective, being able to say that your book won an award is nice for how it looks and sounds in your bio or when you're talking about your book. It may matter to a reader, but lots of readers buy books that don't have award statuses and enjoy them. And tons of great books have never won awards. More importantly, it's best to understand the individual award requirements and process and how a book is deemed award winning. Are you paying to automatically have an award bestowed upon you, and it's not about merit or quality? Is it an individual reader or a committee who is judging the worth of the book? What are those people's expertise in critiquing books, and on what criteria are they judging? The CliffsNotes version: not every award is created equal, so do your research to understand the awards for which you're considering entering your book into the ring.*

Author Virtual Assistants

Virtual assistants have taken the online business world by storm. Many solopreneurs and small business entrepreneurs leverage virtual assistants for a variety of business activities. Like anyone in business, virtual assistants can serve niche markets, and one of those niche markets is authors. Some of them may even specify nonfiction authors, qualifying what genre of author they work with. An author virtual assistant is someone who supports the author in almost any of the book activities with which the author feels a deficit. This could mean tracking sales or shipping the book directly to customers. It could also mean managing the author's online presence by posting for them on social media or responding to emails coming from the website's contact form. An author virtual assistant is an incredible asset to have in managing the multiple responsibilities of being in the book biz.

Publishers

Putting it simply, these are the folks who will actually publish your book—either professionals or yourself. Four publishing models exist—traditional, hybrid, indie, and self-publishing—and employing one of these models is what will ultimately get your book to market. Naturally, there are advantages and disadvantages to each publishing model, so understanding your goals for your book, your timeline, and your budget is beneficial when making decisions about which publishing route to take. No matter what, you cannot get around choosing a publishing path when it comes to writing a book, so this is the one part of the process where hiring support is an absolute must. See chapter 9 for extensive coverage on the different publishing models and appendix A: The Pros and Cons of Each Publishing Route for the advantages and disadvantages to each model to support you as you sort through which route to choose.

QUESTIONS TO ASK WHEN INTERVIEWING PROSPECTS

No matter which publishing professionals you need, there is a handful of things we recommend that you always review while you're interviewing your prospects; we call them the six P's: process, people, (fine) print, pocketbook (or price), property, and portfolio. We've listed specific questions you can ask in appendix F: People on the Publishing Path.

(Pro Tip)

When you're interviewing publishing professionals to work with you on your book, always review the six P's: process, people, (fine) print, pocketbook (or costs), property, and portfolio.

For *process*, you want to know how that provider works. What are the steps they're going to take you through and by what time? Understanding the way they approach the task is helpful to you in not only knowing what to expect for your timeline but also in having a sense of whether you'll work well together and if they have an established plan.

People is our way of saying "know who you're working with." When you interview a potential service provider, are they the actual person you will work with or just the face of a group of people? Is there a team, and could you be working with any number of the team members? Is there a customer representative that stands between you and the person actually performing the work? Understand who is involved in that aspect of your book's life cycle.

The fine *print* is a nod to the contract, and a professional service provider should have one. Read it. Have an attorney read it. Make sure you understand it, and if you or your attorney has any questions at all, ask the service provider for clarity. Be watchful for any hidden costs that weren't made transparent during the conversation about the costs. And don't be afraid to ask for changes to the contract. It's not set in stone until you sign on the dotted line. (And even then, you can request an amendment to the contract if the need arises. But that's another book for another day and for another author.) If you like everything else you hear and see and truly want to work with the service provider that's in front of you, but there are one or two things in the contract that you want changed, ask. The worst thing they can say is no. But they can tell if the two of you are vibin', and the fact that they've presented you with a contract means one thing: you're definitely vibin', and they want to work with you! So, ask for any changes you want, and see what happens.

Did You Catch That?

Don't be afraid to ask for changes to the contract. Nothing is set in stone until you sign on the dotted line.

Pocketbook (or costs) is about understanding the costs for the services rendered—and not just the total cost but also what the payment schedule is and knowing if there is a way of canceling the contract or getting a refund. (And ensure an exit clause is included in the contract that provides you with an out if more than the cheese starts to stink in Denmark.) Essentially, you want to know what the terms and conditions around payment are. You also want to know EXACTLY what you're getting for your money.

Did You Catch That?

You always want to know EXACTLY what you're getting for your money and the terms and conditions of payment.

Property has to do with who owns what. Does the service provider claim any right to your book or what they produce for you by working with them? They shouldn't. But if they do, pass. Move on and find someone else. The one exception to this is if you're going the traditional-publishing route. It's the industry standard for an author to relinquish all rights to a traditional publisher.

> **Pro Tip**
>
> *If someone claims any right to your book or what they produce for you by working with them, move on.*

Finally, *portfolio* refers to getting references or samples of what the service provider has done before. This could mean talking to prior clients, reading case studies or testimonials they have on hand, looking at samples, or inspecting their work by getting a copy of a book they've produced.

For cover designers, you will want to see a portfolio of other covers they've created.

For editors, you will want to see a before-and-after sample of a manuscript they worked on or even ask if they would be willing to demonstrate their work by performing a certain type of editing (developmental or mechanical) on one page of content you provide them.

For publishers you're considering, it can mean asking them what recent favorite books they published and where you can order them. You never know—they may save you time and money and offer to send a complimentary desk copy to you! (As the owner of Press 49, Bridgett and her team will do that in a heartbeat!) For more questions to ask during these prospect interviews, see appendix J: How to Determine If a Publishing Company Is Reputable.

Whether you remember these six P's or not, we encourage you to ask any and all questions that come to mind. Treat these interviews like any other contract-for-hire conversation you would have. If you were going to have someone build you a house, you would ask them ALL. THE. THINGS. to ensure that the house was not only built correctly from the start but also built to last and built to your vision. So, ask! Ask everything you can think of to ask. The quality and success of your book count on it.

TAKEAWAYS AND TO-DOS

Takeaways

- Think about your book like a business. In a business, you would hire, delegate, and/or contract certain tasks that you prefer not to do or that you shouldn't do because you won't get the best results.
- Look for and be prepared to hire additional support when you feel that a part of your book is going to suffer or that it won't get written or published at all because you need accountability.
- Before looking for support, understand *specifically* what kind of support you need.
- Like any new arrangement, or when hiring any service provider, ask a lot of questions, do your homework, read their contract diligently, and have a lawyer do the same.
- When you're interviewing any publishing professionals, be sure to review the process, people, (fine) print, pocketbook (or price), property, and portfolio.

To-Dos

- Audit your strengths and areas where you need assistance. What kind of support might you be looking for when it comes to those things you listed as not being your strengths?
- Start talking with friends and colleagues who have published before to get names and references.
- Identify which of the professionals you need based on your needs assessment, and start reaching out to those you've already been given names of.
- Leverage appendix F: People on the Publishing Path when interviewing prospects.

NOTES

CHAPTER 14

WHEN IT'S TIME TO CALL IN THE PROS

W e've all heard the saying "a magician never reveals their secrets." We know that saying means they're never going to tell you how they make their tricks look like magic. Our approach to this book has been the opposite. We have set out to demystify the writing and publishing process for you so that you don't go after this pursuit thinking you can "abracadabra" your way from blank page to published book. And just as we've told you as much as we can to support your future book publishing endeavor, we also have to acknowledge that our wells of knowledge only run so deep and that there's still stuff we didn't cover inside these pages.

While we are being honest about that, we might as well be honest about something else, too. Even if you understand everything we've said inside these pages, and even if you have all the skills you need to go about writing and publishing a book all on your own, you probably won't want to. You probably won't have the time to. You probably won't get the book written if you fly solo. Plus, we already told you that you shouldn't do that—go it alone, that is.

And because we are bearing all the truths, we might as well tell you that this is the chapter where we tell you that you need us. It also happens that this chapter has been intentionally placed here, following the chapter about getting support and preceding the conclusion and the About the Authors section. (We hope you learn something from this intentional placement. Hint hint. Wink wink. Nudge nudge.)

Before we give away the answer and tell you why we've placed this chapter here, we want to ask you something: can you guess what purpose this very intentional placement serves? Think about everything you've read up until now.

It's okay . . . we'll wait.

drumroll

Your book is a hook. Your hook, specifically. By writing a nonfiction book that directly aligns with your business, industry, expertise, and experience, you've created a tool to funnel people back in your direction. Your book is an elevated business card. It's a way to lead people back to you. To your website, your social media channels, your business . . .

Remember how we've discussed marketing yourself, not your book? Or using your book to illustrate your expertise, experience, or thought leadership? Or leveraging your book to get speaking opportunities that hopefully drive people back to your business and/or back to your book?

Did You Catch That?

Your book is a hook—a way to funnel people back to you.

Well, here it is in action because this book is no exception. You likely weren't conscious of that as you were reading because you were reading with the intention of learning how to write and publish your own book. We are pulling back the proverbial curtain at this moment to say, "See how it's done?"

If you were working with us, we would coach you to ensure that before your book ends, you let the good people who read your book know exactly what you want them to do now that your book is over. In the business world, we call that the call to action. It's asking your people to take the next step in solving their problem that you can help them with.

Now, we could have chosen to hold off on all that call-to-action stuff until the About the Authors section, but then what about those folks who don't read that part? We know there are some of you out there. We couldn't leave that to chance—not if we are thinking with our very savvy author-CEO business hats on (and we assure you, we are).

Instead of waiting to tell you when to call us in to support you, we are seizing the rest of this chapter to do so.

WHEN TO CALL IN SASSY AND BAD-ASSY A. Y. BERTHIAUME AND THE WRITE PLACE, RIGHT TIME

The Write Place, Right Time, is a virtual boutique of book coaching services. A.Y. (known by Ally to her inner circle, which includes her clients) offers private, premium, individual coaching and group coaching programs. Her passion is for the genre of memoir, so she loves to coach authors who want to write in that genre, but she also serves those working in other nonfiction genres (prescriptive, self-help, and personal or professional development).

As a client, you might be calling her in for coaching support if any of the following are true:

- You've been thinking about writing a book but don't know where to begin.
- You have a loose idea of where you want to go but lack clarity and confidence to go further.
- You need a solidified plan for your book—not just an outline of the content but a full and detailed picture, including things like who the book is for, why it is relevant, what publishing options are available, and what an online presence entails.
- You created a detailed outline and have a clear concept but can't seem to hold yourself accountable for the writing.
- You created a detailed outline and are writing regularly but need someone to look at the work as it's developed and provide a developmental editorial review to ensure you're meeting your book's objectives.

One of the main things to know is that A. Y. is not a publisher. She works with authors strictly on developing and completing the manuscript. The kind of publishing support A. Y. provides is publishing education and referrals. She educates her clients on the various publishing avenues, including their advantages and disadvantages, and helps them make an informed decision about which path to pursue that is in keeping with their book's mission, goals, and interests. Once her client has selected a path, A. Y. introduces them to preferred publishing partners, with Press 49 (Bridgett's press) being one of them.

A. Y. works from her office in Vermont but serves clients remotely. Her diverse body of clients is located across North America and Europe. Working with A. Y. is a minimum six-month engagement. People who work with her must be willing to go deep, be vulnerable, and commit to the process. Her programs are collaborative and require active participation and follow-through.

To explore her services and how she works, visit her website, the-writeplacerighttime.com, and you can also book a free call to start the conversation. She loves to hear about people's initial book ideas and better understand where they are in the process and how she can serve them.

WHEN TO CALL IN BIG GUNS BRIDGETT MCGOWEN-HAWKINS AND PRESS 49

If you've read this book and have no doubt that it's time to publish your manuscript, but you simply do not want to do all the work yourself—because, let's keep it real, it's a lot of work—then, let's cut to the chase. Visit press49.com today to schedule your no-obligation call with Press 49.

It doesn't matter if you . . .

- are unsure of where to start.
- are tired of trying to figure out self-publishing on your own, getting burned by professionals who claim they know how to help

you get published but they really don't, or confused by the entire process.

- are overwhelmed by all the work involved with publishing.
- have self-doubt and limiting beliefs.
- don't know who you can trust or if you can trust *anyone* in the publishing industry.

Our award-winning experts at Press 49 will help you get past all this. Once you have an inkling to write a book, don't let it remain an idea; make it a reality. Or once you've done the hard work of drafting your manuscript, don't leave it sitting on a shelf or resting in your hard drive. We take you from a person with an idea to a writer with a completed manuscript to a published author with results you will love and a finished book that makes you beam with pride.

Want to check us out beforehand—try before you buy, if you will? No problem. Some of our favorite projects to date are . . .

- *6 Figures in 12 Months: How to Meet or Surpass Your Revenue Goals as a Real Estate Agent* by Jeff Discher (an Amazon #1 new release)
- *Life After Kevin: A Mother's Search for Peace and the Golden Retrievers that Led the Way* by Susan Lynch (an Amazon #1 new release and a Nonfiction Authors Association Gold Award winner)
- *Making Dollars While Making Change: The Playbook for Game Changers* by Jonathan Quarles (an Amazon bestseller)

(And you should know us by now—we added those details in parentheses only because we know that some peeps find those distinctions kinda sparkly and cool.)

At Press 49, we eliminate the guesswork and get you published in a matter of months, not years. Visit press49.com to schedule your no-obligation consultation today. It will be the best time you ever spent discussing your book idea. Guaranteed.

WANT MORE?

Has this book lit a fire under you, or has it raised more questions? Are you intrigued and want more? We've got you covered!

We love what we do and what we teach and, more importantly, we love connecting and engaging with others who are on the path to being authors and getting published. Contact writing coach and ghostwriter extraordinaire A. Y. at thewriteplacerighttime.com or publishing power-house Bridgett at connectwithb.com to have either or both of us as guests on your podcast, facilitators of an in-person or virtual workshop, or speak to your communities. We look forward to it!

WHAT NOW?

Writing and publishing a book is one of the most important events of a person's life, and if you're not going to do it right, then don't do it at all. But we're in your corner and believe that you should—and, more importantly, that you *can*—get it done and at a high standard. To make that happen, though, you need resources. You need a team. You need experts with you every step of the way, guiding you with what it takes to be an exceptional writer, taking your ideas from a first or second draft to an edited manuscript to a gorgeously published book. So, don't stand there. Call in the pros.

Did You Catch That?

Writing and publishing a book is one of the most important events of a person's life, and if you're not going to do it right, then don't do it at all.

TAKEAWAYS AND TO-DOS

Takeaways

- Even if you understand everything we've said inside these pages and you have all the skills, you probably won't have the time, or you won't want to take the time, to write and publish a book by yourself. Plus, we already told you that you shouldn't do this whole thing alone.
- By writing a nonfiction book that directly aligns with your business, industry, expertise, and experience, you've created a tool to funnel people back in your direction.
- If you're not going to write, publish, and profit from a book the right way, don't do it at all.

To-Dos

- Visit A. Y.'s website, thewriteplacerighttime.com.
- Check out Bridgett and the Press 49 team at press49.com.
- Buy copies of this book for your friends.
- Invite Ally and/or Bridgett to come speak to a community or group near you.

NOTES

SEE THE BIG PICTURE

After engaging in a podcast conversation about writing and publishing, one idea led to another, and we knew we wanted to educate our readers on three main areas: the process of writing and publishing, thinking about their book like a business, and ways to make money from a book outside of direct sales. Before we began, we loosely called this "the trifecta." And we said, "Let's focus on those four areas and see if we can produce a beautiful and compact resource book for authors that sits around 25,000 words—something small and bite-sized."

We stayed pretty committed to the four main focus areas, which you've now digested as individual parts of the book, but we blew way past our word goal. We questioned if we should be concerned, quickly dismissed the notion, and said to each other, "Let's just write." When we finished the first draft (without appendices), we were around 37,000 words. By the time we added all the extra goods to the front and back and handed it over to Press 49, our manuscript was 98,433 words.

We know you probably don't care how many words the manuscript was when we handed it over to the press, so why are we telling you this backstory? To illustrate a point. Several points actually.

We started with the main ideas and arguments we wanted to convey. Still, once we got going, we recognized that to educate our readers on those points in a way that felt informed, thorough, and serving, we knew we had to write as many words as it would take to write this manuscript right. We've preached from the beginning to **A**pproach your **B**ook with a **C**ommitment to **D**oing it right (ABCD mindset), and we abided by that mantra ourselves.

When we began, we knew what we wanted to say, but we also took time-outs to discuss who it was for (which is you) and why it would matter to them (meaning you). We thought about your sticking points. We thought about what we should say to a client, how we would say it, and the "why" behind it. This kind of intentional strategizing is a part of the writing and publishing process even though it didn't involve writing a single word. These were things we needed to know in order to shape the manuscript and to inform our eventual marketing and promotional activities.

When we've told you to think about the long game, think about the big picture, consider your reader and your objectives . . . we've told you because we know that all of these things are critical to the final outcome: the quality of your book, the marketing of your book, and the sale of your book, all of which means the success of your book.

You know what else? We also had really open and frank conversations about the budgetary items involved in producing this book, the timeline, our meeting schedule, and our individual roles and responsibilities. Just like a business needs a financial plan, project management, and administration, so does a book. This book was no exception.

Everything we've preached, we've practiced. Everything we've shared comes from what we've learned from our own experience as authors and from our professional and industry expertise. What we know has served us and our clients; we now hope it serves you.

We want you to feel proud of what you produce. We want you to feel in control of the process. We want you to understand all the stops along the journey. And, honestly, it's all because we have one selfish desire: to see your books out there in the world. We know you've got some important stuff to say and share. We know the world needs more of your fine voices and ideas. If we can offer you what we know so that we get the pleasure of eventually learning from you when your book is finally out there, we'll be really happy readers and better people.

We truly hope that this book has shown you that we're making your book our business as much as we want you to make it yours. And, of course, if you need additional support along the way, we'd be happy for you to reach out and call one of us in as a pro. Check out the About the Authors section to learn more about us and where to get in touch (or go back to the previous chapter and have a look there).

We do want you to write your book. You know that because now you've read this one. You've got what you need to do this right. We believe you have what it takes. Go forth and conquer. Be that book's boss. Make your book your business. We'll be on the lookout for when your book hits the shelves because we know you'll have written, published, and promoted it right.

ACKNOWLEDGMENTS
(THAT YOU DON'T WANT TO MISS!)

W e'd like to start by thanking the Academy. Just kidding, obviously. But let's be real. How many boring acknowledgments have you read or skipped altogether because you've always known them to be boring? We want to spice ours up the way some movies do with their end-of-film credits. Would you expect anything less from us at this point?

First, we are thanking each other. Yes . . . we are.

Coauthoring a book is a very different beast than doing it on your own. It's an all-encompassing creative collaboration and business partnership. It's not just having one CEO for a book, but two. We couldn't have done it if each of us hadn't brought our whole A game and shared equal responsibility of bringing this book from conception to publication.

A. Y.: To Bridgett . . . I couldn't be happier that we had that lightning-strike moment after the live show we did and decided to embark on this journey together. It's been so fun and so easy (and I've never been a fan of group projects, but you've changed my mind!). Thank you for always showing up genuinely over this last year. Your enthusiasm, charisma, and let's-get-it-done personality made you a blast to work with. Paired with all your publishing knowledge that played into not just the writing but also all the strategy and business items we've had to decide on along the way, you've made this book one majorly kick-ass title. I'm so proud of the brainchild we've created.

Bridgett: A.Y., remember when my big mouth proclaimed in the summer of 2022 that we'd get this done and published on August 8, 2023? But as I write this, here we are just days away from the first day of fall 2023, and we are just getting ready to turn this over to a Press 49 editor. Thank you for not immediately saying that there's no way we can make that happen and for not rolling your eyes (or at least not letting me know you were rolling your eyes) when I would pipe up with one suggestion or another. People talk about things running like a well-oiled machine, but that seriously is what this experience felt like. I, too, detest group projects, so maybe that was our secret driving force, eh? And if I had to do it all over again, the only change I'd wish for is that we'd met and started the project sooner! Hit me up when you're ready to start discussing the second edition. (Don't start rolling your eyes now!) I'm here for it!

Next, we must thank a mama. For real. Ally's mom, Anne, was one of our beta readers, and she missed her calling as an editor. Anne's got a laser eye for details, discrepancies, and dissonance. We are so happy she's retired because otherwise she may not have had time to read this book—not once, but twice! Her feedback was just the lacquer we needed to polish this manuscript up and make it ready for the handover to Press 49. (By the way, Anne—Bridgett here. If you have any interest in coming out of retirement and starting a second career in the publishing industry, will you let me know? Asking for a friend.)

To all those who provided accolades and endorsements, which appear in the front matter and on the back cover, we are so grateful that we know so many rock stars across the globe who so quickly and joyfully said YES to our request to review this work and took such care in reading the book and providing beautifully written, praiseworthy testimonials. (Testimonials we thoroughly enjoyed receiving and then texting each other about. "Did you see the one by . . . It's amazing!")

Of course, huge shouts of thanks and kudos to the Press 49 team for turning this manuscript into the dynamite book that it is.

Last, but certainly not least, to our spouses who always have our backs as we work on books (ours and others'), we couldn't do it without your support and belief in us. And, to our sons, who we live to show up for as Ma, Mom, Mother, Mommy, and . . . *Bruh.* You remind us when to put the book down and step into the present moment.

APPENDICES

THE PROS AND CONS OF EACH PUBLISHING ROUTE

B elow is a chart comparing the four publishing routes' advantages and drawbacks and giving you a sense of who each avenue might be good for. Ultimately, we would suggest that you consider the following when deciding on your publishing route:

- Mission (What's the mission of your book? Would a certain publishing route be better for the mission?)
- Vision (Based on what you envision, would a certain publishing route align the most with your vision?)
- Goals (What are your main aims for the book? Which publishing route would help you achieve those goals?)
- Budget (How much are you able or willing to invest?)
- Control (How much control over the process and final decisions do you want?)
- Visibility, Platform, and Experience (Do you already have a following? Do you have anything else published to leverage?)

	TRADITIONAL	HYBRID	INDIE	SELF/DIY
Advantages	• The author does not need to pay any money up front. • The publisher takes care of everything; the publisher edits, formats, prints, markets, and distributes your book. • The book will be published properly. • The author receives an advance against future royalties.	• You can get published quickly—in a matter of months instead of years. • It will be of excellent quality. • It will save you a tremendous amount of time. • They will help you market your book. • You own your content to use to generate revenue through other products.	• You can get published quickly—in a matter of months instead of years. • It will save you a tremendous amount of time. • They will help you market your book. • You own your content to use to generate revenue through other products. • You have major input into your book. • You are guaranteed to get your book published.	• You are guaranteed to get your book published. • You are in control of the timeline for how long it takes to get your book published. • You retain creative control. • You do not have to allow other people to determine your success. • You and your readers decide the worth of your words, thoughts, and ideas. • You do not have to wait to get your book published. You publish it when you are ready. • You get the majority of the royalties. • Successful self-publishing will make it more likely that your book could be picked up by an agent and traditional publisher. • You do not spend a ton of time trying to get an agent's attention. • There is nothing to stop you from using your book content to develop and sell supplemental lines (courses, updated versions, audiobook re-release, etc.).

	TRADITIONAL	HYBRID	INDIE	SELF/DIY
Drawbacks	• There is a one-in-a-thousand chance that you will get a return call from an agent or that the publishing company will provide any feedback on an author's proposal and manuscript. • It can take a long time to get published; it is normally a one- to two-year process. • The publisher makes all the decisions; the author does not have any say in cover design, marketing, or any other aspects of the book's production.	• While your chances of getting published with a hybrid publisher are higher than they are with a traditional publisher, there's still that chance that the hybrid publisher will not accept your book. • If your manuscript is accepted for publication, the publisher may insist on massive changes to the content before your book is published. • There is an up-front investment.	• Because this type of publisher may recommend changes but may not insist on any changes to the content before publishing your book, you may not have the absolute best product possible. • There is an up-front investment.	• You have to pay as you go for services that you contract. • You are working with independent contractors with varying standards. • You have to vet and hire people to perform all the services required to get your book ready and to market, or you have to figure out how to do it yourself. (For more information, see appendix H: The Self-Publishing Checklist.)

	TRADITIONAL	HYBRID	INDIE	SELF/DIY
Would work for you if ...	• You have written a tremendous book that has a good likelihood of getting the attention of a traditional publisher. • You have a platform; you have an extremely large following of tens of thousands, if not hundreds of thousands, of followers; or you are a big name with celebrity or influencer status.	• You see the up-front fee as an investment in your future or the future of your business. • You already have an incredible manuscript that needs little to no developmental or substantive editing, or you are fine with having to make massive changes to the manuscript at the publisher's request. • You do not have the time or an interest in managing all the details and would rather leave it all to the professionals. • You have the money or are willing to pay for a professional product. • You see other avenues for monetizing your book (e.g., speaking engagements, attracting clients for bigger projects, using the book as a basis for leading masterminds or master classes, etc.).	• You see the up-front fee as an investment in your future or the future of your business. • You do not want your work heavily scrutinized, nor do you want to be faced with the possibility of the publisher insisting on extensive changes to your manuscript before you can get published. • You do not have the time or an interest in managing all the details and would rather leave it all to the professionals. • You have the money or are willing to pay for a professional product. • You see other avenues for monetizing your book.	• You have a lot of time to devote to the book. • You want to manage all the details. • You want or need to keep costs down.

WHAT DOES THAT MEAN? THE GREATEST HITS

We've compiled all those What Does That Mean? callout boxes that appear throughout the book in this one place for quick and easy reference.

CHAPTER 1

TRADITIONAL, HYBRID, INDIE, OR SELF-PUBLISH

There are several ways to publish, and each has advantages and disadvantages, which we cover in more detail in chapter 9 (and review again in appendix A: The Pros and Cons of Each Publishing Route). Here is the CliffsNotes version of the most common avenues to bring your book to the marketplace:

- **Self/DIY:** You do everything (or find everyone to do all the things for you)
- **Indie:** Someone else does mostly everything and allows you to retain 100 percent creative license; you pay them
- **Hybrid:** A cross between indie and traditional, the publisher does everything, but they may insist on extensive edits to your manuscript before they will publish you; you pay them
- **Traditional:** The oldest publishing route and the one most people know (think Penguin Random House and the like), traditional publishing is super competitive,

you need an agent (usually), and you might not have much creative control over your project; you don't have to pay them

CHAPTER 2

TEXT-, VIDEO-, OR IMAGE-BASED POSTS

When you post about your book on social media, use text, videos, and images to promote your book. For text-based posts, you can offer an enticing brief synopsis of your book, a provocative direct quote from your book, or a big question that your book answers. If you post a video, it can be a snippet from an interview of you discussing your book, a recording of you sharing some of your favorite lines from your book, or a testimonial from someone who read your book. Finally, in an image-based post, you might have a picture of someone reading your book, a collage of your book as a paperback and as an e-book on a monitor and smartphone, or a picture of yourself at one of your book signings. The options are endless! Regardless of whether you use a text-, video-, or image-based post, aim to promote, inform, or entertain your followers, and always include a link for where people can purchase your book online.

COST VERSUS RETAIL PRICE

Cost: the amount it takes for a publisher, printer, or distributor to produce your book before it's sold

Retail price: the amount your reader will pay for your produced book once it's available for purchase

CHAPTER 3

YOUR BOOK'S IDENTIFIERS AND METADATA

Your book's identifiers are exactly what they sound like: the specific information that identifies your book and that people use to locate (and buy!) your book.

Genre: A classification system that identifies your book's type of content (e.g., fiction, nonfiction, historical fiction, poetry, or autobiography); it's essentially the larger umbrella under which your book falls.

Category: A division within a genre that identifies your book's topical content; after the broader genre is identified, its category is its subsection that informs where your book is placed in relation to other books that are in the same genre.

BISAC Subject Code: A nine-character alphanumeric code from the Book Industry Standards and Communications (BISAC) Subject Codes List that corresponds to your book's category and that tells book retailers, distributors, and librarians where your book belongs on their shelves. They are not going to read the book's description to figure this out.

Title: The name of your book, usually chosen by the author, that should be focused on what would hook their ideal audience's interest.

Subtitle: A phrase following the title of your book that gives the title more context, sometimes conveying the promise of the book and usually rich with keywords for better discoverability.

Pricing: The retail cost for someone to purchase your book.

Publication date: The date associated with the official release of your book to the public.

International Standard Book Number (ISBN): A ten- or thirteen-digit unique product identifier used by publishers, booksellers, libraries, and online retailers for ordering, listing, stocking, and tracking sales of your book.

BISAC SUBJECT CODES

Developed and maintained by the Book Industry Study Group, BISAC Subject Codes are used by all publishers everywhere and are the industry standard for categorizing books. As interests grow, as our lives evolve, and as more content and different subject matters make it into the marketplace, more book categories will develop, and these codes obviously will expand. As a side note, keep in mind that Amazon uses the BISAC codes, slightly altering them for its platform, meaning that the categories you enter and see on the Amazon Kindle Direct Publishing (KDP) platform will not perfectly jibe with the categories you see that are associated with the BISAC codes.

DO IT RIGHT FROM THE BEGINNING AND PURCHASE FROM A LEGITIMATE ISBN PROVIDER

Purchase your own ISBN from the beginning and from a reputable ISBN provider, such as Bowker Identifier Services (also known as simply Bowker), so your book is available everywhere. There are other ISBN service providers out there in addition to Bowker that (claim to) offer ISBNs at price points that are lower than Bowker's prices. Be very wary. Although some of their names may sound legit, some of these providers may not be legitimate at all and may take your money and issue you an ISBN that has already been issued/assigned to a title owned by someone else.

In this case, typically, an author obtains the ISBN early in the writing and/or publishing process, then a lot of time passes before the unsuspecting author uploads their book for distribution, and during the distributor's metadata validation process is when the author finds out that the ISBN is already in use. Oftentimes in these scenarios, the bad actor goes incommunicado, and the author is out even more money with having to go to Bowker to purchase a legitimate ISBN.

The moral of the story? Do not get drawn in by an attractive lower price. Do it right from the start and purchase your ISBN from Bowker.

EMPLOYER IDENTIFICATION NUMBER (EIN)

An EIN, which is separate from your Social Security number, is a step to keeping your personal and business finances from intermingling. Obtaining an EIN is free and can be done online. The Internal Revenue Service's site has information on how to apply for an EIN, plus the Small Business Administration's website contains a wealth of information regarding federal and state tax ID numbers.

DISCREPANCY IN SALES NUMBERS

We have experienced this more than once. As a case in point, Ally had one expectation for what she would receive in a royalty check one quarter, only to be faced with the reality of finding herself in the red. More than a dozen copies of her book had been returned six months after a store had purchased them, reducing what she anticipated she would get paid. Ally ended up having to remit a payment to the distributor instead of the other way around, where the distributor would have remitted a payment to her.

Bridgett had a similar experience. She had received reports of book sales that were looking really solid for the latter part of 2020, but come January 2021, that all turned around for her. She had not one, not two, not three, but four—count them, FOUR!—huge boxes of books placed at her doorstep by UPS due to returns. Conferences Bridgett was slated to speak at in 2020 had ordered them in anticipation of her appearing on their programs, and we all know what happened to in-person events in 2020. Not only did she have to pay the distributor the cost of printing the books, but because the distributor had on file that she wanted returns sent to her instead of having the distributor destroy them, she was also on the hook for the cost associated with the books being shipped to her. (We're talking thousands of dollars here, sports fans.) While she'd been paid a handsome amount of royalties based on the sale of her books to those organizations, Bridgett's profits were handsomely adjusted due to those returns.

THE MOST ACCURATE SALES DATA

If you have an Amazon Author Central account, book sales information is provided from NPD BookScan, and it includes Amazon print book sales plus the sales of your book from more than 10,000 retailers across the United States. However, these data are not accurate. The most accurate data is contained in your Amazon KDP account, not your Amazon Author Central account. Additionally, your IngramSpark account or your publisher-generated reports will contain the most accurate book sales data.

GETTING DISTRIBUTION FOR YOUR BOOK

Amazon KDP and IngramSpark are the industry giants in the book distribution world. If you want to do more than sell your book on your own, and you want to make your book widely available, then you will lean heavily on Amazon KDP and IngramSpark.

Amazon KDP and IngramSpark allow you to self-publish your book and make any updates to it for free. When you publish with Amazon KDP, you are able to make your book available on a global scale, and your book is listed for sale on all Amazon sites.

Like Amazon KDP, IngramSpark makes your book available on a global scale; your book is listed for sale not only on Amazon's websites but also on other online retailers' sites. Your royalties tend to be lower when you publish with IngramSpark than when you publish with Amazon KDP, but your book's reach is faster than if you publish with Amazon KDP alone.

CHAPTER 4

TRADITIONAL STORY ARC

You may have heard about the story arc in high-school English class. The traditional story arc is the three-act plot structure that we see comprising most fiction books. The book begins by setting up the "normal" for the main character, then introduces a turning point (often called the inciting incident), which sends that character on a journey of some sort. That journey is made up of a series of moments that add tension to the story, culminating in a crisis, then a climax, and then falling tension before a new normal is established. This story arc looks a lot like a bell curve.

In nonfiction books, this arc could be looked at as the reader going on a journey. The beginning of the book sets up the problem for the reader, the middle part of the book offers transformation or change that helps the reader see a different way forward, and the final act of the book ties it all together to solve the reader's problem and provide next steps.

SIX-MONTH PUBLISHING WINDOW

So much is happening during this time; it's akin to the duck swimming in the water, gracefully gliding along while its little legs and webbed feet are frenetically moving underwater, trying to get from point A to point B. During this six-month window, everything involved with getting your book to market is taking place. Editors, depending on the type of editing your manuscript receives, are dotting all the i's and crossing all the t's. Designers are creating your cover, typesetting the interior to make it gorgeous, and creating social-media graphics for your book. Proofers are making sure that all errors have been caught and corrected. Administrative professionals are securing identifiers for your book, such as its ISBN and Library of Congress Control Number (LCCN). Other staff members are researching categories and codes for your book, submitting your copyright application to the US Copyright Office (USCO), and submitting your book's details to distributors in preparation for your book to enter the marketplace.

And all the while, you, the author, are being called upon to review the work that's being completed, make decisions, request changes, or give the green light, approving each step in the process so that the publisher can commence with the next step. There is far more behind-the-scenes work taking place during these six months, and much of the timeline is dependent upon the author's responsiveness, but you get the idea. There's a lot going on! As a case in point, at Press 49, we have a minimum of seventy steps that must be completed by our team members to take writing from a manuscript to a published book. Seventy steps. We don't dare to bore you with listing them all here. The point is that those six months are a must!

CUSTOMER FUNNEL

The customer funnel (or purchase funnel) is a model used in business that illustrates the journey someone takes from being a prospect to becoming a client or a customer, and it's applicable to your book business as well. The widest part of the funnel is where prospects become aware of a product or a service, then the funnel is at its narrowest once prospects convert and finally buy.

The widest part of your book business funnel looks the same; it's where the largest number of people become aware of your book. Maybe they are at a conference and hear about it, you appear as a guest on a podcast and they hear about it, you post on social media about the upcoming release, and so on. Next, the customer goes from knowing about a product or service to developing an interest in it. Then, they evaluate whether it's a fit for them and may even engage in negotiation with the seller before finally completing the purchase.

With your book, they hear about it, develop an interest, then go to Amazon (or wherever), read about it to see if it solves a problem they have, and decide if they want to make the ultimate decision to buy. As you can imagine, with each step in the model, the funnel gets more and more narrow as there are fewer and fewer people who move from awareness to interest to evaluation to negotiation, then to a purchase. With your book's customer funnel, you might start with thousands of people who are aware of your book, but as they move through the funnel, only a fraction of those thousands ultimately purchase your book.

CHAPTER 5

DRAFTING VERSUS DEVELOPMENT

Drafting is the act of putting words to paper and getting ideas out of your head and onto the page. Development is all of the parts of the writing process—drafting, editing, and revising—that ensure that the manuscript's content and ideas are organized, cohesive, clear, and specific and that the writing itself is strong, including using active language, having pristine word choice, and implementing accurate grammar, spelling, punctuation, and mechanics. In other words, drafting is one part of development, but development isn't only drafting.

HOW THE COPY EDITOR, LINE EDITOR, AND MECHANICAL EDITORS ARE DIFFERENT

A line editor, copy editor, and mechanical editor perform similar work but are not one and the same. A line editor reviews for creative content, writing style, and language use (at both the sentence and paragraph levels). They focus on the way you use language to communicate to the reader, which might include pointing out run-on sentences, redundancies in repeating the same info but in different ways, unnatural phrasing, confusing digressions, and more. In contrast, a copy editor looks for flaws on a technical level. They correct spelling, grammar, punctuation, and syntax; search for inconsistency in spelling, hyphenation, capitalization, and numerals; and even note ambiguity or inaccuracies in the material (which is pretty darn important for nonfiction books). Last, but not least, mechanical editing is actually the technical and consistent application of a particular style (such as The Chicago Manual of Style). Mechanical editing can be a part of copy editing.

CHAPTER 6

ACCOLADES IN THE FRONT MATTER

When someone opens the front cover of your book, the very first thing they see is a page that contains glowing reviews from your endorsers. Typically titled "Advance Praise," these testimonials come before everything. They come before the title page, any dedication, or the table of contents. This is where those lengthy testimonials you had to abbreviate for the back cover are placed in their entirety, so your readers can see the praise and honor your book received in full detail before it even landed on the store shelves.

CHAPTER 7

SEARCH ENGINE OPTIMIZED

In its simplest terms, to make something search engine optimized means that you design or write material in a way that increases the chances of your work appearing in search results. It's the process of improving your text to include the exact words and phrases people typically use to search for answers to the problems your book (or product or service) solves, thereby increasing your book's visibility in places like Google or Microsoft Bing. You optimize your book so that it has a greater chance of appearing on search engines.

CHAPTER 8

AUTHOR PRESENCE AND PLATFORM

When you have an author presence and platform, you know for whom you're writing, and you know how to market your writing and use your overall visibility to reach your target reader wherever they spend time. It's everything you do online, offline, and in person to create and grow awareness of who you are, what you do, and what you believe in, with the goal of boosting your visibility and making it easier for your ideal readers to find and connect with you, your brand, your business, and your book. You make yourself known for the topic that you write on, so when people think of your book topic, they automatically think of you.

EMAIL AUTORESPONDER SYSTEM

An email autoresponsder system allows you to capture the names and emails of people visiting your site and automatically communicate with them after they've provided that information. For this to work, you need to understand a few of the individual pieces.

- **Email list sign-up:** Put a sign-up form on your website, add a sign-up link to your email signature, and invite people to sign up via social media.
- **Sign-up incentive:** Provide a free PDF, digital download, or coupon code to purchase your book at a special rate; a free fifteen-minute consultation; or some other free content as a hook to encourage people to sign up.
- **Automated emails:** A sequence of pre-written emails that are automatically sent from your email service provider as responses to new email/newsletter subscribers.

CHAPTER 9

A WHOLE PROCESS FOR TRADITIONAL PUBLISHING

Many indie and hybrid presses are pay-to-play models, meaning that if you can afford their services, they'll most likely work with you. This doesn't mean they don't have standards for the quality of the books they choose, but there are no gatekeepers between authors and the publishing team.

With traditional publishing, most often than not, an author has to secure representation via a literary agent. They have to first win over the literary agent, then the literary agent goes to bat for them with the publishers. Researching, querying, and landing a literary agent can be a long and competitive process. Plus, there are very specific submission requirements per agent that must be followed to gain their attention, and even then, there's no guarantee that you'll hook their interest or even hear back from them. And there's no promise that if you do hear back, you'll land them as an agent or that they won't ask you to work on the manuscript some more before taking you on as a client and/or "shopping" your project to publishers.

There are some agents who charge a high reading fee before even considering taking you on as a client. Be wary of those. One way to confirm whether an agent is reputable is to check if an agent is a member of the Association of Authors' Representatives. Vetting and securing agent representation can take years and several rejection letters.

The agent then pitches your manuscript to publishers, which can also take an unknown amount of time. And if you are lucky to sign on with an agent, they can take a 15 percent commission on your published book. (This is on top of the high royalties the traditional publisher retains.) A lot of authors don't want to invest an unknown amount of time trying to jump through the first hoop with no guarantee of securing representation and then no guarantee of securing a press.

CHAPTER 10

YOU ARE RESPONSIBLE FOR EVERYTHING

When we write that you are responsible for taking care of everything when you self-publish in an effort to keep your costs down and your royalties a bit higher, that means that it all falls on you to ensure all the work gets done. You will want to examine if it's really worth it to take on all the work. Some of your responsibilities as a self-publisher include, but are not limited to, the following:

- Decide on your title
- Perform developmental and mechanical editing
- Review edits and make revisions
- Request reviews from advance copy readers
- Secure an ISBN, a barcode, and an LCCN

- Become versed in the more than 1,100 pages of the most current edition of The Chicago Manual of Style to ensure your manuscript conforms to all its rules
- Design your front and back covers
- Engage in another round of revisions because seeing your words in a new (and gorgeous) format will cause it to read differently, and after the passage of time, you will have additional/different ideas
- Engage in a third round of revisions because we 100 percent guarantee that there will be changes you will want to make after seeing the book in print
- List your book on online retailers' sites

You get the idea . . . There's a lot of work involved, and this list is not exhaustive. These are only the main points of what needs to get done. For a comprehensive list of everything you need to do to get your book published, see appendix H: The Self-Publishing Checklist.

TRADITIONAL PUBLISHING COMPANIES' LOW ROYALTY PERCENTAGE RATE

Actually, instead of this being a "What Does That Mean?" it's more of a "Why Is That SO?!" Here's the deal. Authors enjoy much lower royalty rates of 5–20 percent and receive much lower royalty payments from traditional publishers because by not charging the author a fee to publish, the company is assuming all the risk associated with getting a book to market. The same types of costs associated with self-publishing or working with a hybrid or indie publisher are the same costs a traditional publisher also faces with publishing a book. Paying an author lower royalty rates is a means for the company to recoup those monies spent on producing an author's book.

CHAPTER 12

QUANTITATIVE VERSUS QUALITATIVE DATA IN SPEAKING

Numbers tell a story. It's impressive if you can say 96 percent of your audiences have rated your presentation as "very good" or "excellent" or if a company's contract close rate increased by 23 percent within six months of bringing you in to conduct a training on how to deliver effective sales presentations. However, when starting out as a speaker, you may not have quantitative data, numbers that demonstrate your effectiveness as a speaker or the results organizations have experienced because they engaged you. Instead, you rely on qualitative data—written words and video testimonials of those who've seen you in action and who would happily recommend you to others.

GIVE YOUR AUDIENCE A REASON TO LISTEN TO YOU

Using a hypothetical, we will explain what it means to give your audience a reason to listen to you.

The author of a real estate investing book is speaking at an event where people want to learn about a variety of revenue streams they can pursue as side hustles. The author starts with the end in mind, deciding that she wants to take what she knows about real estate investing to have her listeners walk away feeling like they are better educated about real estate investing and energized to further investigate, or, better yet, to get involved with making money in this lucrative industry.

Now that the author knows what she wants as the end product, she has to determine what points she will make that will drive her talk in the direction she wants to take her audience. The three pieces of information that she believes will drive home her point and move her audience to action are the following:

1. The earning potential and how it's calculated
2. The pitfalls to avoid
3. The first three actions one can immediately take to get started

Some of the information she shares will be from her book, but much of it will be from her personal experiences and background knowledge. To give her audience what they cannot get in her book is a bonus; doing so incentivizes the audience to come to hear her talk.

With her audience's takeaway in mind, as well as her three talking points, it's time to create her opening message—one that will draw in everyone, establish a rapport that sends a silent message to the audience that the author understands where they are coming from relative to the presentation topic, and make them say, "This is going to be a good one!"

So, with all this in mind, the opening message the author delivers that gives her audience reason looks like this:

"You've likely seen the house-flipping shows or have friends who have dabbled in real estate, or you may have even looked into it yourself. And you wondered if real estate investing is for you or if it's even profitable. By the time we're done, you will know your earning potential as a real estate investor, the pitfalls to avoid, and the three things you can do right now to successfully get started as a real estate investor."

Constantly focus on why your audience should listen. It is because you know how to help . . . because you understand . . . because you will offer solutions. Always think, "What do I do that makes my audience better?" When you take this approach, this automatically excites the audience and makes them want to hear everything you have to say.

YOUR TAKE AFTER SALES ARE FINAL

Know what percentage of your book sales you will be allowed to retain. An industry standard is the bookseller retains 55 percent of the book's retail price. Considering that a conference bookstore is taking on the responsibility of stocking your book and having staff on hand to handle the sales—tasks you do not have to manage—assume that the bookstore will retain some portion of your book sales. Get in writing what that percentage is, how you will receive your payment after the event concludes, whether they require you to submit an invoice in order for the payment to be processed, and by when you can expect to receive payment.

INTERVIEW YOURSELF: TEN QUESTIONS TO ASK BEFORE YOU START YOUR BOOK

This pairs really nicely with appendix D: Book Planning Scorecard. The whole point of interviewing yourself is to be curious and investigate your book idea. You're asking yourself questions as though you're a third-party observer. You're exploring your book from all angles:

- Your motivation (What's your "why"?)
- The message itself (What are you saying?)
- The way it's told (How is it structured? How does it sound?)
- The reader (Who are you trying to reach and in what way?)
- The end product (What do you envision on the cover? What size do you think the cover should be? What kind of fonts?)
- The end goal (What do you want your book to do for you?)
- The promotional plan (What kind of marketing activities do you want to do?)
- The publishing route (How do you want to bring this book to market?)

You can meditate on these things. Journal about them. Create a vision board. You can even ask yourself the questions out loud, respond out loud, and record yourself so you've got an audio file to refer back to that you can take notes from. The questions you ask yourself are the very beginning of getting all of that stuff out of your head and onto something visible.

Sometimes we need to see what we are thinking before any of it makes sense.

If you've been thinking about starting a book for decades (or even just months), you've got a world of ideas that need to come out. Think of them like seeds, and the vision board or blank journal is the garden bed. You need to plant them, water them, give them light, and see how they grow. As they grow, they'll take shape. You'll be able to see that garden (read: book) blossom, bloom, and show you exactly what it is meant to be.

Here are ten questions to ask yourself during this interview phase, but as you ask yourself these, don't be surprised if others naturally come up. Follow your intuition. Add them to your list. Answer them. You never know what guidance they may offer.

The more you know about this book, the better you'll be able to write it. This is the first step in creating that plan—the plan you need for clarity and control over the book inside you just waiting to flourish.

1. Why are you writing this book? What's your "why"?
2. Why is now the right time to write this book?
3. What are your main objectives or goals for your book?
4. What main message are you trying to offer your reader?
5. How do you want this message to come across (what tone, personality, and voice do you want to use)?
6. What main things do you want your readers to take away from your book?
7. How do you want your reader to feel while reading your book? What impact do you want to make?
8. What do you envision your book will look like when it's done?
9. What kinds of marketing activities do you want to engage in before and after your book is published?
10. How do you want your book to compare to others? What books do you aspire for yours to be like?

BOOK-PLANNING SCORECARD

We promote going into any book project with a plan. The thing is, lots of people who want to write books have never done it before and/or they're not familiar with the publishing industry or the book marketplace. That lack of familiarity and understanding can leave some people really unsure about how to plan out their book and not thinking about a variety of pieces that go beyond just the manuscript itself.

The purpose of this scorecard is to help you identify how much you've already considered about the book you're dreaming about before you actually put pen to paper or fingers to the keyboard to bang out the manuscript.

A score of 1 or 2 for an answer will indicate that there's more thought, reflection, and/or research needed on your part for that piece before you actually begin writing your book.

ANSWER ON A SCALE OF 1–3 FOR EACH ITEM YOU HAVE IN PLACE. 1 – UMMM, NO ... | 2 – SORT OF ... | 3 – HELL, YES!	SCORE:
1. Have you identified your "why" for writing this book? What's motivating you?	
2. Have you determined what type of book you want to write (memoir, teaching memoir, inspiration, business, motivational, collection of essays, etc.)?	
3. Do you know who your book is for? Who is the audience you'll market to?	
4. Do you know what impact you want your book to make on your audience?	
5. Do you know what story you're trying to tell?	
6. Have you mapped your story arc to ensure you have a narrative flow (in the case of a memoir) or outlined your book to guarantee you have an organized structure (in the case of prescriptive nonfiction)?	
7. Do you have a working table of contents or chapter list?	
8. Have you considered additional elements to your book, such as photos, diagrams, case studies, or more?	
9. Do you already have an online platform or presence to leverage for promotion?	
10. Are you comfortable with marketing and promotion (because, no matter what, you'll have to promote your book)?	
11. Do you have a timeline in mind for when you want to complete the manuscript?	
12. Have you set up a writing schedule or established a writing practice for getting it written?	
13. Do you understand the life cycle of a book—the stages it goes through from conception to publication?	
14. Have you considered how much you'll be responsible for regarding implementing tasks yourself versus what you'll outsource?	
15. Have you identified the writing professionals you'll need to support your efforts (editors, cover designers, coaches, typesetters, marketing support, publishers, etc.)?	
16. Have you created a budget for this project?	
17. Do you have goals in mind for what you want your book to achieve for yourself and/or your business?	
18. Have you done any book research to see what kinds of books have already been published that might be similar to yours based on what you *do* know?	
19. Have you explored what publishing direction you would want to take (traditional, hybrid, indie, or self-publishing)?	
20. Do you understand the advantages and disadvantages of your available publishing routes?	

If you scored predominantly 1s, DIG IN.

Just because you scored a lot of 1s doesn't mean you don't have a solid idea or that your idea isn't worth pursuing. We recommend that you don't start drafting the manuscript until you know a little more about what your plan is. However, you can write a few pieces of the manuscript that you *do* know about and see if that helps knock loose any of the other clarity you need.

If you scored predominantly 2s, KEEP GOING.

You're right on the cusp of greatness. We're sure of it. You've already started to think about the right things; now you just have to keep going and finish fleshing out what you're thinking for certain areas. Ultimately, if you've at least started thinking about these areas, you can move toward manuscript development. Some of the things you're not yet sure of may make themselves more clear as you work on the first draft.

If you scored predominantly 3s, WHAT ARE YOU WAITING FOR?

If you confidently scored the majority of the questions with 3s, then you've got a solid plan in place and have really thought about the various elements of writing a book. We think you've done a fine job getting ready to bring this book into the world. So, what are you waiting for? Get writing!

THE COST TO SELF-PUBLISH

We stated in the body that a number of factors determine how much it will cost you to produce your book. Authors who decide to do all the work themselves can expect to spend anywhere from $500 to $5,000, but at the same time, we caution against spending as little as $500 to publish your book. The real starting point is $5,000 (at a minimum) to self-publish your book, and the majority of this cost will be devoted to editing alone.

Below we have provided a high-level self-publishing cost breakdown. This breakdown does not entail every cost you will encounter with publishing your book; these are the minimum expenditures. The minimum. Read: to do it right, it will most certainly cost you more.

- Professional editing: anywhere from $0.01 to $0.12 per word, or $1.50 to $20.00 per page (depending on the type of editing)
- Cover design: $500 to $1,500 and upwards
- International Standard Book Number (ISBN): starting at $125
- Typesetting: $3 to $7 per typeset page
- Marketing: $0 to more than $2,000
- Distribution: free (depending on the distributor you use)

Here is a more detailed and itemized breakdown of each of these things.

Professional editing: as you read in chapters 5 and 13, your book needs more than one type of editor.

TYPE OF EDITOR	SERVICES RENDERED	WHEN TO CONTACT	APPROXIMATE COST
Developmental editor	Conducts an in-depth, big-picture edit	This is the first editor your manuscript needs. While a developmental editor may perform some mechanical editing, the focus is on making sure your manuscript is tight and the ideas are clearly presented.	$0.10 to $0.12 per word, or a range of $7.50 to $20.00 per page
Copy editor or mechanical editor	Fixes mistakes with grammar, punctuation, and mechanics.	This editor should be contacted only after you are confident your ideas are clearly organized and presented in the best fashion possible, as this editor is not responsible for making major adjustments to your manuscript.	$0.04 to $0.09 per word, or a range of $5.00 to $15.00 per page
Proofreader	Conducts a final pass to find lingering errors and typos.	This is the final editor that takes a look at your manuscript. You send it over to the proofreader only when you know you have taken care of carefully crafting your message so that it is clearly written and virtually error free.	$0.01 to $0.03 per word, or a range of $1.50 to $3.50 per page

For more in-depth coverage on what the different types of editors do, reference chapter 13.

Cover design: Book cover design averages $500 but can cost anywhere from $250 to $1,500 and up.

For more on cover design, see chapter 6.

Book formatting/typesetting: The total cost for formatting and typesetting will depend on the experience of the contractor, the length of your manuscript, and the complexity of your formatting. Expect to pay anywhere from $3 to $7 per typeset page. (If your manuscript is 100 pages in length, once it's typeset, it may have a typeset page count of 200 pages, and you will pay $600 to $1,400 for the typesetting.) If you have several charts, tables, footnotes, graphics, images, and the like, and depending on whether the typesetter has to create charts and tables for you, then expect to pay on the higher end. Some typesetters will simply charge a per-page fee regardless of the addition of any visuals, while others may charge the per-page fee plus an additional fee for each visual they have to insert and/or create.

Marketing: Expect to spend anywhere from $0 to $2,000 and up. Some writers have a huge following and can announce their book launch via social media and their author website, spending next to nothing on marketing. If you handle the marketing yourself, then you will stay in the $2,000-and-under range, but if you hire professionals to market your book, expect to spend thousands on copywriting, email blasts, ads, appearances, various collateral for in-person events, and copies of your books. For more on marketing, see chapter 8.

Printing: You can use your publisher, a printer, or print-on-demand services for getting copies of your book, and each will vary in cost. Your publisher will supply you with copies of your book that cost approximately 50 percent to 60 percent less than the retail price, and the cost includes shipping. Publishers typically require a minimum order of twenty-five or so copies and will have your books delivered directly to your doorstep. Most printers require a bulk order, and it might cost you $3 to $5 per copy for 1,000 copies of your paperback book and slightly more for a hardcover book and lower-quantity orders. Finally, a print-on-demand service allows you to get as few copies as you'd like so that you can fulfill orders as they come in. Print-on-demand costs are similar to printer costs.

ISBN: An ISBN is a ten- or thirteen-digit number that is assigned to every published book. It is recommended that you always purchase your own ISBN as opposed to taking the free one offered by the

Amazon Kindle Direct Publishing (KDP) platform, and you can do so online through Bowker Identifier Services (Bowker). At the time of this writing, one ISBN costs $125, ten cost $295, one hundred cost $575, and 1,000 cost $1,500. The barcode may be an additional cost and can be secured from Bowker as well, or, at the time of this writing, you can secure one at no cost by entering your book's details at IngramSpark to generate a cover template that will include a barcode. (There are other ISBN service providers out there in addition to Bowker that offer ISBNs at lower price points. Do your due diligence in researching them.)

Distribution: There are generally no up-front distribution costs with self-published books. At the time of this writing, you can upload your book's files to the Amazon KDP platform for sale on Amazon and to IngramSpark, the distributor that makes books available on Barnes & Noble's and other online retailers' sites, at no charge. (This can change, though. We have seen IngramSpark charge anywhere from $25 to $49 for authors to upload their book to be considered for distribution.) And remember that if you sell your book through an online retailer, the retailer will retain a percentage of the sales.

PEOPLE ON THE PUBLISHING PATH

There are a lot of people in the book industry, and when you have never written a book before, it can seem overwhelming to come across people and titles you've never heard of. Below are lists of various book industry professionals, grouped together by the type of work they do and listed (as a group) in order of when you might work with them according to the book life cycle. This is not an exclusive list by any means, but you'll find a majority of the people you may want or need to employ to get your book from blank page to bookstore. Following these categories of contractors and their general descriptions is a recap of the list of the six P's to ask while you're interviewing publishing professionals to work with you on your book.

COACHES AND CONSULTANTS

Book coach: Works with a specific project; coaching is directed towards the book, not the writer's work in general.

Book doctor: Reads your book and looks for big-picture issues (such as plot, development, structure, organization, and flow); can provide a mix of developmental editing and might serve as a ghostwriter to perform "surgery" on your book and get you unstuck in the manuscript process.

Ghostwriter: Works with outlines, interviews, and revision notes (from you, the author) to sit down and write the words for your book in your voice; tends to not get credited; the stuff they produce is credited to the person for whom they're writing.

Writing coach: Helps you set goals, stay motivated, and stay on track with your writing; this type of coach may not be specific or may be solely focused on book writing.

EDITORS AND REVIEWERS

Beta reader: First-round reader who looks at the early manuscript and gives feedback from the perspective of your target audience.

Copy editor: Corrects grammar and punctuation and checks the text for style and readability.

Developmental editor: Gives feedback to improve high-level elements of your book (such as plot, structure, pacing, clarity, and organization).

Line editor: Works line by line to tighten sentence structure, word choice, and syntax; also pays attention to overall pacing and flow.

Manuscript reviewer: Focuses on an early edit and general manuscript assessment, alerting you to overall weaknesses in your manuscript.

Mechanical editor: Applies technical and consistent style, using a reference such as *The Chicago Manual of Style*. Mechanical editing can be a part of copy editing.

Proofreader: The "safety net" near the end of the editorial process; looks for any mistakes in grammar, punctuation, and spelling as well as any other mistakes that might have slipped through previous edits.

Sensitivity reader: Reviews manuscripts to spot cultural inaccuracies, representation issues, biases, or stereotypes.

PRODUCTION AND DESIGN

Cover designer: Works with graphic design and typography to create a book cover that is both attention-grabbing and represents the contents of the book.

Illustrator: Creates images that add to or help enhance the story (doesn't typically work directly with the author of a book unless you're going the self-publishing route and choosing all your own service providers).

Indexer: Reviews, gathers, and organizes information to compile into an index to make searching for information easier.

Interior/layout designer/typesetter: Works with text layout and page design to create the inside of the book's style and aesthetic (which complements the cover design) as well as make the text easy to read.

Production editor: Manages and reviews publication material, approves final layouts, and works with the various people involved in creating the book's content and packaging.

PUBLICATION PROCESS

Book distributor: Takes on publishers and sometimes individuals as clients to distribute their books to bookstores and other retailers; examples of book distributors include but are not limited to Amazon's Kindle Direct Publishing and IngramSpark.

Literary agent: Focuses on the business side of things; represents writers by pitching unpublished work to publishers, negotiating book deals and being a line of communication between the author and the publisher.

Publisher: Produces and gets distribution for books; they may also provide some media coverage and author promotion depending on their service packages.

Publishing consultant: Serves as the producer of a book; manages your project and advises you throughout each step of the publishing process.

Publishing strategist: Plans out media advertising and marketing and advises on the best strategy for your book's publishing and marketing.

MARKETING

Author virtual assistant: Assists you by tackling necessary but time-consuming marketing (or administrative) tasks so that you can focus on writing.

Book marketing coach: Helps you choose the best marketing route and strategies for your book, then works out and executes a marketing plan; allows you (the author) to professionally market your book without having to learn all the ins and outs of a marketing strategy.

Publicist: Pushes the finished book into the marketplace, including submitting books for book reviews and awards, planning book launches and book tours, and sometimes promoting giveaways.

WHAT TO ASK BEFORE WORKING WITH PUBLISHING PROFESSIONALS

The six P's:

Process:

- How do you work?
- What does the timeline look like?
- What are the steps in your process that I will have to follow?

People:

- Who else might be involved?
- Is it just the individual provider I'll be working with, or do you have a team?
- What are your expectations of me?
- Can you fulfill my expectations?
- Who is my point person?

(Fine) Print:

- Is there a cancellation clause?
- What are the stated roles/expectations?
- What are the conditions around refunds?

Pocketbook (or costs):

- What's it going to cost me?
- What are the terms of payment? When are payments due and by what methods?
- What deliverables should I expect for the cost I'm paying?
- By when should I receive these items?

Property:
- Do you take ownership in any way? Do you have any claim to rights/credit?
- Do you need to be credited? If so, how do you need to be credited?

Portfolio:
- Can I see examples of your work?
- Do you have any prior clients that would be open to speaking with me about their experience working with you?
- Are there any client success stories or testimonials I can review?
- What are some of your favorite projects and where could I view them?

WRITING AND PUBLISHING MUST-HAVE RESOURCE LIST

Presented in alphabetical order, this is a list of websites you will find helpful on your writing and publishing journey. This list is not exhaustive, but it does contain the resources you need to help you set up your book as a business and get through the writing and publishing process. After each URL, we provide a note in italics that gives a brief synopsis of the purpose of the resource, followed by a longer description. Some sites may have fees associated with being able to use them; consult each site for the most up-to-date information regarding any payment requirements.

48 Hour Books
https://www.48hourbooks.com
Order copies of your book.
At 48 Hour Books, you can order copies of your book. The cost will be more expensive than ordering copies from Amazon Kindle Direct Publishing (KDP) or IngramSpark; however, the company has an expedited option for getting your books in a matter of hours or within a few days as opposed to the weeks it can take Amazon KDP or IngramSpark to get them to you.

Amazon KDP

https://kdp.amazon.com

Get distribution for your book, and order author priced copies of your book.

Create an account here to get your book (and e-book) listed for sale on Amazon. Additionally, you can order copies of your book, paying only the cost of production and shipping, and you can track your book sales. Print costs are less expensive than both 48 Hour Books' print costs and Ingram-Spark's costs, and ship times are faster than IngramSpark's ship times.

Book Industry Study Group

https://www.bisg.org

Find the right codes for your book.

In addition to book industry best practices, the Book Industry Study Group's website has a comprehensive list of all the Book Industry Standards and Communications (BISAC) Subject Codes as well as a list of FAQs to help you determine the right codes for your book.

Bowker Identifier Services

https://www.myidentifiers.com

Purchase your ISBN.

With an International Standard Book Number (ISBN) and a barcode, you are able to have your book sold on Amazon and other online retailers' sites. Without it, those distributors will not list and sell your book. The ISBN identifies the registrant, as well as the book's title, edition, and format, and adds a level of credibility to your book. (There are other ISBN service providers out there in addition to Bowker that offer ISBNs at lower price points. Do your due diligence in researching them.)

Editorial Freelancers Association

https://www.the-efa.org/

Find an editor (and more), and budget your costs.

The Editorial Freelancers Association is the oldest and largest national professional organization of editorial freelancers. Their members range from editors to indexers, proofreaders to translators, and more. You'll want qualified professionals working on your manuscript, and this is a terrific place to find them and to understand their costs. The Editorial Freelancers Association has an editing rate list that is handy for understanding the going rate for editorial services at https://www.the-efa.org/rates/.

Google Ads (formerly Google Adwords)
https://ads.google.com/home
Search for keywords for your book.
This is Google's keyword search tool for finding the search words or keywords people use; it helps you with building your book's metadata. You will need to create an ad account to access the tool, but you do not have to spend money to use it. And keep in mind that there are other platforms out there that provide you with this kind of information but that require a fee.

Independent Book Publishers Association
https://www.ibpa-online.org/
This is a valuable resource for the independent author.
This organization solely focuses on leveling the playing field for small and independent book publishers, which is important for the indie author (if you're going that route) and for the author-publisher, which could be you if you decide to author your book and publish it yourself, like a self/DIY model. From events and resources to discussion boards and a directory, the Independent Book Publishers Association has everything you need to learn the complicated publishing business.

IngramSpark
https://www.ingramspark.com
Get distribution for your book, and order author priced copies of your book.
With an IngramSpark account, you can get distribution for your book (and e-book) to include getting it listed for sale on Amazon, Barnes & Noble, and other online retailers' sites. Additionally, you can order copies

of your book from IngramSpark, paying only the cost of production and shipping, and you can generate sales reports. IngramSpark's print costs are less expensive than 48 Hour Books' print costs but are more expensive than Amazon KDP's print costs.

Internal Revenue Service

https://www.irs.gov

Get your employer identification number (EIN).

Visit the site and search for "employer identification number." Having an EIN enables you to set up your business bank account and create accounts with payment processors, such as PayPal and Square, so that you can accept payments.

Library of Congress

https://www.loc.gov/publish/pcn/

Get your book's LCCN.

Your book's Library of Congress Control Number (LCCN), issued by the Library of Congress, makes your book look more official and professional. An LCCN is a unique identification number that the Library of Congress assigns to the catalog record created for each book in its cataloged collections. An LCCN adds a level of credibility to your book.

Lulu

https://www.lulu.com

Get distribution for your book, and order author priced copies of your book.

Lulu Press, Inc., also known as Lulu, is an online print-on-demand, self-publishing, and distribution platform. With a Lulu account, you can list your book for sale on global online platforms and order copies of your book, paying only the cost of production and shipping. Its black-and-white print costs are on par with IngramSpark's costs; however, full-color printing with Lulu can be more expensive than printing with Ingram-Spark. And in all instances, Lulu's print costs are more expensive than Amazon KDP's costs.

Nonfiction Authors Association

https://nonfictionauthorsassociation.com/

Learn from and connect with other nonfiction authors.

This organization focuses on creating a welcoming and supportive community for nonfiction writers. Through its events and programming, writers learn how to write, publish, promote, and profit from their nonfiction books. They also host an award program where you can submit your book for review and have the chance to be dubbed a gold, silver, or bronze winner. (Win an award and be able to say that you wrote an award-winning book, which is great for marketing purposes, remembering, of course, what we said about awards in chapter 13.)

Reedsy

https://reedsy.com/

Meet professionals who can bring your book to life.

Reedsy is a place to meet editors, designers, marketers, and more. You can assemble the team of professionals you need to bring your book to life. As Reedsy puts it, their "community is home to the best publishing talent on the planet." Plus, its blog has a ridiculous amount of content about the publishing stratosphere.

Small Business Administration

https://www.sba.gov/

Start thinking like a small business owner.

The Small Business Administration works to help small businesses start, grow, expand, and recover. If you're going to step into this book-writing thing with your business hat on, you'll value the information that can be found here. This site has a wealth of information, including how to set up a business bank account, in addition to other financial or tax-related things to consider.

Upwork

https://www.upwork.com

Hire expert publishing freelancers and contractors.

Use Upwork to find and hire freelance graphic designers, editors, and other publishing experts. There are other gig/freelancer sites, such as Fiverr and Guru, but Upwork tends to have a better sampling of expert contractors.

US Copyright Office

https://www.copyright.gov

Protect your intellectual property.

Copyrighting your work and including a copyright page in your book puts people on notice that your intellectual property has been protected, and the copyright, once received from the US Copyright Office (USCO), protects you and your book.

Once your book is published, it's important that you remain in control of your work. Officially copyrighting a book with USCO ensures that you are the legal owner of the work you've created in case there is ever a need to litigate in the future.

Word-2-Kindle

https://word-2-kindle.com/

Convert your manuscript to an e-book.

Word-2-Kindle will convert your typeset PDF into a MOBI or EPUB e-book file that you can upload to Amazon KDP and IngramSpark. There are other companies out there that offer this service, but this is one we have vetted, have worked with, and are comfortable with recommending.

THE SELF-PUBLISHING CHECKLIST

We cannot stress enough how much we advise that you do *not* perform this work on your own. Although we provide you with a bit of how-to in some instances, we urge you, whenever possible, to get professionals to perform these tasks for you.

Because this checklist is pretty extensive, here's the *Reader's Digest* version . . .

1. Write.
2. Revise.
3. Edit.
4. Copyright your work.
5. Know and get your numbers (e.g., International Standard Book Number [ISBN], Book Industry Standards and Communications [BISAC] Subject Codes, book dimensions, royalty calculations, printing costs, Library of Congress Control Number [LCCN], and the book's retail price).
6. Get your cover designed.
7. Format/typeset your manuscript's/book's interior.
8. Create your distribution accounts (e.g., with Amazon Kindle Direct Publishing [KDP] or IngramSpark).
9. Publish.
10. Market and get the word out.

Write.

Get your manuscript out of you. If you blog, then that's even better. You own that content and can use it as the basis of a book. If you email people advice all the time, that's your intellectual property. Use it, too! Or if you journal, type up those writings. The first step is to write!

Revise.

After you've drafted your manuscript, read it and note what needs to be revised. You can do this with a red pen on a hard copy or leave your changes and comments to yourself in the digital version.

Edit.

Make sure that you do not skip this step. Even if you believe mechanical editing or proofreading is your forte, get another set of eyes—eyes that belong to an expert editor—to take a (second or third) pass at your manuscript.

Copyright your work.

After you finish the editing of your manuscript, apply for your copyright with the US Copyright Office (USCO) so you can protect your intellectual property. Bear in mind that once you submit your application, payment, and manuscript, this process can take anywhere from two to four months. Additionally, if you are based in a country other than the United States, there are different protocols for copyrighting your work. Be sure to check your local copyright laws.

Know and get your numbers.

Here is what's involved with this step:

a. **Purchase your ISBN:** While your book is being edited, get your ISBN. This is a must if you want to sell your book on Amazon. Visit www.myidentifiers.com, also known as Bowker Identifier Services, to purchase your ISBN. Also, make note that for every format in which you plan to publish your book (paperback, hardcover, or e-book), you will need a different ISBN even if it is the same title.

b. **Get your BISAC Subject Codes:** BISAC Subject Codes are what libraries and booksellers use to categorize your book so that they quickly and easily know where to put it on their bookshelves.

c. **Decide on your book's dimensions and format:** Settle on the size of your book. (Sizes, in order of popularity, are 5 inches by 8 inches, 5.25 inches by 8 inches, 5.5 inches by 8.5 inches, and 6 inches by 9 inches, but there are also dimensions that align with a book's genre.) Now is also the time to decide on the format in which you will publish your physical book: paperback or hardcover.

d. **Understand royalties and printing costs:** When you distribute your book with IngramSpark, author royalties are lower, printing costs are higher, and production times are longer. While it's convenient for Amazon, Barnes & Noble, and the like to do the work of selling your book for you, each of those will retain anywhere from 40 percent to 55 percent of the net profits of the sale of your book. However, if you sell the book yourself, you will stand to make greater profits because you do not have to contend with the 40 percent or 55 percent cut taken by online retailers. At the same time, though, your reach is not as vast and wide as Amazon's or Barnes & Noble's.

e. **Apply for your LCCN:** It is optional to get your LCCN. Getting an LCCN is a two-step process. You first will need to apply to participate in the Library of Congress's Preassigned Control Number program. Then, you apply for the LCCN. Again, this step is optional, and bear in mind that there is a page minimum required for your book to get accepted into the Preassigned Control Number program.

f. **Decide on your book's retail price:** Conduct market research on books similar to yours in genre, topic, and length to gauge how much you should charge. You do not want to have your price so high that you price yourself out of the market, but at the same time, you do not want to have it so low that the cost of production and shipping the book to customers are more than what the customer pays. Find out from

Amazon KDP or IngramSpark how much it will cost to produce your book and for how much similar books are selling, then settle on what you will charge for your book.

Get your cover designed.

A great source for finding professional and experienced graphic designers is Upwork. Getting 3D images of the front cover is your starting point; it's only meant for you to get an idea of how you want your front cover to look. After you finish formatting your manuscript, you will return to your graphic designer with templates you secured from Amazon KDP and/or IngramSpark to have them create the actual cover file that has your front and back cover plus your barcode on the back cover; this is the file you will upload (along with your manuscript saved as a PDF) for the distributor to use to publish your book.

Format/typeset your manuscript's/book's interior.

Your designer or typesetter will have established font pairings for your cover, so you can use those as your starting point for designing the interior of your book. You will want your titles a certain font and size and your body a certain font and size. Additionally, before turning over your interior for typesetting, you need to ensure that the book contains all the parts that readers have come to expect to see.

To that end, here is the order of the parts of a nonfiction book:

a. Book cover
   i. Title
   ii. Subtitle
   iii. Author
   iv. Artwork
b. Front matter
   i. Advance praise/testimonials (optional)
   ii. Half title page
   iii. Title page

    iv. Copyright page

    v. Dedication page (optional)

    vi. Table of contents

    vii. Foreword (optional)

    viii. Introduction (optional but highly recommended)

    ix. Acknowledgments (optional and can appear in the back matter instead)

    x. Preface (optional)

c. The body of the book

    i. Sections/parts

    ii. Chapters

d. Back matter

    i. Afterword/epilogue (optional)

    ii. Acknowledgments (optional and can appear in the front matter instead)

    iii. Author's bio

    iv. Appendices (optional)

    v. Glossary (optional)

    vi. Coming soon/read or learn more (optional)

    vii. Index (optional)

e. Back cover

    i. Synopsis and/or advance praise/testimonials

    ii. Author bio and headshot (optional)

    iii. Barcode containing ISBN (may also include price and genre)

Remember, if you do the typesetting yourself, each chapter should begin on an odd-numbered page, and you need to have a total number of pages that is an even number. So, if you have a chapter that starts on an even-numbered page, insert a blank page before the start of the chapter so the chapter can start on an odd-numbered page. Similarly, for example, if you finish formatting your book and it's 213 pages long, insert a blank page at the end to make it an even number, 214.

Finally, if you want to have text on your book's spine, then your book needs to be at least 112 pages in length. If the book is any smaller/shorter than that, then the graphic designer will not have enough room to put your title and name on the book's spine. But when you have an expert do the typesetting for you, they already know all of this.

Also, with formatting, if you plan to offer your book as an e-book, too, then this is the point at which you need to convert your manuscript file into a file that can be uploaded and consumed as an e-book. It is not as simple as just converting your Microsoft Word file into a PDF. Enlist a professional to take care of this for you.

Create your distribution accounts.

You're just about ready to publish! Create your Amazon KDP account and your IngramSpark account. Follow the prompts to create a new title, and enter the information requested.

It seems redundant, but because different distributors will use different paper, which can have different thicknesses, you will need to have two cover files, one to upload to Amazon KDP so that you can sell your books on Amazon and one to upload to IngramSpark so that you can have your books sold on Barnes & Noble's site and the sites of other online retailers. To have your books also sold on other sites, such as Target and Walmart, ensure that you select the expanded distribution option when uploading your book for distribution at IngramSpark. (Bear in mind that you can select the expanded distribution option for either Amazon KDP or IngramSpark but not both. If you do, not to worry—nothing will implode; one platform or the other will contact you and let you know that you need to remove the expanded distribution option from your title.)

Return to your graphic designer with the templates, clarifying which is for Amazon KDP and which is for IngramSpark, and finish getting your cover designed.

Request a proof of your book from Amazon KDP or IngramSpark so that you can see it, ensure that it looks the way you want it to look, and make sure that there are no errors before you release it to the world.

Publish.

All that's left to do is upload your files to Amazon KDP and IngramSpark. Enter the information that's requested of you, such as genres, keywords that people would use in searches that would lead them to your book, and information about the book (such as the description); add pricing; and publish your book!

Market and get the word out.

Now you need to get the word out to everyone and encourage them to buy copies for themselves and everyone they know. Actually, you should get the word out *before* you publish. Create the necessary assets to tell the world about your new book.

DEVELOPING YOUR WRITING PLAN

Your book won't write itself. Planning, outlining, envisioning, thinking—all the conceptual work *is* important; don't get us wrong. But at some point, you've just gotta get your butt in the chair and your fingers moving. It doesn't matter what kind of chair or where the chair is . . . It doesn't matter if you're holding a pencil or a pen or if you're pounding on the keyboard. But you do have to stare down the blank page of death and get on with it.

So, these exercises and questions aim to help you craft your own road map to success that feels good to you and is realistic.

Here's the process:
A. Answer the questions.
B. Build the plan based on the answers.
C. Calendar your deadlines.
D. Do it. Actually follow your plan. Get your butt in the chair.

A – ANSWER THESE QUESTIONS
1. I would like to complete a full draft of my manuscript by _____, which is _____ months away.
2. I am the most productive in the . . . (morning/afternoon/evening).
3. Based on my schedule, a _____ (insert a number) minute writing session feels doable to me.
4. Based on my schedule, writing _____ days a week feels realistic.

5. On average, I can write _____ words per writing session. (You may need to actually clock yourself a couple of times to get your average if you don't have one already.)

6. If I write _____ words per writing session, I need _____ writing sessions in order to reach roughly 60,000 words. (This is the average length of a full-length nonfiction book, but feel free to play around with other word counts).

7. If I need _____ writing sessions to reach 60,000 words, and I have _____ months, I need to factor in _____ writing sessions per month.

8. I like to set daily, weekly, or monthly goals. (Circle one.)

9. Based on how I like to set goals, I will set a daily, weekly, or monthly goal of _____ words or _____ writing sessions.

10. I will hold myself accountable by . . .

11. I will celebrate my accomplishments by . . .

B – BUILD THE PLAN

Once you have identified your answers to the previous questions, use them to create a daily, weekly, or monthly plan. You'll know how often you're writing, for how long, and how many words you're shooting for during each writing session. You'll know when you aim to write. Plus, you'll have a sense of how you intend to hold yourself accountable and ways you can celebrate when you do.

C – CALENDAR YOUR DEADLINES

Block off in your calendar the times and days of the week you're going to write. Consider noting in those blocks what your goals are so that you keep them fresh. Consider even creating a tracking sheet for yourself to help with accountability and progress, and put in your calendar a time to update it each week.

D – DO IT!

Execute your plan for one week, then evaluate if you need to make changes. You reserve the right to adjust your plan at any point if you need to so that it feels good and to ensure that you are making active progress on your book.

HOW TO DETERMINE IF A PUBLISHING COMPANY IS REPUTABLE

Here are six areas to help you determine the trustworthiness of a publishing company as well as questions to ask as you meet with and vet potential publishers.

1. **Service:** Has a commitment to openness, accessibility, and being authentically helpful without a further agenda.
   - Will you put me in contact with a few of your authors or clients to have a conversation with them about their experiences working with your company?
   - With whom do I work during my project?
   - If I have questions during and after the publishing process, how do I get them answered?
   - How do you support authors after they're published or after the project is completed?
2. **Leadership and excellence:** Has a commitment to providing expert perspectives and guidance to aid the author in reaching the goal of getting published and pursues editorial, design, and production excellence.
   - Will you offer guidance in the areas of cover design, typesetting, and simply making my book a success, or will you take my ideas, even if they are not in the best interest of my book, and just do as I ask?

- If I have an idea that is not an industry standard or that will not serve my book well, then will you steer me in the right direction?
- May I see a sample of before-and-after editing and typesetting, as well as multiple cover design concepts you've created, for one or more of your titles?

3. **Standards:** Upholds the highest standards in the publishing industry to create works of lasting financial and/or cultural value; does not publish works of hate speech or works that encourage discrimination, oppression, or violence; respects the rights of authors; observes all copyright laws and conventions; and never knowingly publishes plagiarized work.
   - How do you remain abreast of industry standards?
   - Do you publish or work with everyone and all kinds of content? What or who, if anything or anyone, will you turn away?
   - How do you ensure a manuscript is in compliance with copyright laws?
   - How do you deal with plagiarism?
   - Do you have a guide or manual you use for certain aspects of the publishing process? If so, then what do you use?

4. **Integrity:** Does not mislead readers or buyers with false promises or inflated or manipulated data, rewards authors and contributors for their work, is honest in financial dealings, writes contracts in understandable language, and promptly and fairly resolves all disputes.
   - May I review a contract and/or have my lawyer review it before signing it? What if I want changes to the contract? Will you oblige?
   - How are royalties calculated?
   - How often do I receive sales and/or royalty reports, and what's included in the reports?
   - How do you handle issues if or when they come up during the publishing process? Describe a time when you did have an issue and how you handled it.
   - Is there an exit clause in your contract?

5. **Inclusivity:** Strives to publish people from all communities with differing viewpoints and works with publishing partners from all backgrounds (you are able to see yourself in their roster of authors and/or in their team members).
   - What are the names of some of your authors?
   - What are the names of some of your titles?
   - Have you published a book like mine or that's on the same topic as mine?
   - Who is on your team? What's their background?
   - Will you send or show me one of your favorite projects to date and tell me why it's your favorite?

6. **Professional development:** Has a commitment to growing and learning.
   - What professional development do you engage in?
   - What professional organizations are you a member of?
   - What are the names of podcasts, periodicals, or other materials you consume?
   - How do you stay up to date on the trends and changes in the industry?

THE BOOK'S LIFE CYCLE (THE RECAP)

In chapter 4, we discussed understanding the book's life cycle and why it's important. Here's the bird's-eye view of each phase of the life cycle and what occurs in each phase.

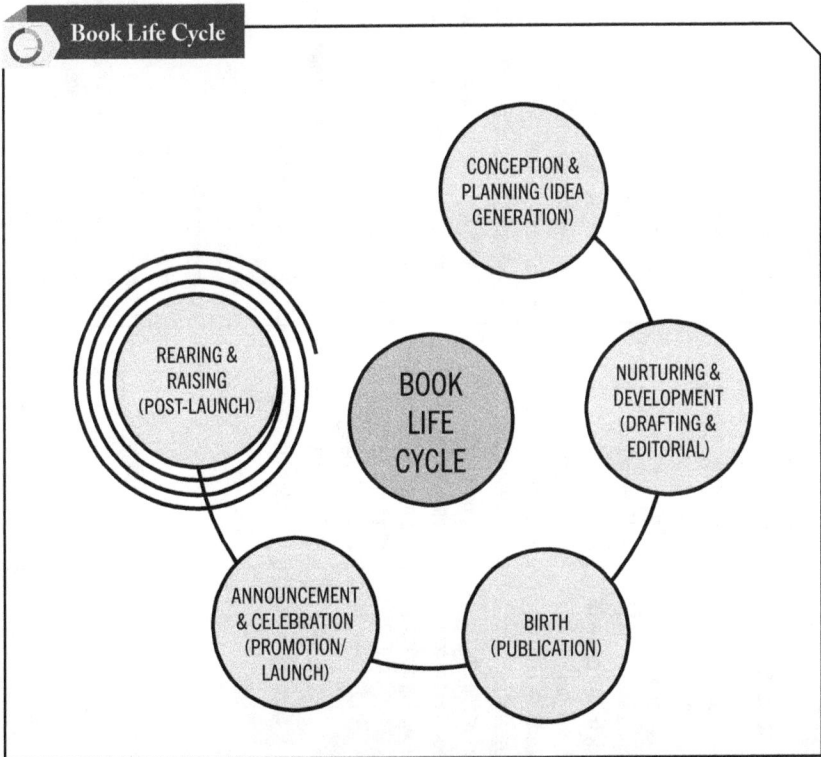

Book Life Cycle

- CONCEPTION & PLANNING (IDEA GENERATION)
- REARING & RAISING (POST-LAUNCH)
- BOOK LIFE CYCLE
- NURTURING & DEVELOPMENT (DRAFTING & EDITORIAL)
- ANNOUNCEMENT & CELEBRATION (PROMOTION/ LAUNCH)
- BIRTH (PUBLICATION)

IDEA GENERATION	DRAFTING AND EDITORIAL	PUBLICATION	PROMOTION/LAUNCH	POST-LAUNCH
• Vision or spark of an idea, needs clarity • Needs outlining and organization • May need a proposal (if going with a traditional publisher) • Researching might be needed (for the book itself or for your publishing options)	• Drafting • Revising • More drafting • More revising • Beta readers' assessments • Developmental review/edit or manuscript assessment • Copy/line/mechanical editing • Proofreading • Gathering endorsements	**If using a traditional publisher:** • Researching comparable books • Researching agents • Querying agents • Pitching agents • Reviewing contracts • Editorial changes • Approvals and proofs • Creating metadata (including ISBN, LCCN, copyright, keywords, categories, and BISAC subject codes) • Distribution **If using another publishing method:** • Choosing a press • Cover design • Interior layout/design • Preparing final files • Uploading final files • Reviewing final files • Creating metadata (including ISBN, LCCN, copyright, keywords, categories, and BISAC subject codes) • Distribution	• Marketing plans • Landing pages • Online platform/presence (beyond website) • Social media postings • Advertisements • Assets and collateral • Launch parties • Putting your sales hat on	• Continued marketing • Continued leveraging • Continued selling

SELF-EDITING CHECKLIST

Before you send your last manuscript draft to any editor or to a publisher, you should actually have been editing the earlier drafts yourself. This will ensure that you're sending the cleanest possible "last" draft of your manuscript to your editor when it's time. Presenting the cleanest manuscript you can will make everyone's life so much easier. When you edit your manuscript according to our suggestions below, it will read so much better, the editor will have fewer markups and questions for you, and you will not have as many edits to make in the end, thereby making the editing process exceedingly smoother for everyone involved.

LEVELS OF EDITING – QUICK GUIDE

TYPE OF EDITING	TIMING/DRAFT STAGE	POSSIBLE FOCI
Developmental (macro level) *The BIG stuff that holds the story or argument together*	• Early draft stages. • There can be more than one developmental review/edit.	• Organization • Flow • Clarity • Specificity • Structure • Living up to its promise • Plot holes or gaps in the narrative or argument
Line/copy/mechanical editing *The sentence-level stuff that makes the work sing*	• Later, more revised drafts. • When the big stuff is taken care of, now you can look at the sentence-level items.	• Sentence structure • Grammar • Punctuation • Word choice • Syntax • Cadence • Rhythm
Proofread (micro level) *The tiny stuff that polishes the work and makes it shine*	• Final draft. • This is the last look before send-off.	• Errors that were overlooked during the sentence-level editing • New errors that have been created by fixing the last wave of revisions • Typos • Extra or missing periods • Extra spaces • Capitalization errors

At a minimum, here are ten things you should consider doing in the self-editing process:

1. **Review a hard copy.** It's funny how you can see content totally differently when it's in print, so print out your manuscript and read it over again, checking for style and grammar. Watch out for split infinitives, word usage (e.g., *loose* versus *lose*), passive voice, dangling modifiers, and any other mistakes that you commonly make. If you are unsure of the mistakes you most commonly make, look back at some of your

past work that has been edited or proofread by an editor to identify your most common errors.

2. **Remove all unnecessary information.** Take a first pass at your manuscript to eliminate any sentences or paragraphs that do not contribute to your book's main idea. To feel better about these deletions and to ensure you do not lose any writing you may want to use later or elsewhere, save two files, one with the manuscript in its original state, then a second one from which you will work to make your eliminations.

3. **Reorganize.** Rearrange the content of your chapters, or even the chapters themselves, to make sure you have presented your ideas in the best order possible. At a minimum, find the thesis paragraph in each chapter, take it out, and create a separate document with just the thesis paragraphs. Rearrange the thesis paragraphs to ensure that they are in the best order. You may opt to go the extra mile and do the same for each paragraph in each of your chapters. Find each paragraph's thesis statement, take it out, and create another document with just the thesis statements. Does the order of those thesis statements make sense?

4. **Check construction.** As you put your chapters (and/or paragraphs) back into your book in their new order, make sure that each chapter and each paragraph follows its thesis paragraph and its thesis statement, respectively. Sometimes you may need to add new information; other times you will have to merge two chapters. And in yet other instances, you will have to split a chapter or paragraph into two when you see that you have two main ideas in either instance.

5. **Check for missing information.** Look at your rearranged list of thesis paragraphs and make sure that you have filled in all gaps and have left no room for ambiguity. Pay particular attention to areas where you may need to add an example or where you need to develop an argument or a critical point better.

6. **Check transitions.** Make sure that each of your chapters flows together. In places where they do not flow, move paragraphs around or add transition phrases or sentences to ensure that the flow and connection of thoughts are evident to the reader.

7. **Read your document aloud.** Reading aloud forces you to slow down and hear your words, and it ensures that you find errors that you might not otherwise see. It really does work! Bear in mind that reading aloud is time intensive. As you read, you can search for the things listed in steps 8, 9, and 10.

8. **Review each of your sentences.** Make sure that you have some variety in the lengths of your sentences. Incorporate a combination of lengthy and short sentences.

9. **Check your word choices.** Look out for the same word used repeatedly in a paragraph, on the same page, or in the document. It is fine to use the same word, for example, twice throughout the book, but not so much if it's used twice in the same paragraph. If you use strong words, such as *appalling*, use them sparingly, opting to use words with differing degrees of strength, such as *striking* or *unfortunate*, and saving *appalling* to make a more forceful point.

10. **Check for spelling and punctuation.** While your word processing software can be helpful, and you are encouraged to use its spelling- and grammar-check features, do not fully rely upon those features. Check for comma placement, semicolon and colon usage, and quotation mark and apostrophe placement.

EDITORIAL TRICKS TO TRY

Developmental Editing

- **Cut and rearrange.** You can physically cut and rearrange portions when you think something is out of order by printing a hard copy, cutting the sections (or sometimes individual paragraphs), and rearranging them to see how they could flow differently. There's a different way of seeing your chapter when you have a physical copy to play with than just having the one-dimensional scroll of a document on the computer.

- **Highlight/color-code.** Look for the pieces at the beginning of a chapter that identify the focus of that chapter and set up the premise (also known as a thesis) for that section. Underline or highlight that thesis. Then, highlight or color-code any piece that supports the thesis to ensure that you haven't missed the main point altogether. If you do find that you've stated three things but only addressed two, then you've identified a gap. Leave yourself a note inside the chapter, signaling the need to go back and fill in that gap.
- **Use your senses.** It can be helpful to conduct a sensory audit when you include stories to illustrate points. When reviewing a personal anecdote/story or perhaps a client case study, look for what sensory details you have provided to help place the reader in the moment; can you taste, hear, smell, see, or feel what's happening? You don't always need all of the senses to be present, but having some will help enrich the writing and make the scene/anecdote more powerful and impactful.

Line/Copy/Mechanical Editing

- **Look at first words.** Go through the document, only looking at the first word of each paragraph and then the first word of each sentence. Circle any repeated words when they appear in a row. You want to avoid having three or more sentences all beginning with the same word unless the repetition is stylistic and purposeful.
- **Consult with a style guide.** When you're in doubt of how something should be grammatically structured, punctuated, or formatted, consult with a style guide. *The Chicago Manual of Style* is the one typically used for publishing in the United States.
- **Spot the vague words.** Replace vague, unspecific words with better ones. Search for words with superficial or flat meanings with the intent on replacing them. Unspecific and passive words don't illustrate what's really happening or what you truly mean and leave the reader wanting more or sometimes not understanding fully what's being said.

Replace lackluster words with strong, active, illustrative words. As an example, think about how little the word *good* evokes in comparison to *exquisite, excellent,* or *high quality.* Grab the thesaurus if you need to. Similarly, look for "filler" words that unnecessarily crowd and elongate sentences and eliminate or replace those, too. Words such as *that, this,* and *like* are often overused and not needed.

Proofreading

- **Read backward.** Most of us are used to reading right to left, and once we have read our own work several times, we can no longer see minute errors because we know what we mean even if that's not what is happening on the page. So, begin at the bottom, right-hand corner, and read from the bottom of the page up, right to left. You'll be shocked how many new things you find while reading your words in the opposite direction.
- **Search for words with more than one spelling/meaning.** Built-in tools in Microsoft Word or Grammarly extensions that show us the little squiggly line indicating errors can be useful but aren't always 100 percent accurate. They may not pick up on the fact that you used the wrong form of *there* because it was spelled correctly. Do your due diligence and search within your document for words with more than one spelling/meaning and ensure you have the correct version.

HOW TO GET TESTIMONIALS AND ADVANCE PRAISE

Make getting testimonials and advance praise for your book part of your marketing plan. Having testimonials from those who your potential readers know and trust puts your book in front of people you would not be able to reach on your own, and it helps sell your book. Note how the words *recommendation*, *testimonial*, and *endorsement* are used interchangeably.

1. Identify Your Targets

This is where you think about the big names associated with your book's topic as well as the people who will read your book. The goal is to acquire the greatest testimonials you can from the people who are at the top of their games in terms of fame and influence over the people who are most likely to purchase your book. (You may think that big-name authors and influencers are outside of your reach, but asking never hurts. The worst they can say is no, but what if they say yes? The only way you'll know is if you ask.)

Think of known authors in your book's genre or prominent figures in your book's field as well as anyone who influences your ideal audience. You can also turn to those who have endorsed books that are similar to yours.

Think of people who are connected to the topics covered in your book and ask them to each write a testimonial for your book.

Don't be afraid to ask a lot of people. If you need three to five testimonials, plan on asking six to ten people, with the hopes of getting at least half of them to follow through; you may have some who will commit to writing a testimonial but who never get around to it, or you may have some who simply do not respond for one reason or another. Make a list of people you want to contact, then have a strategy to contact each of them, which is covered in step 2.

2. Reach Out with Your Requests

Show up like a pro. Do not beg, suck up, or tell your entire life story. Also, do not tell someone that you have no clue whether anybody will even buy your work. Imagine if you received a message that was worded like that. You'd think twice about wanting to offer an endorsement.

Keep these pointers in mind when you reach out to people with a request for a testimonial. (Following this list are two sample messages for you to edit and use.)

- **Keep it short.** The people you're contacting are busy. They do not have time to read a tome. Keep your message as short as possible while still getting the job done.
- **Introduce yourself.** Introduce yourself with a brief background and why you're qualified to write your book. Explain in a few sentences what you want to achieve with your book, the problem your book solves, and why readers will be interested in it.
- **Find a shared cause/interest.** Find a point of connection between yourself and the person from whom you're requesting the testimonial. This should be relatively easy if you did a good job of creating your target audience. It's also a nice touch if you mention the person's work in your book or if you quote them. If you do, then it'll be crucial to indicate this when you reach out. Flattery goes a long way, right?

- **Be specific.** Your request must specify what you want and what you intend to do with what you're asking for. In short, ask, "If you love my book, will you write a positive testimonial, fifty to one hundred words long, that I may use to market my book?" Also, explain that you can edit the length of their testimonial.

- **Pick a due date.** Let them know by when you need to receive the testimonial, allowing yourself some wiggle room. If you know you need to get the testimonials to your publisher by March 1, then ask for them by February 20, with the hopes of getting them by February 25. You might add something like this: "It would be really helpful if you respond by February 20, but I am happy for any replies received beyond that date if your schedule prevents you from meeting that deadline."

- **Make it simple.** Make your book or a few of your best chapters (remember that these people are busy) available via a link. If time permits, you may be able to provide them with a physical copy of the book to review as they write their testimonial.

- **Don't get in your feelings.** Be mindful that there may be valid reasons why a specific individual will not write a blurb for your work, and that's fine. Don't take it personally. The individual might just be busy, on their own deadline, traveling, or have other personal reasons for not coming through for you.

The goal is to invite enough people so that even if a few don't reply, you'll end up with a number of fantastic testimonials.

Some people may want access to the entire book, but the majority just want to see a table of contents and a few sample chapters. If you provide the entire book, though, be prepared for the great majority of people to not read it from beginning to end. Don't take it personally!

Some people may respond with the request that you write the testimonial for them and send it over for their review, then they will make a few tweaks, give their blessing, and add their name to it. This is a win! You get to write exactly the type of endorsement you want for your book—and in glowing terms—while having the credit go to someone who's considered an influencer! They may modify a few words, but you'll be writing your own recommendation. The people who see the endorsement only know that this big name person thinks your book rocks.

3. Follow Up

Approximately one week prior to your due date, send a friendly reminder to those who have committed to reviewing the book.

Thank anyone who sends you a testimonial you can use, and as an additional thank-you, send each of them a final autographed copy of your book.

Email Templates for Your Book Testimonial Request

TEMPLATE 1

Hello, [author/influencer].

I enjoyed and learned a lot from your book, [*book title*]. I especially liked the part where you talked about [explain briefly].

This spring, I'm releasing my new book entitled [*your book title*], published by [insert publisher's name]. It's about [explain in two to three sentences].

Will you write a testimonial for me? If it's a yes, then I'll provide you with sample chapters or the entire book for evaluation.

Thank you so much! [Your name]

TEMPLATE 2

Hi there, [author/influencer].

Would you be willing to write a testimonial for my new book that's coming out this fall? It's entitled [*your book title*], and it includes a foreword written by [big name that's committed to writing the foreword]. I've also received commitments from powerhouse authors [provide the names of two to three other big authors/influencers] to write testimonials. I've provided a brief description of my book at the end of this message.

If you respond in the affirmative, then I'll promptly provide you with the table of contents, one chapter from the book (because I know you're busy and do not have time to read all 62,055 words of the book!), and my bio.

All you have to do is write a quick testimonial—100 to 150 words will do—about what readers will get from the book, what makes me an authority on the topic, and why [*your book title*] is a must-read, then send it over to me by [month and day]. Your testimonial, along with your name and title, will appear on the cover, in the book's front matter, and/or on the book's Amazon product page.

As a thank-you, I will send you an autographed copy of the finished book.

I have been a fan of yours since seeing you present at [event] in [city and state] in [month and year]. I immediately purchased your book, and I regularly reference it [give brief details]. As a matter of fact, I mention it in [chapter/section of your book]!

I hope this is a yes! Please let me know by [month and day], if you're willing to do this for me, okay?

Thanks!

[Your name]

Here's a quick description of [*your book title*]:

Notice that the first message begins by praising the author's work or making note of a shared connection. This isn't flattery. It expresses that you admire their work and establishes a direct relationship. But the second template gets right to the point—recognizing that people tend to operate off the first few words of a message—and later creates a connection.

You can use this same approach in social media groups. Make a post asking for volunteers, and send a DM to anyone who responds to your request. Granted, you may not get "big" names, but a good mix of testimonials is great to have.

THE LOGISTICS OF BOOK PRESALES

The sooner you start preselling your book, the better. And bear in mind that you do not have to have a completed book before you start selling copies of it. As a matter of fact, starting presales can motivate you to get your book finished! This list is here to support you as you navigate the logistics of selling your book before it officially hits store shelves.

Get the word out: Post your book for sale on your website—just as you would post any other item—indicating that you are accepting pre-orders, and include an anticipated release date that gives you wiggle room. Create a product entry on your website's store page, or if you're working with a publisher, add a link to your site that directs your community to where your book is sold on your publisher's site.

Calendar it: Set a date for the last day of presales that's at least six to eight weeks before your publication date. For example, if your book will officially publish on September 15, then your last day of presales should be no later than August 1. That way, you have time to order your author-priced copies (plus 10 percent to 15 percent more copies because you will have stragglers), get them shipped to you in time for you to autograph them, and put them in the mail in time for people to receive them before September 15. Wow them with the earlier arrival date because who doesn't love getting goodies in the mail earlier than they anticipated receiving them?! (Remember to advertise the special presale price on your website with verbiage such as "Only $19.99 until

August 1!" And remember to charge each book order a flat domestic shipping and handling fee of $6.99 or so. Research the fees for shipping internationally and settle on that rate as you see fit.)

Place your order: Within a day or two of the conclusion of your preorder period, order the number of author-priced copies you need based on the number of sales you made.

Sign and ship: Autograph and mail your books. If you choose to ship them yourself, we recommend using the US Postal Service as opposed to UPS or FedEx because the latter two do not offer a media mail shipping option, a cost-effective way to send educational materials. Ensure that you either write "media mail" on the packaging or use a media mail rubber stamp, and let the postal clerk know that you need the media mail rate. Alternatively, you may sign your books and send them off to an order fulfillment service along with a mailing list to have the service provider take care of the packing and shipping for you. (Don't forget to add a snazzy "autographed by the author" sticker to the cover!)

Follow up: Approximately two weeks after sending out your orders, follow up with the readers, asking them how they enjoyed your book. (And if you have another action you would like them to take that directly connects to your book's content, such as applying to be a part of a mastermind you're leading or joining a social media group, then extend an invitation to them to further engage with you accordingly.) If they loved your book, then invite them to post a review on Amazon and provide them with a link to your book for ease in doing so. Keep in mind that, as of the time of this writing, Amazon has limitations on posts from non-verified purchasers, meaning it's harder for folks who didn't buy the book on Amazon to post a review. Check with Amazon on those limitations so that you do not find yourself in a situation where you've asked several people to submit reviews only for the bulk of them to get denied and never posted to your book's product page on the online retailer's site.

WHAT YOU NEED ON YOUR BOOK'S WEBSITE OR WEBPAGE

It is not absolutely mandatory that you have a website or a webpage for your book, but it is one of the marketing pieces that you will find invaluable. Imagine being able to send people to www.[yourbookstitle]. com; there's something sexy about that.

On your book's website or webpage, the least you need to have is the following:

- Your book's information: an image of the book cover; reviews, if you have them; and links to purchase your book online from all outlets that carry your book
- A brief bio and a picture of yourself
- An email sign-up form (to capture those names and emails for your contact list)
- Links to your social media accounts (so people can connect with you)
- The ability to purchase an autographed copy of your book directly from you (Remember that you will need an employee identification number [EIN] to be able to establish accounts with payment processors so that you can accept payments online and in person. And bear in mind that unless you have made the necessary arrangements to make autographed copies available to retailers, the books are not autographed.)

But you can also include the following on your book's webpage or website:

- A video trailer for your book
- Bonus content/free downloads, such as checklists, journal activities, or book club discussion questions
- Links to interviews, podcasts, or other media connected to you and your book
- The option to book you for a speaking engagement or some other appearance
- Information about upcoming book signings and/or other events
- A link to your sell sheet
- A link to your blog

WHAT YOU NEED ON YOUR BOOK'S SELL SHEET

Your book sell sheet is your book's résumé. You can use it in a multitude of ways, but the most common way is to provide it to brick-and-mortar bookstores that you want to stock your book.

Your sell sheet must include the following:

- A high-resolution image of the cover of your book
- An excellent, succinct description of your book
- Relevant purchasing information, which should include the format in which the book is sold (paperback or hardcover), the price, the International Standard Book Number (ISBN), and the name of the distributor (book buyers prefer IngramSpark, so it's a wise decision to not just offer your book on Amazon but also to make sure it's distributed with IngramSpark as well)
- Your book's Book Industry Standards and Communications (BISAC) Subject Codes
- Your or your publisher's contact information

Additional items you can add to your book sell sheet include the following:

- Any key endorsements or recommendations your book has received
- A succinct tagline that gives the full essence of your book in one sentence
- An author photo and a brief bio
- Comparisons to other titles that are similar to yours
- Links to additional resources, such as a reader's guide or journal questions

PODCAST GUEST BEST PRACTICES

Here are steps for getting yourself scheduled on podcasts, what to do while you're on the show, and what to do after your episode is released.

1. Look for podcasts that appear to be good possibilities, listen to a few episodes, or at a minimum, read the show's description. Try your best to listen to an episode or two; it'll be a good indicator of what you will experience as a guest. Is the host all about himself, or does he really give the guest a chance to talk?
2. Next, locate contact information for the show's booker or host; if you have trouble quickly locating that information, then check hunter.io or LinkedIn Premium.
3. Then, post a positive rating and review of the podcast on its platform.
4. Finally, pitch yourself, sharing what you do that connects to the show, how you believe you could offer something new to the show, and the fact that you've written a book. Also explain that you're a fan of the show, attaching a screenshot of your review. Consider going the extra mile by including in your pitch a few examples of episodes you liked. And it's always a plus if you add how happy you'll be to promote your episode. All that's left to do is to wait for a yes, then charm the listeners with expertise from your book.

While you're on the show, don't worry about thinking that you'll give away too many details of your book and people won't want to buy it. Quite the contrary. First, you won't be able to give away all the details in the course of one show episode, and second, if your show content is rich, people will definitely want to get your book! So, don't hold back.

Whether it's in-person, live, or a recording, be a pro. Arrive to the show early (not on time), and where and when applicable, make sure your surroundings are quiet, check that you have a strong Wi-Fi signal, and stand for the interview if you can. (There's a different energy in your voice when you stand while you speak.)

Once your episode is released, share it across all your social media channels, tagging the host. Also consider sending a thank-you email or a small gift. Who knows? You might receive an invitation for an encore conversation!

SPEAKER CHECK-IN EMAIL TEMPLATE

When you are confirmed for a speaking engagement, a best practice is to send a check-in email at least one week before the date of the engagement to put the event contact's mind at ease, letting them know you're on top of things and that you will be there.

Use this email template with "Check-In" as the subject line:

[Salutation]

I will arrive at [venue name], located at [venue street address, city, state], by [local time] on [month, day, year of presentation]. I am preparing for up to [number] participants for my presentation, taking place from [start time] until [end time].

Thank you for providing [list equipment and/or supplies that the organizer promised to supply]. I will have [equipment and/or supplies you promised to supply] with me.

If you have questions, or if any of this is incorrect, then please let me know by [month, day, year that is three business days from the date of the email message].

Looking forward to it!

Thanks so much, [organizer's name]!

[Signature]

ABOUT THE AUTHORS

Alyssa Berthiaume (usually known as Ally and published under A. Y.) is the founder of The Write Place, Right Time, her virtual boutique of book coaching services. Ally Berthiaume has been braving the blank page and the writing path her entire life. She was five when she was bitten by the passion for the pen and the page. She was eleven when she wrote her first memoir. At twenty-two, she completed a double bachelor's degree in psychology and creative writing, and at twenty-five, she completed her master of fine arts degree in creative writing and two graduate certificates (in English composition and women's studies). At thirty-two, she figured out how to turn her passion for writing into a living by starting her own business. Finally, at thirty-five, she pushed through her own limiting beliefs, applied everything she had learned, and published her first memoir, *Dear Universe, I Get it Now: Letters on the Art and Journey of Being Brave and Being Me*, which has won a Gold Award from the Nonfiction Authors Association.

As a writing coach and ghostwriter, Berthiaume serves leaders, entrepreneurs, and visionaries across North America and Europe who know they have the power to heal the world by sharing their stories and spreading their message. Her most profound belief is that when we tell our stories, we activate our own healing and allow someone else to activate theirs. The more healed humans we have on the planet, the more our world becomes healed. It all begins with the willingness and vulnerability to speak our truth.

Ally is also a tenacious, focused, and heart-centered champion for loving and kind humans pushed to the margins and the causes she cares about. She approaches her work with clients in equal doses of straight-forwardness and warmth while upholding a standard of developing organized, authentic, interesting, and powerful books that come straight from the deep hearts and brilliant minds of those she works with. Ally has a superpower for hearing between the lines and capturing the voice of her clients.

Behind the scenes, there are also plenty of bloopers on her reel as a boss, mom, wife, and writer who is really just human like everyone else. If you can catch her away from the keyboard, she's probably drinking maple lattes, watching *The Princess Bride* for the thousandth time, solving the latest Hunt A Killer case, or having fun with her husband and son. She lives in Vermont.

To keep up with the evolving happenings of Ally business, The Write Place, Right Time; to sign up for her emails; or to be in the know, visit her website, thewriteplacerighttime.com. And, of course, don't forget to grab your copy of her award-winning memoir, *Dear Universe, I Get it Now: Letters on the Art and Journey of Being Brave and Being Me* (which can be found on Amazon, Barnes & Noble, Bookshop, and a number of other online retailers), or buy additional copies of this book for all the aspiring authors you know. They'll thank you.

Bridgett McGowen-Hawkins (also known as Bridgett McGowen—more on that later) grew up loving to read, write, consume Stephen King thrillers nonstop, and crank out notes on her personal typewriter as early as the age of eight. So, if someone had told her way back when that she would one day be a publisher, it would not have been a far-fetched idea. However, her initial career aspirations put her in front of a camera and a teleprompter instead of in front of a team of editors and typesetters.

In high school, in addition to winning University Interscholastic League competitions in newswriting and headline writing, Bridgett also saw success in the areas of spoken prose and poetry. She earned a bachelor of arts in communication from Prairie View A&M University, then a master's degree exactly one year later. Her original goal was to appear in people's homes every evening at 6:00 p.m. as an anchor for a major network—likely in the Houston area. But instead, she attended law school for a year and a half and quickly learned that a career in courtrooms was not her shot of tequila.

Having always been a great student and a fan of school (as a child, she was miserable when she saw summer breaks approaching), she taught for a total of sixteen years, starting at Lone Star College in the Houston area in 2002, eventually returning to her alma mater to teach there as well, then adding to her curriculum vita (CV) teaching at the University of Phoenix from the spring of 2006 through the summer of 2018.

In 2009, she became a faculty development consultant for an educational technology company while continuing to teach online as she traveled the country, presenting workshops and conferences for audiences of college, university, and career school faculty, staff, and administrators. The door closed on that consulting position in 2016, at which time she founded BMH Companies, the parent company of Press 49, and shifted to full-time speaking, then publishing in 2019.

Since 2001, Bridgett has been an award-winning international professional speaker, appearing at conferences, conventions, and summits alongside the likes of former President Barack Obama, Oprah Winfrey, Amy Cuddy, Serena Williams, Deepak Chopra, Katie Couric, Alex Rodriguez, Mel Robbins, and far too many more to name. (Yes, we're name-dropping here.) When she's on those stages, she uses her maiden name, Bridgett McGowen, as her professional speaker name because her full legal name is simply too long and has too many syllables for any audience to remember.

After a confluence of events that took place in 2019, Bridgett wrote and self-published two books in the course of six months, one of which, *Real Talk: What Other Experts Won't Tell You About How to Make Presentations That Sizzle*, won a Best Indie Book Award in 2020 and a silver BookFest Award in 2023. Other books she's authored and compiled include *Rise and Sizzle: Daily Communication and Presentation Strategies for Sales, Business and Higher Ed Pros; Own the Microphone: How 50 of the World's Best Professional Speakers Launched Their Careers (and How You Can, Too!); Redesign Your 9-to-5: Advice and Strategies from 50 of the World's Most Ambitious Business Owners and Entrepreneurs;* the award-winning *A Collective Breath: Stories of Being Black in America and Visions of Change;* the award-winning *Upward: Leadership Lessons for Women on the Rise;* and the award-winning *Show Up and Show Out: 52 Communication Habits to Make You Even More Unforgettable.*

It was the publication of that award-winning book, *Real Talk,* in April 2019—having it sell out at an international conference in Washington, DC, the very next month and successfully collaborating with forty-nine professional speakers in the fall of 2019 for an anthology—that moved her to establish the hybrid publishing company, Press 49. With a roster of more than 160 authors and coauthors who hail from the United States, India, and the United Kingdom, Press 49 partners with publishing experts from all over the globe.

When she's not deep into a publishing project or speaking on a stage, she's on her seven-speed, biking her little heart out. Bridgett lives with her husband and son in the Phoenix, Arizona, area, and she loves beautiful sunsets.

When you're ready to put your brilliance out into the world in the form of a paperback, a hardcover, or an e-book, Bridgett and the Press 49 team are also ready. We will serve as your consultants, walking you through how to get it done right, or we can take on the entire project and perform the work for you. Visit www.press49.com to schedule your no-obligation consultation. It'll be the best time you ever spent talking about getting published. Guaranteed.

INDEX